Studies on the History of Musical Style

Studies on the History of Musical Style

by

Arnold Salop

with a Foreword by

John W. Grubbs

Wayne State University Press
Detroit 1971

Copyright © 1971 by Wayne State University Press,
Detroit, Michigan 48202. All rights are reserved.
No part of this book may be reproduced without formal permission.

Published simultaneously in Canada
by the Copp Clark Publishing Company
517 Wellington Street, West, Toronto 2B, Canada.

Library of Congress Catalog Card Number 78-155673
International Standard Book Number 0-8143-1449 X

table of contents

FOREWORD

Although the major shaping of Arnold Salop's *Studies on the History of Musical Style* took place in 1965 and 1966, the genesis of the book is inseparable from the studies he undertook and continued from about 1957. A focal point for the author's application of his ideas concerning musical style was his Ph.D. dissertation "The Masses of Jacob Obrecht: Structure and Style," which he completed at Indiana University in 1959 under the supervision of Willi Apel. This dissertation and the subsequent article "Jacob Obrecht and the Early Development of Harmonic Polyphony" (*Journal of the American Musicological Society*, 17 [Fall 1964], 288-309) thus formed the basis for Chapter 3 of the present work.

From 1959 onward the author became increasingly interested in finding more meaningful ways to study, write, and talk about music as a communicative art. It was his firmly held belief—a belief stemming perhaps in part from his own experiences as a composer—that music must be approached as a "humanistic phenomenon," an art in which a composer either hopes or expects that some human beings will respond to his musical expression in certain predictable ways. And so over a period of years, in his musicological research, as well as in his teaching, Arnold Salop again and again dared to ask such questions as (1) If we know the musical resources and techniques available to a composer in a given musical era, can we determine the kinds of decisions he would have to make in the compositional process? And (2) if we can make such a determination, can we draw conclusions from the choices a composer has actually made in a composition—conclusions that will enable us better to understand the composer's intentions, as well as the essence and significance of his music and musical style? Arnold Salop's own answer to both of these questions was "Indeed, we can!" And he set out to substantiate his belief.

Shortly after he finished his dissertation, Mr. Salop began to apply some of his ideas to renaissance-baroque stylistic consider- ations. And in February of 1960 he read a paper entitled "The Element of Fantasy in Renaissance-Baroque Distinctions" at the Southeastern Chapter Convention of Music Teachers National As- sociation held at the University of Louisville in Kentucky. This paper was later expanded for the article "On Stylistic Unity in Renaissance-Baroque Distinctions," published in *Essays in Musi- cology, A Birthday Offering for Willi Apel,* edited by Hans Tischler (Bloomington, Indiana: University of Indiana, School of Music, 1968). This material was not included as a chapter in the present book, but it did strengthen the author's belief in the validity of his ideas.

Next came studies dealing with the eighteenth, nineteenth, and twentieth centuries. The first of these was perhaps the author's study of Schoenberg, for in April of 1964 he read a paper entitled "Schoenberg the Prophet" for the Detroit Musicians League. Later restructured and expanded to become Chapter 9 of the present book, this material deviates somewhat from the analytical tech- niques applied in other chapters of the book. In essence, it probes and challenges the ideas of Arnold Schoenberg, and in particular it questions the listener's ability to respond in accordance with the composer's intentions. Thus, although some of the original readers' reports suggested that the chapter be omitted or excised (due to the different approach), it is altogether appropriate that the ma- terial has remained in the book. What we see in this chapter is not only an important commentary on Schoenberg and the twentieth century, but also the personal testimony of the author as a twentieth- century composer and a statement of his belief that music can be a "humanistic art" in our own time.

Also in 1964 Arnold Salop applied his ideas to the classical and romantic eras and published his results in the article "Intensity as a Distinction between Classical and Romantic Music" (*Journal of Aesthetics and Art Criticism,* 23 [Spring 1965], 359-371). This material eventually formed the basis for Chapters 7 and 8 of this volume. The essential ingredients for the concept of a book on the history of musical style were now at hand.

Having had the opportunity to explore his ideas on musical

style for seven or eight years, by 1965 Arnold Salop had conceived the idea of the present book. And one must also note that in March, 1965, he read a paper entitled "Two Motets by Josquin des Prez" at the University of Illinois in Urbana which was the basis for Chapter 4. The material for Chapter 6 was evidently close to completion by the spring of 1966, when the author presented a paper entitled "The Exuberant Bach" at the University of Texas at Austin.

The book was completed by the fall semester of 1966, and accepted for publication by Wayne State University Press on March 14, 1967, with the understanding that the author would be willing to undertake some suggested recastings. Although he had expressed his willingness to undertake some of these changes, Arnold Salop was killed in an airplane crash in Lexington, Kentucky, on April 3, 1967, only a few weeks after his book had been accepted for publication.

It is indicative of the importance attached to this book by Wayne State University Press, that despite the author's tragic death, which made impossible the kinds of changes that the author and the Press might have wished, the editorial staff of the Press has remained firm in its decision to publish the book and has sought the help of the author's family and friends to insure that the book remain as faithful to his intentions as possible.

At this point, some comment is needed concerning the subsequent editing of the manuscript. After reading the masked copies of the readers' reports, the author wrote to Dr. Harold A. Basilius, then director of the Press, on March 21, 1967, indicating that he was amenable to the major revisions that had been suggested: deletion of the last chapter, rewriting of the introductory chapter, and even elimination of the term "humanistic." Other changes, however, he viewed less enthusiastically, and in a fuller draft he had made for the letter—a draft later furnished to Dr. Basilius by Mrs. Arnold Salop—he explained his objections more fully.

Chapter 1 was recast by Professors Herbert Schueller and Ruth Wylie, former colleagues of the author at Wayne State University. And at the request of Mrs. Salop this material, together with the entire manuscript, was sent to Professors Dr. Hanns-Berthold Dietz and the present writer, colleagues of the author at the University of Texas at Austin. Emendations were returned to Dr. Basilius, particularly in relation to the introductory chapter. These emendations were based both on our knowledge of what Arnold Salop was trying to convey in the chapter, as well as on a statement made by him in the draft of his letter:

... my entire approach is based upon the conceptions of communication put forth in the first chapter. If I were to eliminate these, or even water them down, I think I could be criticized for not setting forth the rationale upon which my analyses are based.

Later, when the directorship of the Press passed to Dr. Herbert Schueller, the copyediting was assigned to Miss Sandra Yolles, who is to be commended for her sensible grammatical and stylistic alterations. At her request, I have furnished translations for a number of German quotations and read galleys in the author's place.

Those of us who were fortunate enough to know Arnold Salop well are gratified that his book will now reach the reading public. And our belief in the importance of his contribution could not be better stated than a comment in one of the original reader's reports:

> ... Here is a book which deals with music itself, not with its cultural or biographical background, and it deals with the most important things about music, things which distinguish period and personal styles, rather than superficial statistical or abstract concepts. The author obviously knows what he is doing, and shows what he has done in an interesting yet rigorous way. At best, the book will be a truly important contribution and perhaps even a landmark in the history of musicology. At worst, it will provoke controversy, which I would also regard as a service.

Arnold Salop was born on June 30, 1927, in New York. He was raised in New York and later in Southern California. He received his university education at U.C.L.A. (B.A., 1952), Claremont Graduate School (M.A. in composition, 1957), and Indiana University (Ph.D. in musicology, 1959). His Ph.D. dissertation, "The Masses of Jacob Obrecht: Structure and Style," was supervised by Willi Apel, who considered the work to be outstanding.

He served as assistant professor of musicology at George Peabody College for Teachers (1958-1960) and at Wayne State University (1961-1964), as associate professor of theory at the University of Mississippi (1964-1965), and as associate professor of musicology and theory at the University of Texas at Austin (1965-1967).

Aside from his activity as a musicologist, he also maintained a continuing interest in composition. Among his compositions are a *String Quartet* (1953, rev. 1963), a *Symphony for Brass Instru-*

ments (1956, rev. 1964), an *Adagio for Piano* (1960, rev. 1966), a *Symphony No. 2* (1966), and incidental music for the plays *King Lear* (1961), *Julius Caesar* (1963), *As You Like It* (1963), *Romeo and Juliet* (1963), and *Antony and Cleopatra* (1963). These and other works have been performed at such places as New York, Detroit, Los Angeles, Atlanta, Austin, San Antonio, the University of Alabama, and Ohio State University.

His promising career as musicologist, composer, and teacher, came to a premature end at the age of less than forty. Those of us who were favored to be his colleagues and friends are each marked by the personality and intellect of this gentle man, and we continue to ponder our immeasurable loss and yet our immeasurable gain.

John W. Grubbs
Department of Music
The University of Texas at Austin

INTRODUCTION

With all that has been written about the history of Western music, it has seldom been treated as the essentially humanistic phenomenon that it is. There have been attempts to describe its effects in terms of some kind of natural law, to view its development as the working out of an evolutionary process, to draw parallels with other arts, even to correlate stylistic traits with philosophical and theological currents of thought, as well as with sociological conditions. To the best of my knowledge, however, no one has seriously attempted a systematic approach to music as a product of human ingenuity, of that mixture of assumptions, aspirations, and limitations that we call the human condition.

Each of the following essays represents an attempt to come to grips with this most important problem. The aim has been to treat music as an aspect of human thought and behavior. I have tried to figure out, as well as possible, the assumptions, values, and beliefs that lay behind the various kinds of styles discussed.

To do this, I have assumed that a composer's choice of materials and means of organization is governed, at least to some extent, by the belief that he is doing something that will be appealing to other people. This does not mean that every detail of a composition necessarily reflects an attempt to create appeal, but only that the composer must believe that somewhere in his style are certain phenomena that will prove attractive to his intended audience.

This is no more than to suggest that a composer's thought is necessarily concerned not just with acoustical materials, but with the ways of producing psychological effects by means of these materials. His fundamental aim, after all, is not merely to produce sounds, but rather to call to mind certain qualities by his choice of sounds. Any composer must assume that he commands a store of musical stimuli that, applied in certain contexts, can induce something approximating particular states of mind in his audience. In large measure, indeed, his claim to recognition must be based upon this ability to influence his audience's state of mind in fairly specific ways.

All this, it seems to me, is virtually self-evident and generally accepted. The entire activity of composition in the context of Western culture of at least the last seven or eight centuries would make little sense in the absence of some such fundamental belief in the psychological powers of various kinds of musical effects.

Less generally recognized is the possibility that there may have been considerable divergence of opinion concerning what constitutes the store of effective musical stimuli. Some composers, for instance, might well have believed that the value of their music (i.e., its ability to induce and modify particular states of mind) could be traced to its projection of certain kinds of eloquent harmonic effects, while others may have been more interested in melodic design, color effects, etc.

It would seem only reasonable, then, to begin a study of this kind by attempting to reconstruct various composers' beliefs concerning these sources of value. While this might seem a hopeless task—it is difficult enough to piece together a living composer's attitudes in this respect—I would suggest that a viable approach can be formulated by considering the ways in which different composers went about solving certain common problems imposed by the need to make their music communicate. It is to the formulation of just such an approach that the first of the following essays is devoted.

Each of the remaining essays represents an attempt to apply the principles derived in the first chapter to a body of music or musical thought on which they seemed capable of shedding some new light of understanding. In all but one case, the material lent itself to fairly broad coverage. I felt in a good position to discuss large repertories of works as wholes because of some very clear uniformities of practice in the aspects treated. In dealing with the works of Josquin, however, the sheer amount of music involved and the stylistic diversity it contains, along with the unresolved questions of authenticity and chronology, led me to narrow my discussion to just two works. In the chapter on Schoenberg, finally, I have dealt not so much with the music as with the ideas set forth in some of his writings on music. I did this not merely because these ideas embody such an interesting intellectual development, nor even because Schoenberg's theories so obviously influenced his composition, but rather because his whole thought structure seems a logical outgrowth of the assumptions underlying romantic music which I have attempted to formulate in Chapter 8. Thus, this last chapter is something of a postscript to the essay on romanticism.

ONE

The Narrative Element and the Study of Musical Style

*I*T IS NO EXAGGERATION to say that many of the current methods of studying musical style reveal as much about their authors as about the music being examined. For instance, the enumeration of easily observed characteristics that so often passes for style analysis today betrays a state of mind that might well be termed analytical pessimism. Such a position seems to imply that the processes of creation are so complex that they can never be formulated in understandable terms, and that we may understand the art work as experience, but we cannot hope to reconstruct the composer's creative thinking, even in an approximate way, by studying his music.

On the other hand, the many interpretations of style based on preconceived ideas of correct harmonic, metric, or formal practice, or of evolution by way of reduction to very general outlines, often seem to become mere attempts to defend theories rather than reasonable explanations of thought processes embodied in the music. The principles developed usually have been more in the nature of inspirations—interesting ideas—rather than carefully formulated and tested hypotheses. As a result, we know a good deal about Riemann's attitudes, or Gombosi's, or Schenker's, but really very little about those of Beethoven, Obrecht, or Tschaikowsky. To one degree or another, each of these scholars—and their names are only representative—has allowed a personal belief to color his interpretations, often to the point of obscuring the innate intentions of the composers.

If there is to be a significant evaluation of music as a humanistic phenomenon, however, it almost certainly will have to rely upon evidence gleaned from a study of the music itself. For there can be little certainty about the extent to which such things as personal circumstances, environment, or historical currents may have entered into the formation of a composer's style. We may learn a great deal about the composer and his circumstances without in the least understanding the workings of his mind during the process of creation. Even a composer's own direct statements of intent—like those of any creative artist—must be held suspect; it is conceivable, after all, that a composer might not have been aware of his innermost motivations and values—that he might have imagined a source of interest quite different from that which actually accounts for the appeal in his works.

My aim, ideally, is to formulate some criteria for the evaluation of styles that would facilitate a recognition of the composers' assumptions and beliefs about musical structure and effect instead of imposing dogmatic preconceptions upon the music. In practice, however, such an approach is impossible. The simplest judgment drawn from a set of facts requires some presuppositions. Even a judgment of relative lengths in physics requires assumptions concerning constancy of temperature, the behavior of solids, and indeed the nature of matter in general—perhaps of the universe.

The problem, then, is not to eschew presuppositions altogether, but to adopt the right ones—that is, those that will prove most useful in describing the positions of the various composers without imposing irrelevant views upon their arts. Although this would seem to present an impasse—I would suggest that certain assumptions can be made about a composer in the Western tradition, at least about composers who have contributed at all significantly to this tradition.

The first assumption is that the fundamental purpose in writing music in the Western tradition has been to evoke certain kinds of conditions in men's minds. Whether these desired conditions have been formulated in terms of beauty, elevation, affect, or any other category, the fact remains that the fundamental aim in writing music has not been to achieve any kind of practical result (such as influencing a divinity or causing rain), but rather to exert an effect on human modes of thought or feeling—which is no more than to say that music has been considered an aesthetic entity in Western civilization.

This means that music must involve "communication," however unverified. One cannot bring about a desired state of mind in another human being—one cannot amuse him, edify him, elevate his spirits, or bring him to rapt contemplation of the divinity—without one in some way attempting to create the impression that the succession of sounds in a composition is something more than a mere succession of sounds; that is, it is saying something which is intended to be meaningful. This is a different type of communication, however, from the semantic kind which is more familiar to us. Reference to dictionaries or established codes and rules of syntax is of very limited usefulness in producing recognition of the meaning intended by the composer.

Thus any body of conventionally agreed-upon symbols and relational practices can play only a partial role in establishing meaning. For the response to musical materials is in some measure involuntary: the meaning is evoked as much as it is designated. The sound contains peculiar powers of suggestion that lead a reasonably sensitive and sympathetic listener to draw some kind of analogy with mood or idea. A loud, percussive effect almost unmistakably suggests forcefulness. A soft, legato passage has gentler connotations. A major triad may sound "bright," "brilliant," or "sweet" (depending upon such factors as loudness, instrumentation, execution, and so forth); a minor triad ordinarily will have somewhat "darker" feeling-tones. A flute in its upper register may seem "brilliant," whereas a clarinet would be termed "shrill." Each of these represents the association of an emotional response—a feeling-tone—with an acoustical phenomenon.[1] Why such responses are made is a matter for conjecture. The point is that such analogies can be drawn, and indeed have been drawn for a very long time.

The idea of evoked responses as the primary basis for communication, then, can be taken as a second assumption common to Western composers.

It is very clear, however, that music consists of something more than a series of isolated evocative effects. Suppose that all of the effects contained in a Beethoven sonata were presented, but in some kind of random order. Let us say that a tape recording of the sonata could be cut into foot-long segments, the segments thrown into the air, and then the whole reassembled in whatever order the segments fell to the ground. Almost certainly such a patchwork opus would lose a great deal of the sense of coherent meaning so obvious in the original version. Thus there must be a second factor contributing to meaning: a thread of logic that ties the individual moments together and draws a more general meaning out of the many individual impressions. If the evocative effects may be compared to words, this thread of logic might be compared to some kind of syntax, a relational system designed to turn individual meanings into a generalized conception.

Furthermore, the relations between the effects must be assumed to be understood by a listener as automatically as are the meanings of the individual sounds. Otherwise, if understanding depended entirely upon convention, appreciation would be restricted to those persons aware of the syntactical usages underlying a composition. This would be equivalent to saying that only someone who understood the workings of sonata-allegro form and of phrase-sentence structure could appreciate the creations of Beethoven. It makes more sense to postulate that the attentive human mind tends to compare the musical impressions presented so as to draw more and more generalized meanings from the flow of effects. Such a predisposition would account neatly for the human ability to follow the thread of musical logic intuitively.

Here, then, are three presuppositions which seem to form the intellectual basis underlying Western music:

(1) Music is a form of communication.
(2) In the process of communication, a meaning is evoked (as opposed to designated), at least in some measure.
(3) Also in the process of communication, there is a tendency to compare impressions and draw more generalized meanings as a piece progresses.

These three propositions can be used as the key to the formulation of a system of analysis, the first task of which is to attempt to determine the composer's decisions by selecting a range of effects which have evocative powers and by comparing the musical moments on the basis of these evocative effects.

It is quite likely that any given composition will contain both individual effects which are evocative of meaning, and attempts to establish syntactical relationships between these effects. It is easily conceivable, however, that a particular composer may place more emphasis on one or the other of these factors. He may count upon a series of highly meaningful individual effects to convey his meaning, or he may use more commonplace effects but count upon building the impact by the juxtaposition of ideas and the development of a train of thought. The latter approach might be said to resemble the thinking of a dramatist who arranges effects so as to produce a mounting sense of suspense while leading up to a critical point. The former, on the other hand, might be said to resemble the type of thought behind a set of loosely related character-sketches or mood-descriptions in which the charm of the momentary evocation virtually makes one overlook the entire question of logical development.

Thus two distinctly different types of structure are possible. In some styles, the appeal may come primarily from the inherently attractive or meaningful qualities of certain effects; while in others, appeal and meaning may be the result of the logical sequence into which the individual effects are arranged. To be sure, these are extremes, and composers have achieved any number of intermediate positions. But there is a strong likelihood that one principle or the other will predominate in the style of a given composer.

The two principles are of course somewhat antithetical. A really stunning effect tends to draw attention to itself and thus to disturb concentration upon the way this event relates to what already has happened and upon what are to be its consequences. On the other hand, preoccupation with the sequence of the events may well draw attention away from the impact of individual effects, since the listener may be concentrating on how each effect fits into the established context and conjecturing about its influence on the subsequent course of events. The idea of an art equally balanced between these two principles, then, seems more a theoretical than a practical possibility.

The two stylistic types may be termed "narrative" and "picturesque." A picturesque style would draw its appeal primarily from individual effects or relatively small groups of effects, while the attractiveness in a narrative style would reside more in the sequence into which the individual effects are arranged.

Obviously it would be sheer folly to judge narrative and picturesque styles in exactly the same way. It would seem reasonable, in conducting an analysis, to assume that the predominant elements of a composer's style represent a more accurate reflection of his intentions than do the secondary ones. Hence, one of the first steps in analysis would be to determine just what are the principal aspects of a style. Or at least the aim would be to determine roughly the extent to which a composer relied upon each of these principles for communication and appeal.

But how is it possible to decide which of the many effects contained in a composition seem highly evocative, and just which of the many lines of development to be observed were intended to carry a sense of narration? Music, after all, is a complex art. At any given moment, many different events and effects may occur: a new harmony may be introduced, a motivic reference may be made, a rhythmic pattern may unfold, a new accent pattern may begin, the key may be changed, a voice may be added or dropped, motion may speed up or slacken in one or several of the voices, a crescendo or diminuendo may be in effect in any or all of the parts—and these are just a few possibilities. Surely the listener cannot long follow every minute event introduced in each and every element of music without suffering a complete breakdown of memory and attention. And it would be folly to assume that composers called for such total absorption of all details.

One must assume that a composer would have considered only a certain range of effects to be highly evocative, and only certain methods of organization to be proper for the suggestion of narrative flow. One composer, for example, may have considered particular types of harmonic configurations and relationships to be his main evocative resources. In a similar way, another composer may have assumed that narrative flow should be suggested by means of the rise and fall of melodic curves, while another may have counted upon the general rise and fall of intensity to propel the action along its course. I am considering intensity to be a complex entity influenced by such factors as rhythmic activity, speed, volume, rate of recurrence of accents, number of voices, degrees of dissonance, harmonic and melodic tensions, pitch levels, and so forth. (As the term is used in this book, it should not be construed as a synonym for loudness.)

In each of these cases, it is assumed that the composer has decided only certain effects should claim the listener's primary attention, the rest being relegated to the background of consciousness. Obviously, then, one of the first necessities for reconstructing the composer's line of thought is to determine what his decisions were: which of the elements in a style were designed to stand in the foreground of attention, and which were supposed to fade into the background? It is easy to see how a miscalculation on our part could result in serious errors of judgment. A composer who has taken considerable pains to fashion a narrative flow in the element of harmony may seem to be essentially uninterested in the sense of narration if his work is judged from the standpoint of melodic organization. It is clear that the distinction between foreground and background elements is a matter of great importance—one of the first objectives in any process of analysis.

Yet it should be borne in mind that the mere presence of an effect or type of organization—even its consistent use—does not necessarily imply that the composer expected it to be the main appeal to an audience. It is easily conceivable, for example, that a particular procedure may have been utilized, not because it held promise of being attractive, but because it was convenient to use. It represented, perhaps, a standard way of arranging unimportant details. Determining foreground elements is not merely a matter of finding any and all of the procedures the composer uses consistently; rather, it is a matter of deciding which of the many things that can be observed seem to reflect the composer's aims directly.

The significant interpretation of evocative effects is largely a matter of attempting to gain an awareness of the general state of musical taste during a given period. In general, the question is whether or not a particular effect may have been apt and striking enough to an audience of the time—whether by virtue of novelty or metaphorical implication—to constitute a major point of appeal.

Evaluation of this kind of course represents a rather knotty problem. It is not always an easy matter to capture enough of the frame of mind of a given time and society to be able to judge with any certainty which of the effects attracted their intended audiences. And it might prove quite laborious to apply these somewhat sociological tests to the many kinds of phenomena to be found in a specific body of compositions.

On the other hand, the procedures designed to produce a sense of narrative flow are relatively easily recognized. Composers interested in this phase of composition attempt to create, not a conglomeration of individual effects, but a pattern of events. The pattern, being a larger entity than the individual effect, is much easier to perceive. The judgments, furthermore, will be in terms of something like consistency or adherence to a scheme—much easier entities to evaluate than the historical and sociological considerations bearing upon the appeal of individual effects.

It may be suggested, then, that analysis could well begin with the study of the narrative organization. If there is evidence of a composer's great care in narrative composition, there would seem to be little reason for going into the whole question of evocative effects. It seems safe to assume that a "narrative" composer would have counted but little upon picturesque strokes, since, as pointed out earlier, a striking effect tends to draw attention away from the flow of the events. But if the sense of logical flow seems to break down occasionally, or if the connections between some of the effects seem awkward at best, it may well be judged that the composer had a minor interest in narrative organization, and that he considered his main interest to lie elsewhere. In such a case the next step would be to go into the question of which effects might have seemed evocative to an audience of his time.

But how can one judge either that the sequential logic has been carefully organized or that it breaks down at certain places? Music criticism of the past century or so is full of attempts to demonstrate or to disprove the existence of sequential logic. What kinds of criteria can be used here?

Is it enough to refer to some form of standard practice? Has logical flow been demonstrated merely if one points out that such and such a problematical place in a musical composition is actually the beginning of the second theme in the recapitulation? Or if, by a series of clever reductions, this actually can be interpreted as supertonic in an unfolding, but much prolonged II-V-I cadence?

Solutions of this kind imply that the sequential logic is primarily a matter of conditioning: Beethoven seems logical because his audience has come to know approximately what to expect in any one of his compositions and can measure what actually occurs against what it has learned to expect (owing to familiarity with his harmonic idiom, his formal procedures, and other factors).

Although the influence of conditioning should not be underestimated, particularly in the arousing of short-range expectations, something more seems to be involved in the kind of long-range planning that would help to create a narrative style. It may be helpful to attempt to construct a model of the kind of thought processes that would be involved in the suggestion of a logical sequence of events.

Obviously the sense of logical progress in music rests upon the action of memory. An impression must first be stored in the mind before other impressions can be compared with it and before judgments can be made about connections between them. Any action of memory, of course, involves an initial establishment of a quality in the mind and an introduction of another quality, different in some way and to some degree from that first implanted.

Yet one cannot go on repeating exactly the same quality (for instance the pitch E) for very long and still give the impression that something meaningful is being said, or is going to be said, any more than one could go on repeating a single word indefinitely and still leave the impression of rational discourse. The established impression must be built upon, in lingual as well as in musical communication, and the building requires a departure.

There is a third element in the memory process—one that is often overlooked, namely, a tendency to condense thoughts, to substitute larger, more general impressions for the more minute and more numerous ones that bombard our ears directly. When one considers how many significant changes may occur within just a few seconds, it becomes clear that nothing short of a freakish memory is capable of retaining all of the individual details. For most of us there has to be some process of simplification; we are literally forced to substitute a general impression for a multitude of smaller ones every so often. This process of reduction, furthermore, must go on continually as the piece unfolds, so that ever larger stretches of the composition are stored in memory in ever more condensed states. This is what must happen if the sense of logical flow is to seem unbroken.

Thus, the action of memory in a narrative piece could be described as follows: first, the establishment of some quality; next, a departure from it—the following of many qualities; and then a reduction of the many particulars to a more general impression. This more general impression, once established, can then lead to another departure. The resulting combination of a larger general impression and the ensuing departure once again would be subject to a reduction—and so the process would continue.

A few examples may help clarify the picture. Suppose, for instance, that a monophonic piece (in which rhythmic values are assumed to be equal) begins with the pitch E followed by the pitch F. At once a listener would sense and remember both of the two individual pitches and another, more general impression, of a rising line. The addition of a G would tend to reinforce the impression of a rising line while it weakens the memory of the individual pitches, since more time would have elapsed and there are more entities to crowd into memory. That is to say, a listener would look for the gist of the passage—the *Gestalt*—because of the increasing difficulty of retaining all of the individual impressions in mind. The addition of an F, making the sequence E-F-G-F, would further weaken the memory of the individual pitches, and thus cause a listener to attach even more importance to the *Gestalt*—now no longer a direct rise, but a curve, an asymmetrical arch.

Suppose that, at this point, something were done to suggest

25

the end of a train of thought: a pause, a rest, a repeat of the last note, even simply making that last F a turning point for the line— any of these expedients might serve the purpose. The impression left in memory quite likely would be of this asymmetrical arch. There might be a more or less vague idea of where it ended, where it had begun, and what its high point had been, but the strongest impression left probably would be of its general contour and scope. Whatever followed would be compared with this shape. If the subsequent unit took the form of the same generally arched shape, but with a rise to a higher pitch level, or with proportionately more time spent in the higher reaches of the gamut, comparison of these two shapes would lead to the general impression of increased emphasis on a higher register—a rising line once again. If a third curve went still higher, or stayed high still longer, the impression of a rising line would become even stronger.

Thus, as curve blended into curve, the qualities of the separate arches would gradually be forgotten, at least to some extent, while the individual events which went into forming the curves almost certainly would fade from memory. All of these events would be reduced to a general but increasingly strongly felt impression of a rising line.

Suppose, however, that one of these arches did not fit comfortably into the series. Let us say that it did not place appreciably greater emphasis on the upper register than its predecessor, or even that it may have represented a lesser emphasis on the high range. Needless to say, if the hearer now sensed the beginning of what he recognized as a downward trend, he would possibly continue to make the necessary reductions: the rising line would be converted into the shape of an arch, just as was done in the case of the individual pitches which formed each of the separate curves.

But even if the upward trend were to be resumed after the one deviation, there would still be a possibility that the process of reduction of impressions might function effectively. The deviant curve might well be interpreted as something of an interruption; with the resumption of upward motion, the manifold impressions again would be related to the sense of the rising line, with cognizance being taken of the detour that had been encountered on the way. The question, after all, is not how rigidly a trend is carried out, but rather how well the individual events can be reduced as they are related to an overall pattern of events. An interruption conceivably could be just as well related as could a direct continuation. The reduction process would be likely to break down only when the interruptions became so numerous, extensive, or striking in effect as to make it difficult to perceive any underlying trend.

Similar patterns could be established through the organization of the harmony. The first impression might be of a triad, F-major, for instance. The departure might take the form of a move to the dominant. A return then to the F-major triad would suggest the ending of an excursion. If what follows is a longer-lasting departure, say a I-VI-IV-V-I progression, there would be a tendency to compare this with the original I-V-I, resulting in the judgment that the scope of the departure had grown considerably. A third excursion which involved a momentary change of key, such as I-VI-IV-V of V-V-I, would seem but another step in this direction.

Suppose, however, that the E-F-G-F melodic curve were followed, not by a curve similar in shape though larger in scope and dimension, but rather by a radically different type of figure—for instance by a slightly inflected monotone in a higher register. Suppose, also, that the third curve also was quite different in character from the others, perhaps a straight descending line into a low register. The listener would then relate the three curves (that is, reduce the manifold impressions) by a sense of contrast: section B as contrast to section A, and section C as contrast to both A and B. If this stream of novelties were kept up for some considerable time, the early impressions would begin to fade from memory without having contributed to a more general quality brought about by a line of development. The impression would be one of general contrast: every event would seem different in essence from every other event. In a situation of this kind the assimilation and reduction of events to more manageable proportions could not well take place, since there would be no line of development to which the individual effects could be related. Events would have to be evaluated without considering their place in the movement as a whole, and without taking into account the ways in which all of the preceding events might have contributed to and modified the meaning and significance of current happenings. Since the earlier events would not have contributed to a line of development, they would simply have to be forgotten eventually to make room for new impressions.

It is clear, then, that the possibility of suggesting logical development derives from the formation of what might be termed "trends." Wherever a trend can be sensed, there is a possibility that the many individual events can be reduced effectively to progressively more general impressions. Where no such line of development is apparent, the listener is free to simplify in whatever way he sees fit, usually by dropping events from memory.

This is not to say that the presence of a strong contrast, or even of a set of strong contrasts, precludes a sense of logical flow. Indeed, the contrasts may well be used to establish something like a quality of conflict, or at least of opposition of forces. If such an opposition is to seem to contribute logically to the flow of events, however, it eventually must give way either to attempts to reconcile the extreme positions, or else to manipulations designed to strengthen the sense of conflict. Either of these alternatives involves the emergence of trends: a gradual movement from one extreme to the other in the former case, and a gradually widening scope to the opposition in the latter.

Here, then, is a useful criterion for evaluating a given style: What element in the style is most strongly responsible for suggesting trends? Harmony? A melodic line? Intensity? And how far are these trends carried? If it seems that the individual events all can be related to a reasonably simple pattern of trends, the first guess might be that the composer sought to exploit narrative possibilities. If, on the other hand, the various trends cannot be reduced to a reasonably simple pattern—simple enough to allow for consistent substitution of more general impressions for the many particular ones—the style probably tends toward the picturesque source of meaning. To use simpler terms: Does the evidence indicate that the composer is asking his listener to remember the gist of what has already happened in the piece, or does it imply that the composer expects him to forget a good deal of what has gone before in his preoccupation with present effects?

The mere presence of a reasonably simple pattern of trends, however, does not in itself constitute evidence of narrative intent. For another element—one that derives directly from the second of the basic assumptions mentioned at the beginning of this chapter—is involved in the suggestion of logical connection: the assumption that musical responses are largely evoked rather than designated, that the recognition of meanings and relationships is largely automatic and intuitive. This means that no matter how clearly a piece of music can be dissected into trends, there will be no quality of logical connection unless those trends can be sensed and followed almost involuntarily.

Now any event which draws a great deal of attention to itself, whether because of an intrinsic sense of its significance or by virtue of an element of surprise, could have the effect of precluding such an intuitive following of the trends. For by drawing attention to itself, that event could erase the past context from memory; there would be a tendency to overlook what had been felt earlier in the surprise at, or delight in, the immediate present. The chain of reductions (by means of which the memory is able to function efficiently) would be broken, or at least impaired. Ordinarily it takes only a few such impairments to bring on an attitude of listening for the next shocking or immediately appealing event as something of an end in itself. When this happens, one no longer follows the line of development, but merely seeks to absorb the pleasures offered by each of the highlights. Thus, the suggestion of a logical line of development requires the creation of a sense of smoothness and naturalness.

The problem of fashioning a flow of events that would seem "natural" obviously is related to the question of expectations. A flow is natural when the event introduced at any given point seems consistent with the expectations generated by the events preceding. It may not fulfill these expectations exactly as might have been predicted, or it may even inject new and unexpected elements; but the result must seem a plausible outcome for the moment, or at least an infusion of a new line of thought at an appropriate place, a line to be developed and assimilated in the coming moments.

In recent years, the possibilities of commitment and expectation usually have been examined from the point of view that expectation derives solely or primarily from experience and conditioning—"we expect what we know." A more sophisticated formulation involves the notion that an event gives rise not to a single expectation, but to a range of possible continuations of varying degrees of probability. It is the degree of probability in this formulation which is determined largely by cultural conditioning.[2]

Although positions of this kind would seem to be supported by the findings of many comparative musicologists, the history of Western music provides much evidence that the assignment of overriding significance to cultural influences is not entirely justified. Composers, after all, often have proceeded with little regard for established norms—the habit-responses of their intended audiences. And this has not usually involved novel solutions to familiar problems, but rather the establishment of new types of problems for which the established habits have little or no relevance.

This is not to suggest that conditioning plays no role of any consequence in raising musical expectations. One must be sufficiently conversant with Western traditions to be willing to fuse separate sounds into harmonies; for instance, in order to follow the music of many composers. In other cases, it is necessary to follow the outlines of a particular voice, paying only minimal attention to the other voices and to the "harmonies" which are formed. In still other styles, one must be able and willing to follow the play of intensities, and to interpret influences on intensity in certain ways (for example, associating high intensity with speed, loudness, high pitch, and so forth). But to consider such entities as the most important influences upon expectation is to limit oneself from the start to an area of investigation so general and fundamental as to preclude any degree of deep understanding.

It makes more sense to consider that the composer, in fashioning his style, was attempting to take advantage of the tendency of the human mind to respond to logical form as well as of the responses his culture has made into habit. If anything, the natural responses would seem to have played the larger role in fashioning stylistic novelties. Thus the expectations engendered by trends would seem the most significant focus for study, inasmuch as it is the pattern of trends that is mainly responsible for the suggestion of a logical sequence in the events.

The perception of a trend may lead to three types of expectations: that the trend will continue in its original direction; that it will be changed by a reaction; or that it will culminate in some appropriately significant way. Once a trend has been perceived, a listener probably will be willing to concede that a continuation in the same direction seems plausible. Having heard two links in an ascending sequence, he is willing to interpret a third as a reasonable subsequent event; having heard three links, he will so interpret a fourth.

But this is true only for a time; beyond a certain limit, further motion in a particular direction seems artificial. A mechanical element creeps into an unduly prolonged trend, interest is lessened, and absorption in the art work destroyed. When this becomes the case, what is expected is no longer a continuation, but a reaction.

The same type of reaction is engendered by a turn of events that contains an element of surprise: a sudden fortissimo outburst or a piano subito, for instance, or else an abrupt raising or lowering of the pitch level, or a quick rise in rhythmic activity. In all of these cases of surprise, the sudden departure from an established trend works to destroy the sense of logical flow, since it focuses attention upon the event causing the disruption. Unless this disruptive event can be incorporated once again into the sense of unfolding flow (for example, by becoming a part of an antithetical opposition of forces that is later resolved in one way or another), a listener is forced to conclude that the previously established context really has had little to do with the events now taking place. This may eventually induce the mind to forget that earlier section, thus leading to a breakdown in the sense of narration. The listener probably would be first inclined to view the disruption as a temporary thing, however, and to look for verification of this guess in the form of either a quick or a gradual return to the previously established quality. Thus, the introduction of a surprising event leads not to the expectation of continuation in that novel vein, but rather to the expectation of another specific type of reaction: a return to something similar to the original context.

The expectation of culmination is simply a judgment that a trend should at some time issue into a significant result as in the achievement of a goal or an outcome to processes long in evidence. If this does not happen, there must be some sense of disappointment. For the listener tends to assume that the composer had an objective in mind when he fashioned the trend.

Three possible types of expectation can therefore be engendered: continuation, reaction, and culmination. Furthermore, they cannot be considered mere abstract possibilities, but must be taken for reflections of psychological principles with which the composer must deal insofar as he wishes to invest his composition with a sense of logical flow. Consideration of these expectations, inasmuch as they depend upon fundamental psychological predispositions, could well form a practical basis for judgments about the means and the extent of narrative organization in a given composition. This would be especially true of the way in which changes are introduced. Such changes must occur in a narrative composition because the trend into which they are introduced must seem to unfold "naturally," that is, more or less according to expectation. And one can only count upon the expectation of continuation to function for a limited time; beyond this time, the expectation of a reversal comes more and more into the foreground.

In particular, the care with which the break is made and the attention given to the new expectations it brings into play provide the most important clues in judgments concerning narrative intent. It should be decided, at this point, whether the reaction takes place rather early (that is, before the expectation of a change has developed to significant proportions), at an appropriate time (when such an expectation has developed, but before it has become overripe), or too late (after a sense of mechanical, contrived motion has set in). In the last of these cases, of course, the judgment will be that the narrative sense has broken down. In the first case, on the other hand, judgment would usually lead to an expectation that compensatory moves will follow. If such a return ensues, the judgment probably would be that the composer was attempting to organize this element into narrative patterns, at least up to this point. If no such return follows within a reasonable amount of time, the judgment would have to be that the narrative connection had broken down.

If the reaction occurs at an appropriate time, the new expectations generated by it will depend upon the nature of the reactive step taken. The break, of course, might take the form of an abrupt change of some kind (from fortissimo to piano subito, for instance), or of a change in the general direction of the trend (for example, allowing the pitch to sink back gradually after a rise or allowing a crescendo to give way to a diminuendo). An abrupt change, because it involves an element of surprise, would bring into play the principle of reaction and generate expectation of a return to roughly the original quality. If a seemingly significant event took place immediately beforehand (perhaps a cadence, a modulation, or a fortissimo statement of a significant and well-remembered theme), the expected tendency would be to continue presenting this newly introduced quality for a considerable amount of time.

What is established in such a case by the reduction process is an antithetical relationship, a relationship that one would now expect to develop in favor of one element or the other. When a program occurs that seems designed to keep clearly in balance all the relationships, factors, and influences (for example, without such lingering on the abruptly introduced quality that the antithetical sense is forgotten), it seems fairly certain that the structure is narrative. Although there is some subjectivity in a judgment of this kind (How, after all, can one determine just what amounts to too much delay?), the evidence is often so massive that one can hardly overlook signs of breakdown or of smooth connection.

If no significant event immediately preceded the change, the expectation would be of a quick return to the quality from which the departure was made, or at least of a start in that direction very soon. If the return is abrupt, a listener probably would tend to think of the whole deviation from the trend as something of a detour, and would then expect to see the original trend resumed, and (by the principle of culmination) led to its goal—perhaps with further detours along the way. On the other hand, if the return is gradual, the abrupt change which marked the original reaction would come to seem little more than a regrouping of forces for another assault on the way to the significant outcome of the original trend—as though the first attempt had failed.

If a composition gives easily perceived evidence of following one or the other of these programs, it would seem safe to infer that the composer was interested in the narrative facet of his art. If, however, the changes and reactions in a movement do not seem to follow out these commitments consistently, it would seem reasonable to conclude that the composer in question did not expect the events to be compared on this large a scale. He obviously did not expect that a continual process of reducing impressions would be carried on by his audience; he would be content if many of the earlier impressions were simply dropped from memory and attention were focused on the events now unfolding. His art, in other words, would be picturesque. It would then be time to look for a range of effects which might seem intrinsically attractive to an audience of his time, something that might seem powerful because of its novelty and aptness.

The narrative composer, then, works somewhat as follows. First, he organizes some particular musical elements (like harmony, melodic line, or intensity) into an easily perceived and reasonably simple pattern of trends. Second, some time after the initial trend gets under way, he may introduce either a reversal of its direction, or an abrupt change to a quality quite different from that which has been reached. Either of these would be introduced, furthermore, before the trend has gone so far as to acquire a sense of contrived, mechanical motion. Third, the composer would continue and culminate the program to which his choice of digression has committed him. I do not mean to imply that these should be considered rigid commitments; there are many fine shadings of timing, as well as of degrees of contrast, all of which would influence the expectations concerning what is to follow. In addition, there are many situations where several different moves would seem equally plausible. Nevertheless, there is a range of possibilities beyond which the composer could not well go without causing the narrative sense to break down; and as the number of events grows in the unfolding of a composition so that more and more happenings must be stored in memory, it often becomes quite clear whether or not reductions can be made efficiently.

Analytical procedure—the test for narrative organization— would involve: (1) determining the main element in which consistent patterning of trends can be found; (2) deciding whether these patterns would have been perceivable to the intended audiences; (3) judging whether reactions are introduced consistently before the trends acquire a mechanical quality; and (4) examining to see if the changes in direction or quality lead to appropriate types of programs, such as those outlined above, at least reasonably well.

By proceeding through a process of this kind, it is possible to get some idea of how far a composer carried his narrative organization, and, by inference, of how much he depended upon it to produce appeal. Knowledge of this kind can reveal something of the intellectual substance behind a style, as well as provide some valuable information concerning interpretation.

Suppose, for instance, that the works of a certain composer show great care taken to create a sense of trend and culmination within individual phrases (perhaps by means of an harmonic and rhythmic drive to the cadences), but little or no evidence of intent to combine the separate phrases into a larger pattern of trends. In a case of this kind, it would seem reasonable to conclude that the composer was counting upon each individual phrase to create the sense of appeal, without much concern for heightening the appeal as the piece unfolded. In this style the build-up and resolution of harmonic and rhythmic tensions constitute a "picturesque" point of appeal. On the other hand, if the style of a composer displays consistent attempts to combine all of the separate phrases into a large pattern of trends, reactions, culminations, etc.—all following one of the program types outlined above—one cannot help concluding that the composer envisioned a dramatic line of development, by means of which the appeal would be intensified as the movement progressed.

Still another program might involve a picturesque approach in which the point of appeal is a reaction. In this structure, the composer would establish either a trend or a situation which will set the stage for a reaction to seem more agreeable than it otherwise might have. For instance, an amorphous melodic curve, a curve that seems to wander aimlessly, could set the stage nicely for a subsequent clearly directed curve (perhaps a descending sequence). The intrinsically attractive qualities of the sequential descent would be enhanced by the fact that they emerged from so nebulous a background, a background in which all sense of purpose and orientation threaten to disappear. In this reactive art, too, knowledge of the treatment of the narrative element obviously is required for an understanding of the composer's position and for the formulation of reasonable performance standards.

This is still a rather rough outline of an approach to the diagnosis of narrative structure. To refine it further requires a discussion of one more concept which may be termed the critical point. There are certain times in a composition when a particular event assumes, or should assume, considerable significance. Sometimes the sense of significance is intrinsic to the effect employed; for example, a cadence, particularly when it defines a new key, or a return of significant and well-remembered thematic material, or a climax.

The sense of added significance also can be achieved by means of narrative organization by inserting what might be termed a countercurrent into an unfolding trend. Suppose, for example, a particular portion of a composition were dominated by an intense downward motion. If a brief flareup were to take place—nothing extensive enough to wipe out the memory of the descending trend —then a return to the downward tendency would seem all the more significant for having conquered an obstacle thrown in its way. The line of reasoning might be formulated as follows: Where there is an expectation, a degree of tension is set up in the mind. Will the expected actually occur as our cultural conditioning leads us to anticipate? In this process, the listener predicts and then becomes curious to determine whether his predictions will be realized.

As long as the expected event actually comes to pass without significant delay, the tension generated by curiosity remains moderate in degree. Otherwise, the first reaction probably involves some degree of shock. The second reaction might be a reevaluation: Was the situation which led to this prediction interpreted erroneously? Then a third reaction might follow in which the listener will begin to wait for the event he was expecting earlier to occur in the further course of the musical flow.

The last of these reactions sets up something like a goal in mind. The listener is no longer merely absorbing impressions from the musical flow; nor is he merely predicting events yet to come. Rather he is matching the accomplished event retained in memory against the impressions introduced by the subsequent flow of the music. And he is not idly engaged in this matching process. For if he does not find what he is looking for, he must admit that he does not understand the composer's organization of events; he must admit that the second reaction mentioned a moment ago was the correct one, namely, that he has erroneously interpreted the situation which led to this prediction. To do this, of course, is to abandon hope of understanding and enjoying the composition.

Thus, there is not only a curiosity, but a desire to hear the event which the listener has come to expect. Anything that does not match what he is looking for may well be overlooked, unless an effect is sufficiently striking to make him forget his search and start calculating in a new direction (in which case, of course, the narrative connection would have broken down). The listener begins to have a goal in mind as he listens. What was at one time merely an expectation now has come to have a value attached to it and its eventual manifestation would seem all the more significant. The longer he goes on without discovering his expectation, tension will mount. The greater the degree of tension, the greater will be the sense of relief when it is resolved, and the more significant will seem the event capable of suggesting such a release.[3] It is because the countercurrent comes to seem an interruption, then, and generates a tendency to view the return to the original direction or quality somewhat as a goal achieved, that it is able to heighten significance.

The technique of heightening significance by inserting countercurrents has several applications. Composers often treat the ending as such a critical point. It is obvious, of course, especially if one has worked at all with composition students, that there is a problem involved in suggesting termination; mere cessation of activity does not always suffice. In a narrative style, the problem of termination relates to the process of culminating a trend. By the principle of continuation, it may be expected that the trend leading to an ending will continue, unless it has been so long under way as to set up a demand for a reaction. Neither continuation nor reaction, of course, would foster the sense of resolution of issues that might make for a quality of termination. Inserting a countercurrent into a dominant trend, however, could bring about interpretation of the subsequent return as a goal achieved—a resolution rather than merely another link or another reaction. In addition, the delay would tend to heighten the significance of the return, so that in both of these ways a feeling-tone of termination may be brought about. These actions and the impressions they convey could tend to create the sense that the play of forces has reached an outcome and has been resolved in a way significant enough to carry a sense of finality.

The reversal of a trend, particularly if it is large-scale, also could involve a critical point. This is true because the narrative composer's aim must be to avoid the impression that there is an element of the arbitrary in the arrangement of the events. So momentous a change as a reversal of a large-scale trend is not to be undertaken lightly. A listener wants to believe that such a turn of events was not introduced capriciously, but can be traced to some cause. Such a cause might be a significant event, and the sense of significance may be defined partially by a countercurrent. In a situation of this kind, the insertion of a countercurrent acts in yet another way to make the reversal of direction seem smoother: it plants a seed of that reversal—a seed that seems lost for the moment as motion in the original direction is resumed, but one which, in retrospect, seems to become the germ from which motion in the new direction has grown.

A third type of critical situation is the moment when the play of narrative forces seems to issue into an outcome, or at least a provisional outcome. The reentry (i.e., the beginning of the recapitulation) in the classical sonata-allegro movement often offers a prime example of this type of critical point. Again the countercurrent often is used to enhance the sense of significance.

The conceptions of the critical point and of the use of the countercurrent to enhance its significance are most useful, indeed necessary, refinements in the understanding of musical structure. Where a series of trends might be judged to be too complex—to contain too many turnabouts—to be perceived as a narrative structure, it may actually represent a simple scheme, the apparent complications being introduced by countercurrents inserted to underline the significance of the main critical points.

With this possibility in mind, then, one can begin asking questions of a given style: Can the piece be reduced to a reasonably clear and simple pattern of trends? Were the trends found in the various elements perceptible to an audience of the time? Do the changes in direction and quality follow a reasonable program of fulfillment of expectations?

On the basis of questions like these, we can find evidence presented in various compositions which helps us to gain insight both into the creative procedures of many composers and into the assumptions underlying these procedures.

I should perhaps note at this point that I can see no reason for attaching either a high value or a stigma to one or another of these art types. They merely represent different approaches to the problem of creating meaning and value; the one is as legitimate as the other. To be sure, it is fashionable today to consider what I have called the narrative element a *sine qua non* of musical value. A composition that does not embody an exemplary organization of the flow of time is often considered the inferior work of a second-rate composer who really did not know his business. Leaving aside the fact that this judgment calls into question many works of proven and enduring value, I should like to point out that I am not implying that a picturesque style necessarily involves deficiencies in the organization of the flow of time. Rather, I would suggest that a picturesque composer is allowing a different element to enter into his calculations governing temporal organization; he perhaps feels that he can take more liberties with the sequence in which events are arranged because he knows his audience will find enough delight in certain of the events to overlook any discontinuities or lack of overall direction.

If at times it seems that I am somewhat critical in my descriptions of temporal relations in picturesque compositions, it should be borne in mind that this is not a judgment about aesthetic worth, but rather the reflection of the approach employed. For I have measured these picturesque compositions against a narrative yardstick, purposefully not taking into account the degree to which attractive events tend to make one overlook questionable connections. I am really not reflecting upon the correctness of the composer's calculations, but only on how far from right he would have been had he relied primarily upon narrative resources. If the result often seems a caricature, it does show quite graphically the extent to which the procedures of a given composer deviate from strictly narrative requirements. This method of ignoring the influence of picturesque effects on the sense of logical sequence, then, provides a most useful means for demonstrating the degree of dependence upon, or independence from, the organization of the flow of time for creating musical value.

TWO

The Secular Polyphony of Guillaume de Machaut

ITH THE DEVELOPMENT of a polyphonic approach to composition in the ninth century or even earlier, a whole new range of musical resources was put at the disposal of the composer. No longer were attractive effects and the suggestion of narrative connections restricted to what might be projected in a single line. Now the evocative qualities of harmonic intervals could be exploited; a decorative melody could be added to an already familiar one; indeed, the relations of the separate voices could serve to generate and release tensions in various ways.[1]

Although all of these considerations may have entered into aesthetic calculations at one point or another in the early development of polyphonic conceptions, it may well have been a byproduct of the growing complexity of polyphonic relations that provided the main impetus for the artistic developments of the fourteenth century; namely, the emergence of the more precise and flexible rhythmic organization which probably can be traced to the need for coordinating independent lines. At any rate, the more delicate, complex, and precise rhythmic patterns made possible by the notational innovations of the early decades of the fourteenth century (the so-called *Ars nova*) led to the emergence of a new type of polyphonic style, a style dominated by a florid but still fluid and beautifully shaped melodic line. The new rhythmic differentiations, of course, were what made it possible to suggest broad general directions to the line despite its floridity. It is this practice that forms the basis for Guillaume de Machaut's secular polyphonic art.

Before going into a study of this art, it may be well to call attention once more, as Besseler[2] and others have done, to the fact that there is a distinct difference between the styles embodied in the secular compositions on the one hand and in the motets on the other. In the secular polyphonic pieces, for the most part, the treatment of the rhythm is flexible and complex, with a good deal of syncopation and pronounced independence of the parts. Where the prolation is perfect (that is, where the quarter-notes are divided into triplet eighths, as Ludwig[3] transcribes them), there is a free mixture of the long-short (♩ ♪) and short-long (♪ ♩) patterns that might be considered the equivalents of the first and second rhythmic modes. The motets, on the other hand, are characterized both by a far simpler rhythmic organization in which syncopation does not play so large a role (but hocketing is frequently found), and by a lesser degree of independence between the freely composed voices. (There is, however, a considerable degree of rhythmic independence between these freely composed voices and the virtually always more slowly moving tenor.) In all but nine of the twenty-three motets, the upper voices are so consistently organized into the long-short pattern of triplet eighths that they seem very distinctly reminiscent of the first mode. Of these nine exceptions, furthermore, only four (numbers 14, 15, 20 and 22 in Ludwig's edition) contain a mixture of the first and second mode patterns, while the other five (numbers 7, 8, 11, 16 and 19) are in imperfect prolation and hence do not fall into these triplet divisions at all. As a result, the motets seem rather simple and perhaps a little stiff in character—quite in contrast to the air of sophistication which attaches to the secular works.

To be sure, not every motet is written in this simple style, nor does every secular piece contain a highly sophisticated rhythmic organization. Some secular works, such as *S'Amours ne fait*[4] and *Helas! tant ay dolour,*[5] show more than a trace of the old modal patterns, while motets such as *Lasse! comment oublieray-Se j'aim mon loyal ami-Pour quoy me bat*[6] and *Martyrum gemma latria-Diligenter inquiramus-A Christo honoratus*[7] show some degree of rhythmic flexibility. Drawing the distinction between the styles of motet and secular composition seems justified, however, both because the examples cited are clearly exceptional, and because the degree of complexity in the motets never does approach that in even the simpler secular works.

There has been some feeling in recent times that the motets are the most significant of Machaut's works. Perle, for instance, maintains that: "The motet is the form that defines the period." [8] I would suggest, however, that this is pure surmise. What little evidence there is could easily be interpreted as pointing toward just the opposite conclusion. For one thing, the motets are so obviously in what must have seemed an already archaic style by fourteenth-century standards, what with the relatively simple rhythmic organization frequently bordering on modal patterns. For another, it has been shown quite conclusively that all but a few of the motets are early works.[9] The biographical picture that emerges from Machabey's study,[10] furthermore, as well as the predominance of the themes of courtly love in Machaut's poetry, indicates that his heart was more devoted to the court than to the cloister. All of which makes it at least seem plausible that the motets may have been written as if on demand, as the fulfillment of a duty, rather than as an expression of deep personal belief. It may well be that the secular pieces called forth an artistic ingenuity greater than that applied in the motets. At any rate, if a reasonably accurate picture of the creative personality that was Guillaume de Machaut is to be reconstructed, there would seem little justification for disregarding the secular polyphonic works, or even for minimizing their importance.

Some idea of Machaut's conception of texture in his secular polyphonic works can be gained by examining the virelai *Dame, mon cuer emportes*[11] (Example 1). If the reader will take the time to sing through each of the two lines in this composition, he certainly cannot but be struck by their differences in quality. The upper voice obviously is smooth, clearly outlined and directed, and ingratiating. It is shaped so as to generate expectations (for example, the rather mincing, low-lying, and indecisive motion of measures 5-10 clearly is setting the stage for a reaction), and these expectations are either modified in a plausible manner or realized in the further course of developments. This is a tune that could be sung and enjoyed whether or not the second voice were performed with it. It is the sort of melody that one might find oneself remembering and whistling some time after originally hearing it.

The lower part, on the other hand, is no pleasure to sing or to play. For long stretches it moves so slowly that one can hardly avoid becoming bored. At several points, to be sure, a little rhythmic

Example 1. *Dame, mon cuer emportes* (virelai No. 32).

activity begins to be felt (measures 5-6, 8, 17, 21-24, and 26-27), an activity that suggests drive and hence leads us to expect motion toward some sort of goal, perhaps a cadence. In all but the last two of these cases, however, the sense of drive leads into, not a goal, but a rest. We certainly expect, then, that the drive will be continued after the rest since its energy has not been released. Instead, the line reverts to slow motion. The expectations aroused by the drive are ignored rather than consummated; it is as though the speedup had never taken place. In each of these cases, we are left somewhat puzzled; we might be inclined to ask: What was that all about?

It should be pointed out, furthermore, that there does not seem to be any effect within the line so striking as to take our minds off this question or the sense of puzzlement that goes with it. We cannot but feel a sense of dissatisfaction with the rhythmic organization.

Aside from these points of increased rhythmic activity, little sense of directed motion is to be found in this line. This results partly from the slowness of the motion which tends to focus attention on individual notes rather than on the curves to which they might contribute. It can also be traced, however, to a considerable degree of repetitiousness: the pitches F and C monopolize measures 1-5 and 14-20, while G and D dominate measures 7-13. And, in spite of the activity in measures 22-28, there is no significant sense of progress; the line simply goes over basically the same set of pitches a few times and then moves one step higher (to A). With all of the repetition up to this point, a far stronger move certainly would be required to suggest any appreciable progress.

Thus, in the whole of the composition, the tenor develops a sense of direction only occasionally, and, at most of the few points where directed motion is suggested, the directional implications are ignored rather than consummated. There is no getting around it; we cannot but feel a sense of dissatisfaction with the way the events in this line are put together.

All of this discussion is designed to show, not that Machaut was a poor composer, or even that he did not master the art of combining equally attractive voices, but rather that the shape and attractiveness of this voice was not particularly important to him. His main aim in this composition must have been to project an appealing melodic line; the other voice probably was designed to add occasional interesting sonorities and to act as something of a rhythmic counterpoise to the flow of the main melody.

The situation is much the same in the compositions with more than two voices. In the three-voice ballade *Mes esperis*,[12] for instance, the cantus (i.e., the voice underlaid with text) obviously was designed with great care. It flows fluidly from point to point, has several most welcome reactions (for example, in measures 11 and 16), and in general has a sense of purposeful, directed motion at all times. Such is not the case, however, with the contratenor. Although this line gives promise of logical development at its beginning, signs indicating lack of design eventually turn up, signs such as the sudden and inexplicable breaking off of the fast motion in measure 16, the seemingly arbitrary changes in register, and the relative slowness of the motion at many points (for example, beginning at measure 30). The tenor is even more clearly not a product of careful design, what with its frequent abrupt register changes and its general sense of redundance. Again, then, there seems no getting around it, only one of the lines shows evidence of careful design; the others are of subsidiary importance, providing rhythmic impulse or interesting sonority as required.

One may well ask whether the primary appeal was in the harmony in this case. With three voices, after all, the succession of sonorities may well have been sufficiently striking in itself to attract and hold interest.

And, indeed, there are most interesting harmonic effects in *Mes esperis*. The "colors" range from the open intervals (fifths and octaves) at the beginning and at almost every cadence, to the "sweet" parallel thirds in measures 40-41, to the parallel seconds in measure 9. Every so often, furthermore, what probably should be interpreted as a double leading-tone cadence (i.e., a cadence with a halfstep approach to the fifth as well as to the root of the next chord:) injects something of a quality of surprise (for example, in measures 16-17, 27-28). Certainly the change from an agitated motion with much dissonance to a complete stop on an empty fifth at the numerous cadences provides a very striking and agreeable effect of clarity emerging from confusion.

On the other hand, however, many of these effects may not have been perceived by the intended audiences. For the performance practice of the time probably did not embrace the idea of blending of the separate voices, but rather of a distinct contrast between them.[13] Indeed, free and *ad libitum* mixing of voices and instruments seems to have been the general practice, with the instruments usually being of quite diverse timbres. Thus, the three notes sounding simultaneously probably would have been perceived more as separate entities—as parts of separate lines—than as constituents of a single impression (i.e., of a harmony). In general, then, the play of consonances and dissonances would have been deemphasized, and might indeed have escaped perception. The "shock" value of the double leading-tone cadence, however, probably would still make it stand out clearly, particularly since it is generally followed by a complete cessation of motion on an empty fifth—a most impressive effect after the preceding bustle and clashes.

If the harmony was intended as a primary point of appeal, its attractiveness was probably conceived somewhat in terms of the picturesque. Possibly the intent was to introduce a colorful and variegated succession of sonorities, each sound being so provocative as to constantly renew interest. Or it may have been to bring a sense of clarity out of the bustle and confusion from time to time. There is, however, no evidence of any large-scale planning of trends implemented by the harmony. The performance practice, indeed, makes it doubtful that the harmony provided much more than an occasional interesting effect.

In this piece, then, as well as in *Dame, mon cuer,* it is clear that the narrative function is primarily a result of linear construction; the shape of one voice, the cantus, is responsible for the sense of logical progress throughout the course of the composition.

And this seems to be the case throughout Machaut's secular polyphonic works: one voice gives evidence of careful design; the others, with but a few exceptions, do not. These subsidiary voices, furthermore, usually move so slowly that they could not possibly compete for the listener's attention. The harmony, so far as it may have entered into aesthetic calculations at all, could have assumed a sense of drive only occasionally. Certainly no organizational scheme emerges from the play of harmonies with sufficient force and clarity to impress itself upon a listener. Machaut must have believed that his audience would derive enjoyment primarily from following the main melodic line, and that it would become aware of the contributions (harmonic and rhythmic) of the other voices only intermittently.[14]

In order to deal with Machaut's conception of narrative organization, then, it is necessary to study his treatment of the single line which dominates the texture. For his is an art based upon melodic design.

Underlying Machaut's melodic style seems to be the assumption that even rather florid lines can be constructed to suggest a basic sense of direction. For these lines give evidence that considerable care was taken to create the impression that what seems an elaborate play of curves, leaps, and scale passages amounts to little more than a highly decorated rise or descent. One senses, for instance, that the general level of tension associated with the higher register is ebbing all through a given passage, even though the passage may contain a number of returns toward the higher register or abrupt moves in one direction or another.

A simple case of this kind is shown in Example 2. Here the direct line of descent is broken only by the two circled notes C($\sharp$) and D, omission of which would leave a descending scale over the gamut of an octave. Certainly so brief an interruption hardly would

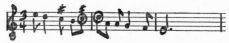

Example 2. *Se quanque amours* (ballade No. 21): Cantus, m. 3-5.

suffice to destroy the general sense of descent. Similarly, the decorative moves to neighboring notes do not conceal an octave descent in Example 3. (The notes of the descent are marked.) In some cases, a descent seems to take place in two stages, the second retracing

Example 3. *Une vipere* (ballade No. 27): Cantus, m. 1-4.

some of the ground covered by the first, but placed at a generally lower pitch level (Example 4). In retrospect, the relation between

Example 4. *Se pour ce muir* (ballade No. 36): Cantus, m. 25-28.

the low point of the first descent and the lower point reached at the end of the second is so clearly perceived that the intervening notes all come to seem little more than a delay. Even when the two descents begin at the same pitch, the reaching of a lower level by the second one provides a quality of continuation strong enough to impart a sense of general descent to the whole passage (Example 5).

Example 5. *De petit po* (ballade No. 18): Cantus, m. 1-5.

In many instances, long and leisurely descents are suggested by a series of curves rising to successively lower peaks. Such a passage of moderate length is shown in Example 6; a more extensive

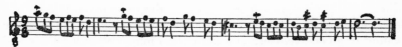

Example 6. *Ploures, dames* (ballade No. 32): Cantus, m. 41-46.

one is reproduced in Example 7. A similar technique is used to create a general sense of rise in Example 8.

Example 7. *Nes que on porroit* (ballade No. 33): Cantus, m. 30-41.

Example 8. *Pour ce que tous mes chans* (ballade No. 12): Cantus, m. 3-6.

It is clear, however, that Machaut was thinking of something more than merely imparting the suggestion that the line should at times develop a sense of direction despite a considerable degree of floridity. For the various sizes and types of curves so formed (the rises, descents, arches, etc.) give evidence of having been arranged in a succession designed to create an impression of dramatic development—of the growth and decline of tensions in a logical way. As the various ascending and descending passages (carrying connotations, respectively, of the generation and resolution of tension) are played off against each other, what might be termed a stressful situation seems to emerge, to unfold plausibly, and to reach resolution. The use of melodic decoration, then, probably can be viewed as an expedient designed to implement such a program; a technique of this kind, after all, would make it fairly easy to fashion the various sizes of curves required to suggest different rates of growth and decay of tension.

In order to give some idea of the means employed to effect a sense of logical sequence and of the extent of their application, I should like to present a number of studies of specific compositions. To lessen the tedium always involved in descriptions of music, however, I shall limit detailed and reasoned study to the ballades, and merely sketch the procedures to be found in the virelais and rondeaux.

Ballades

By the fourteenth century, the ballade had assumed a standard structure of three verses set to the same music, with each verse consisting of an opening couplet and an additional line (or set of lines), the last part of which served as a refrain (i.e., presented the same text in each verse). Since the two lines of the couplet invariably were set to the same music (with *ouvert* and *clos* endings, of course), the musical structure of the verse could be represented as A A B, with the B section containing the refrain. In just a few of Machaut's ballades, the last section also is repeated, so that the form becomes A A B B.

Machaut seems to have seen just two dramatic possibilities in this type of formal arrangement. Both, of course, are based upon the idea of establishing a sense of conflict between forces adding to the tension and others easing it—essential elements in any dramatic situation. In most cases, this conflict is made to seem more or less provisionally resolved at the end of the first part (i.e., after the repeated line of music), with a more serious challenge to the resolution offered and eventually overcome in the second part. In several ballades, on the other hand, the program involves an obviously most inadequate sense of resolution of tension at the end of the couplet, with steps taken to produce a more final-sounding impression by the end of the refrain, often despite the fact that couplet and refrain end with identical passages (the device sometimes called musical rhyme).

These two programs are implemented in so wide a variety of ways that generalization of any kind almost necessarily would involve oversimplification. At the risk of bogging down in detail, then, I shall present a fairly close study of a sizeable number of the ballades, describing the relations of the separate curves and attempting to piece together something of the underlying dramatic rationale.

A most frequently employed scheme involves the use of climax to suggest the greater challenge to the forces of resolution found in the second part of the ballade. In most of the compositions organized in this way, the climax comes at or near the beginning of the second part (i.e., immediately following the repeated section). Such is the case in the settings of *S'amours ne fait* (ballade No. 1 in Ludwig's edition), *On ne pourrait penser* (No. 3), *Biaute qui toutes autres* (No. 4), *Doulz amis* (No. 6), *Ne penses pas* (No. 10), *N'en fait, n'en dit* (No. 11), *Pour ce que tous mes chans* (No. 12), *Esperance qui m'asseure* (No. 13), *Dame par vous-Amis dolens-Sans cuer m'en vois* (No. 17), *De petit po* (No. 18), *Se quanque amours* (No. 21), *Tres douce dame* (No. 24), *Nes que on porroit* (No. 33), *Gais et jolis* (No. 35) and *Ma chiere dame* (No. 40).

The appropriateness of such a scheme is readily apparent. For the conclusion of the first part carries some connotation of restored equilibrium, of a stressful situation resolved to some extent. It is only natural to expect, then, that the conflict will become more serious if the piece continues at all, since it is suggested that the dramatic situation has not just been resumed, but has actually carried farther. There would hardly seem any reason for reopening a question that has been more or less resolved, after all, unless there was an intent to draw more significant consequences from it. The repeat of the first part, however, seems to run counter to this commitment in that it suggests that very little has been done to heighten the conflict of forces already presented. As a result, the expectation of intensification is even stronger; to avoid such a move now would be to introduce a distinctly anticlimactic element, leaving the listener puzzled about the purposes served by the second presentation of the conflict of forces. If the composer had no intention of eventually going farther—the listener might well ask—why did he bother to repeat the first section and thereby implant the whole pattern of growth and decay of tension so firmly in memory? He might be tempted to reach a judgment, intuitively, somewhat in the vein of the saying: The mountain labored and brought forth a mouse. Certainly there would be something of a comparable sense of incongruity in a tame ending to what had promised to develop into a highly dramatic situation.

It becomes clear, then, that something more significant probably should happen in the second part of the ballade—perhaps something that would act to bring the conflict to a point of crisis. Thus, a reasonable continuation might involve a sterner test of the will to resolve tension. A climactic passage appreciably overshooting anything found in the first part would fulfill just such a function, with a following descent easing the tension and establishing an atmosphere appropriate for the suggestion of termination.

The mere presence of a program of this type does not suffice to demonstrate primary reliance upon narrative resources. It still remains to be shown that the individual events contributing to the build-up of the dramatic structure flow smoothly into each other or create the illusion that each event represents a plausible continuation of the line of development. A convenient point of departure for the study of this question is provided by the problem of closure: what evidence is there of care taken, not only to fashion a smooth and logical flow of events, but also to create the impression that the conflict of forces represented is resolved, if only provisionally, at the end of the first part?

In the case of *N'en fait, n'en dit* (No. 11; Example 9) and of *Pour ce que tous mes chans* (No. 12), the play of forces is fashioned into a single curve which occupies the entire first part of the ballade (an inverted arch in the former and an arch in the latter). In view of the simplicity of the organization, there can be no question of either logical connection or provisional resolution of tensions. For a certain amount of complexity is required to make the relation between moments problematical, while the symmetrical quality of these two curves tends to suggest closure in itself.

Example 9. *N'en fait, n'en dit* (ballade No. 11): Cantus, m. 1-8.

In the remainder of ballades noted on pages 48-49, the play of forces is considerably more complex. In all but one of these compositions (*De petit po;* No. 18), a climax is placed near the end of the first part. A late climax of this kind, of course, is a move very well suited for suggesting closure, since it creates the impression that the conflict of forces has been brought to a head, at least for the time being, so that virtually any reasonably extended gesture toward easing the tension (a fairly prolonged descent, for example) would seem a resolution rather than merely a continuation.

There is one provision, however. That is that the climax itself must seem well motivated and a plausible outgrowth of the preceding sequence of events. It is to this question, then, that the study should now be turned: Is there evidence of care taken to build up a dramatic situation that would make the turn to climax seem an appropriate move?

In order to avoid needless repetition and unduly prolonged descriptions, it might be well to observe that there is no need to begin evaluating the sense of logical connection right from the beginning of the composition. For virtually any opening motion probably would prove acceptable to a listener as the starting point for the dramatic action. The only provision would be that the passage not be so long, complex, slowly moving, or redundant as to draw attention from the curve or direction being outlined and focus it upon the individual notes. That Machaut avoids these conditions is, I think, perfectly obvious. Only a very cursory inspection is required to verify that the opening of the main melodic line in each of the ballades quickly creates the impression of purposeful, directed motion.

The same applies to the second curve as well. As long as it manages to suggest a sense of direction, virtually any passage will be interpreted as a plausible response to the atmosphere established by the first. One might judge, for instance, that the second curve represents an amplification of the first (for instance, a longer descent or a broader arch), or a continuation of it, or a contrast or reaction to it. A reasonably sympathetic listener certainly would be willing to make the attempt—involuntarily, I would suggest—to find some means of relating almost any diverse action at this early stage in the dramatic development.

It is, then, the way the subsequent curves fit in with expectations engendered by the first two that determines whether or not the dramatic course of events will seem to proceed smoothly and logically. Thus, if the climax late in the first part of the ballade is itself to seem a natural turn of events, it must flow plausibly out of the commitments generated by the relation between the opening curves, taking subsequent modifications into account.

In Example 10, for instance, the appropriateness of the climax derives from the fact that the curves preceding it so unmistakably suggest a closed-off unit. The first appreciable motion (measures 2-4) forms an arch, but an arch whose close (on the pitch A)

Example 10. *Esperance qui m'asseure* (ballade No. 13): Cantus, m. 1-11.

seems anything but final since it collapses downward so suddenly at the end. It is quite in line with expectations, then, to go over the descent again, this time in a less precipitous manner. Such fulfillment of expectation lends something of a goallike quality appropriate for suggesting the close of a train of thought. The impression of close is reinforced in this case by the final coming to rest on the pitch D which is so clearly established as what today would be called a tonic at the opening of the piece. Where so strong a quality of close occurs, of course, it always seems appropriate to follow it with a sterner test of the will toward resolution. It is because the climax following represents just such a move, I would suggest, that it seems so well in place.

A similar type of organization is to be found in *Ne penses pas* (No. 10), where the first fourteen measures contain the obviously closed-off unit. In this case, however, the climactic high point near the ending (measure 15) does not really suggest a higher level of tension than that attained in an earlier peak reached in measure 6. But since the amount of time separating these two climaxes is quite long, and since the line lies rather low during the intervening period, the late move to the high note does not seem so much an exact return to a pitch touched earlier as it seems an independent gesture. As a result, it is still able to carry the suggestion that the conflict of forces has been brought to a head, to some degree, so that the following descent represents a tentative resolution.

The appropriateness of the climax in *S'amours ne fait* (No. 1; Example 11), on the other hand, can be traced to the fact that it

Example 11. *S'amours ne fait* (ballade No. 1): Cantus, m. 1-17.

provides a plausible reaction to the situation as it has been developed up to that point. That is to say, the climax is preceded by three separate descents (measures 1-3, 4-5, and 6-7), each suggesting some increase in intensity. (Although the first two of these traverse roughly the same gamut, the greater rhythmic activity of the second and the more tentative quality of its ending clearly indicate a decline in stability and hence a rise in tension.) Thus, by the time the third descent gets underway, it has become clear that a sense of close will virtually require the easing of tension such as might be provided by a long and leisurely descent. While the beginning of the third descent gives promise of fulfilling this commitment, the fact that it is so soon cut off suggests that the attempt at resolution has been thwarted. A situation such as this carries some connotation of deadlock: neither force seems able to overcome the other. One way of breaking out of such an impasse— a situation fraught with frustration—would involve a bold stroke, such as is here provided by the immediate move to climax. That this is a plausible turn of events may be judged easily by an observation of human behavior: where frustration occurs, the consequence is usually some sort of affective reaction[15]—perhaps in the form of colorful language or in a violent act. The abrupt move to climax at this point, I would suggest, seems most appropriate because its highly impassioned quality bears such a distinct resemblance to an affective reaction of this kind.[16]

In *Doulz amis* (No. 6; Example 12), the opening situation is established by two descents (measures 1-4 and 5-6) separated by the upward leap of a tritone. Because the second of these lies

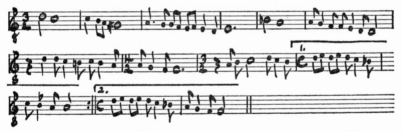

Example 12. *Doulz amis* (ballade No. 6): Cantus, m. 1-13.

generally lower than the first, it seems merely a delayed continuation of a general descent, leaving the impression that the tritone leap—the only significant motion upward in these measures— represents an attempt to break away from the prevailing downward motion. Since this attempt obviously has been less than successful, one is well prepared to hear the stronger attempt presented in measure 7. The descent following, however, seems cut off prematurely; it is called to a halt before reaching the lower portions of the gamut, setting the stage nicely for a subsequent climax and resolving descent (measures 9-13) almost exactly as described in connection with *S'amours ne fait.*

A rising trend gives rise to the climax and makes it seem plausible in *Gais et jolis* (No. 35; Example 13). The first two curves are descents (measures 1-6 and 7-12), the second of which lies generally higher than the first. The third curve contributes to the sense of rising intensity by opening with the first steady motion upward: a rise of a sixth, mostly along the scale, to the climactic note in measure 14. Because of the exertion implied by this type of motion, the following descent represents a most welcome easing

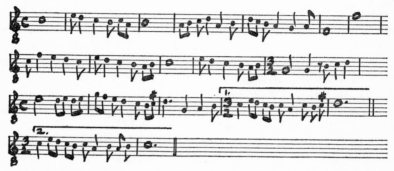

Example 13. *Gais et jolis* (ballade No. 35): Cantus, m. 1-19.

of tension, so welcome that it seems to bring the implied conflict of forces to a close, at least provisionally.

The easing of tension, however, is not permitted to run the course now expected. What has promised to be a long descent, with internal twists, is interrupted by a rather sizeable leap downward (measure 15), and this is followed by a general rise toward the cadence. Thus it seems that the descent has encountered an obstacle (since the line turns back upward just before the leap), the over-coming of which has led too far, that is, to a too sudden quitting of the pitch area around middle C. In order to restore the sense of stability required to suggest finality, then, some motion toward accomplishing a compromise would be in place—essentially what the rise accomplishes.

The climax also seems a natural outcome of a rising trend in *Nes que on porroit* (No. 33; Example 14), but the sense of rising intensity is achieved in quite a different manner. In this piece, the recurrence of a little melodic figure (each recurrence is marked in Example 14) cuts the melody into a rondolike series of excursions. These excursions, then, are what reflect a trend toward

Example 14. *Nes que on porroit* (ballade No. 33): Cantus, m. 1-23.

greater intensity: the second (measures 5-6) lies higher than the first (measures 1-2) and uses more dramatic leaps; while the third (measures 10-14) hits a still higher note, remains more stubbornly in the high register before descending, and lasts considerably longer, so that it assumes something of the function of a climax, bringing the situation to a head so that a resolution can be effected. At the end of this section an application of what I have termed the countercurrent can be seen: a brief flare-up (measures 17-18) before the final descent.

The tension leading into the climax is generated by the juxtaposition of passages in contrasting registers in *On ne porroit penser* (No. 3; Example 15). Here the first curve lies mostly at or above

Example 15. *On ne porroit penser* (ballade No. 3): Cantus, m. 1-15.

the pitch D (measures 1-3), while the second curve, rhythmically very similar to the ending of the first, lies mostly a fourth lower at or below the pitch A, leaving a sense of antithetical relationship and hence of unresolved tension. The following passage (measures 6-8) represents an attempt to ease this tension by effecting a descent that should unite the high and low registers in a single curve. Still the low register is approached and left by a leap (measures 7-8), implying that this attempt has not yet been fully successful. Once again, then, there is some sense of deadlock—of inability to accomplish the expected. Thus, the bold move to the climax that follows (measure 9) would seem well in place, as explained in connection with *S'amours ne fait,* as a plausible reaction to the sense of frustration inherent in the situation. The following descent, of course, serves to ease the tension considerably, both by virtue of its own downward direction and because it finally seems to fulfill a long-sensed commitment. The result is some quality of provisional resolution of the conflict of forces.

A similar establishment of tension by juxtaposition of contrasting registers can be seen in *De petit po* (No. 18; Example 16). In this case, indeed, the sense of close depends almost entirely upon the suggestion that the tension generated in this way is

Example 16. *De petit po* (ballade No. 18): Cantus, m. 1-20.

resolved, since no move to a climax is involved. The passages in the low register in this work (measures 8-10 and 14-15) are exceedingly brief and develop little sense of directed motion, quite in contrast to the clearly shaped and directed curves in the higher portions of the register. As a result, they sound like interruptions of underlying motions rather than logically motivated continuations. What is expected after each one, because of the element of surprise that goes with the sense of interruption, is a return to something like the qualities in evidence before the interruption occurred; in this case, to a higher register and to a fluid, directed line. This is the pattern of events that unfolds twice: the first time leading to a cadence that seems inconclusive, and the second time with a more final-sounding cadence, bringing the conflict of forces and the opening section of the ballade to a close.

It is clear, then, that there is abundant evidence of care taken both to imbue the flow of events with a sense of plausibility and to create an impression of at least provisional resolution of the conflict at the end of the first part of these ballades. Indeed, by means of calculations such as these, I would suggest, this can be shown to be true for each of the ballades noted on pages 48-49. The general impression is much the same in each case: establishment of some kind of situation involving what might be termed a conflict between forces tending to generate and ease tensions, and a working out of this conflict to the point where it can be resolved provisionally. With the literal repeat of all but the last few measures of this first section, the stage is set for the sterner test of the will toward a resolution posed by the climax at or near the beginning of the second part.

The sense of climax for the ballade as a whole (i.e., after the double bar) is achieved in most cases by qualitative means, that is, by reaching a pitch appreciably higher than any found in the first part.[17] Such is the case in *S'amours ne fait* (No. 1), *Biaute qui toutes autres* (No. 4), *Doulz amis* (No. 6), *Ne penses pas* (No. 10), *N'en fait, n'en dit* (No. 11), *Pour ce que tous mes chans* (No. 12), *Dame, par vous* (No. 17), *De petit po* (No. 18), *Tres douce dame* (No. 24) and *Gais et jolis* (No. 35). In some ballades, however, the sense of climax is brought about quantitatively. That is to say that the highest pitch reached is no higher than the climax in the first part, but the line remains at or around that pitch appreciably longer. In a vocal style, of course, this would produce a sense of increased strain just as clearly as reaching for a higher pitch. Included in this category are *On ne porroit penser* (No. 3), *Esperance qui m'asseure* (No. 13), *Se quanque amours* (No. 21), *Nes que on porroit* (No. 33) and *Ma chiere dame* (No. 40).[18]

In each of the ballades in these two categories, the climax that opens the second part is followed, as is only to be expected, by some kind of descent or an easing of the tension. Again, however, the treatments are highly individual. In some instances, indeed, the descents are turned to entirely different purposes.

Perhaps the simplest program of this kind involves a leisurely, decorated descent from the climactic pitch. The decoration is usually rich enough to create a series of internal curves, descents, twists and turns, so that the outline of the descent is recognizable only by means of the successively lower high points reached. Such is the case, for instance, in Example 17 (the notes outlining this descent are marked, where, in addition, a final flare-up in the last three measures acts as a countercurrent, enhancing the sense of finality in the following cadence.[19]

Example 17. *N'en fait, n'en dit* (ballade No. 11): Cantus, m. 9-19.

In *Tres douce dame* (No. 24; Example 18), a clearly sensed commitment to descent is thwarted by the introduction of a brief

Example 18. *Tres douce dame* (ballade No. 24): Cantus, m. 13-26.

rising trend. This trend is formed by a series of descents placing progressively less emphasis on the motion downward: the descent in measures 18-20 is shorter than the one preceding and does not reach as far downward; the next one (measures 21-22) is even shorter and shallower. Once again, then, there is a suggestion of the frustration of a clearly expected move, making the subsequent move to a higher pitch (measure 22) seem most appropriate. What follows, of course, is now sensed as a resolving descent. The program seems quite clear: the brief deemphasis of descent in measures 18-22 is an interruption of the will toward resolution or another test of the determination to resolve tensions, though not as strong a test as was offered at the beginning of the second part of the ballade.

A similar thwarting of expected descents creates quite different consequences in *S'amours ne fait* (No. 1; Example 19). Here the climax is followed first by a descent, as might have been expected, but then (from measure 26 on) by an obvious attempt to return to the high register. Clearly, the descent was too direct and open-ended to impart any sense of finality. The determined rise of measures 26-30 suggests that the battle to achieve resolution is not to be won so easily; there is still a good deal of energy left in the forces testing the will toward resolution. A reasonable expec-

Example 19. *S'amours ne fait* (ballade No. 1): Cantus, m. 18-41.

tation, then, would be that another attempt to ease tension by means of a descent would take place, as is indeed the case beginning in measure 30. This attempt is thwarted also, however, in that the line is turned back upward to form an inverted arch (measures 31-33), implying that the disruptive forces (i.e., those opposing the sense of resolution) still have not given up. A reasonable general expectation now would be of an alternation of descents and rises, with the former gradually gaining ground—essentially what is provided in measures 34-39.

Interestingly enough, the ballade ends not with a full realization of the commitment to descend, but rather by using this commitment as a foil. Knowing how heavy the downward pull must now seem, Machaut turns to a high, strong, almost heroic sounding ending (measures 40-41), an ending probably designed to reflect the resolve implied by the text of the refrain: "*qu'en ma dolour languir jusqu'a la mort.*"

Viewed in retrospect, then, the entire second part of this ballade could be interpreted as an attempt to create the kind of atmosphere in which the final statement would seem most heroic and most resolute. Suggesting that a descent was imminent and then running counter to this implication could well have been an expedient designed to achieve this end. That this reflects careful planning in terms of commitments and trends generated by linear curves, just as well as if the commitment to descent had been realized more fully, seems beyond question.[20]

A much simpler dramatic program by far is to be found in *Biaute qui toutes autres* (No. 4; Example 20), a program which

Example 20. *Biaute qui toutes autres* (ballade No. 4): Cantus, m. 11-22.

involves placing progressively greater emphasis on the descending element. At first, the element of descent is restricted to a downward leap (measure 11). In the following curve it takes the form of a slightly decorated scalar descent (an obvious amplification of the descending motif); a descent, however, that is balanced to some degree by a turn back toward the upper register making it into an inverted arch (measures 13-14). The next descent has no such turning back (measures 15-16), while the last one is considerably longer and thus realizes the commitment to suggest resolution more fully. This final descent, indeed, is most striking in effect, partly because of the clarity of outline and direction associated with the sequential motion it describes—a clarity all the more impressive because of the rather hazy, nebulous way in which the other curves are outlined—and partly because, as is the case in many other ballades, it represents a return of the musical segment which has already twice brought the first part of the composition to an end. All of this merely serves to enhance the significance of this descent, making it more capable of suggesting termination convincingly.[21]

Each of these fifteen ballades, then, (the ones with a climax placed at or near the beginning of the second part) reflect a considerable degree of planning in terms of generation and release of tension, as well as in terms of providing moves reasonably well in line with expectations. Unless I have misjudged completely, the evidence suggests that the first part probably was designed, not only to present a smooth and convincing flow of events in its own right, but also to set the stage for the main climax that follows. The remainder of the piece is devoted to bringing the tension suggested by the climax to some kind of resolution. What might be called the dramatic program is clear: generation of tension—provisional resolution (all repeated)—crisis—final resolution.

A similar dramatic program is to be found in five more of the ballades, the only difference being that the climax is placed, not at the beginning of the second part, but somewhere farther along in it. Such is the case in *Helas tant ay dolour* (No. 2), *De desconfort* (No. 8), *Je ne cuit pas* (No. 14), *Je suis aussi* (No. 20) and *De toutes flours* (No. 31). The rationale is much the same as in the compositions discussed up to this point: a more or less provisional resolution to the conflict of forces at the end of the first part, and a sterner test of the will to resolve tensions in the second. The only thing is that this sterner test takes shape gradually, after some additional play of forces, instead of being introduced immediately after the second ending. It is clear, furthermore, that steps were taken to make the additional play of forces seem somehow more significant and more critical dramatically than the conflict presented in the first part of the ballade. This is accomplished either by placing greater emphasis on the high register, or by a freer mixing of rising and descending passages.

A typical case of this kind can be seen in *De desconfort* (No. 8; Example 21). The first part obviously represents a fairly well closed-off unit, what with the emphasis on descent from the climactic pitch reached in measure 4 and again in measure 6. In the second part, a rising trend begins to be felt for the first time in the

Example 21. *De desconfort* (ballade No. 8): Cantus.

composition; it is effected by means of a series of descents which are cut off in one way or another. Thus, in the first of these descents (measures 14-16), the line turns back upward, but only at the last moment; in the next one (measures 16-18), a similar return is more fully developed into the shape of an inverted arch; and in the last one, the descent is not just turned upward, but abandoned in favor of an abrupt move to the high register followed by a direct rise to the climactic note (measures 20-22). In this way, the climax is made to seem a plausible outcome to a rising trend. At the same time, the increased emphasis on motion upward has the effect of making the conflict of forces seem more powerful, more significant, than it did in the first part of the ballade. The whole, then, resembles a drama in which the conflict of forces is gradually more sharply outlined until it is brought to a head by this late climax.

By calculations such as these involving the placement of the climax, I would suggest that a clear dramatic organization can be found in twenty of the forty-one [22] ballades: in Ludwig's order, numbers 1-4, 6, 8, 10-14, 17, 18, 20, 21, 24, 31, 33, 35, and 40. In the remaining ballades, the sense of unfolding drama does not depend upon the suggestion of climax. In ten of these, however, the scheme employed seems most closely related to those described above; it involves a similar suggestion, although by means other than climax, of a greater challenge to the will toward resolution in the second part. Something of this sort is to be found in *J'aim mieus languir* (No. 7), *Il m'est avis* (No. 22), *Honte, paour* (No. 25), *Donnez signeurs* (No. 26), *Une vipere* (No. 27), *Ne quier veoir* (No. 34B [23]), *Je puis trop bien* (No. 28), *De triste cuer* (No. 29A [24]), *Phyton, le mervilleus serpent* (No. 38), and *Mes esperis* (No. 39).

In all but the last four of these, the sense of greater challenge results from a more serious upward motion to the line in the second part. Since the first parts of these ballades consist almost entirely of descents—even brief upward moves are generally incorporated into larger descending patterns—the introduction of a rising line in the second part suggests a new degree of determination and hence a greater challenge to the will toward resolution.[25] In *Honte, paour,* for instance, the first part consists essentially of three descents (measures 1-3, 4-9, and 10-14) plus a fourth in the second ending (Example 22). The brief upward moves in measures 5 and 6 do not really serve to break the general sense of descent; they merely seem part of a process designed to embroider the line and to delay the inevitable descent. Even the more extended rise in

Example 22. *Honte, paour* (ballade No. 25): Cantus.

measure 8 is cut off abruptly by a reversion to the low register. In none of these instances did the rising element assume anything more than a function of contrast to the prevailing tendency toward descent. Thus, when a direct rise of an octave is spread over some three measures in the second part (measures 18-21), the sense of increased challenge is unmistakable. What follows is an eventual reassertion of the will toward resolution by means of a series of descents. Because a more powerful challenge has been overcome, the sense of resolution itself seems considerably stronger than it was at the end of the first part.

In addition, it may be noted that the arrival at the cadence on B♭ seems far more final in the second part than in the first, in spite of the fact that the same closing formula is used in both sections. This can be attributed, in large measure, to the fact that the formula fits into a general pattern of descent in the second part —its high point F (measure 28) is a step lower than the high point of the curve preceding (measure 25)—while in the first part no such relation can be observed. Thus there is a greater degree of momentum to the downward motion to B♭ in the second part and a greater feeling of propriety at the arrival there. The factor of added momentum works together with the overcoming of a greater challenge to suggest a more final resolution.[26]

In three of the other four ballades in this category (*Je puis trop bien, De triste cuer* and *Phyton, le mervilleus serpent*), the greater challenge in the second part is suggested not by a rise, but by a passage which develops little sense of direction. The lack of direction in *Phyton, le mervilleus serpent* (Example 23), for instance, can be traced partly to an almost redundant hovering about the pitches D, C, and B in measures 26-32 (notice that even the

Example 23. *Phyton, le mervilleus serpent* (ballade No. 38): Cantus.

brief flare-up in measure 29 issues back directly into this environment), partly to a lessening of rhythmic activity, and partly to the series of quick and abrupt shifts in register in measures 32-35. Obviously, passages like these pose a problem in interpretation to the listener. The whole sense of logical progress threatens to disintegrate into a series of effects without much suggestion of a thread of connection between the events. With the return of clearly directed curves—a sense of return strengthened by a clear reference to the passage that ended Part I (from measure 36 on)—this threat of discontinuity seems to have been overcome, allowing the line to settle into the ending with a quality of finality.

The effect is reinforced by cadential practice in *Je puis trop bien* (No. 28; Example 24). With the exception of the first ending, each of the phrases in the first part of this ballade issues into a cadence on C. The directionless passage (measures 17-23), then, heightens the sense of tension and is followed by an obviously

Example 24. *Je puis trop bien* (ballade No. 28): Cantus.

feeble attempt (feeble because of the brevity of the approach) to return to definition of C and thereby ease the tension (measures 24-25). With the restoration of a sense of direction (measure 26) comes a move into a cadence on what is obviously the wrong pitch (D). The quality of resolution imparted by the descent of the last phrase is then reinforced by the sense of return to definition of the well remembered tonal center C.

A similar sense of increased challenge is achieved by a suggestion of greater freedom and scope to the motion in *Mes esperis* (No. 39; Example 25), the remaining ballade in this category. Here all the motion in the first part is circumscribed; it is clearly directed and purposeful but yet held within a narrow range, often going over the same small group of notes several times. At the beginning of the second part are to be found the only bold steps taken in this melody, including a downward sweep over the range of a ninth and an immediately following upward leap covering the same interval. The more circumscribed motion gradually sets in again, leading to a clear sense of relief—an easing of tension —appropriate for the suggestion of termination.

In nine more ballades, the dramatic structure is brought about in quite a different way. It is the result not so much of a suggestion of greater challenge in Part II, as of one of more adequate resolution. In each of these pieces, something is done to undermine the sense of finality at both endings of Part I, so that not even a tenta-

Example 25. *Mes esperis* (ballade No. 39): Cantus.

tive sense of resolution is created. In some cases, the occurrence of
rather exciting events just before the ending accounts for this
unsettled feeling. In *Riches d'amour* (No. 5), for instance, an unexpected and most dramatic upward leap of an octave creates the
excitement—appropriately enough between the phrases of text
povres d'espoir and *et garnis de desir*. The descent that eventually
sets in is both too rapid and too brief to suggest even a provisional
resolution adequately. In other cases (e.g., *Se je me pleing;* No.
15), an obvious commitment to a lengthy descent is simply not
fulfilled. In still other cases (e.g., *De fortune;* No. 23), what
promises to be an ending descent is turned back upward into an
inverted arch.

During the second parts of these ballades, steps are taken
to bring about something like an adequate sense of resolution.
Some idea of how this is worked out can be seen in Example 26. In
the first part of this piece, considerable significance is imparted
to a sojourn at a climactic pitch level (measures 13-15), both
because it is approached by means of a deliberate rise and because
there is an implication of a stubborn unwillingness to relinquish

the high pitch-level so painstakingly achieved. The first ending contains a descent that is both too brief and too shallow to suggest even tentative resolution adequately. Although the descent lasts longer in the second ending, it is not much deeper and it is accomplished with a considerable increase in rhythmic activity—all of which compromises the suggestion of resolution; there seems to be more of a drive into this cadence than a drift. After the second ending comes a passage obviously designed to provide some relief

Example 26. *Ploures dames* (ballade No. 32): Cantus.

to the high tension resulting from the inadequate suggestion of resolution, with the remainder of the second part given over to achieving a more satisfactory sense of release. This more satisfactory release is accomplished despite the use of a climax (measures 30-33) very similar to that found in Part I and an ending passage identical to that which brought the first part to a close. The reason this rhythmically driving descent now seems so much better able to suggest resolution is that it is serving to resolve not just the tension suggested by the climax (as was the case in Part I), but also the conflict of forces that sets in after the climax. For between the climax and the ending descent is inserted a rather long curve (measures 33-39) moving first down, then up again (though not as high), and then down once more—suggesting some additional conflict between rising and descending forces—a type of conflict in which the descent at the end seems to offer a perfectly appropriate resolution. It is, then, by separating the descent from the climax—by making it seem that it has been withheld until the time grew more ripe for it—that the sense of finality is achieved.

Something quite similar can be seen in five more ballades: *Dame, de qui toute ma joie vient* from the *Remède de Fortune*, *Dame, comment qu'amez de vous ne soie* (No. 16), *Amours me fait desirer* (No. 19), *Pas de tor* (No. 30), and *Se pour ce muir* (No. 36). In each of these, the device of musical rhyme is used (i.e., the same passage brings both the couplet and the refrain to a close), but actions are taken in the second part to convert the passage that seemed to effect so inadequate a sense of resolution at the end of Part I into a genuinely final-sounding close.

The sense of inadequacy conveyed by the second endings in the first three of these works can be traced to an unexpected turn to a cadence on B♭. In *Amours me fait desirer* (Example 27), for instance, the move to B♭ in the second ending to Part I seems

Example 27. *Amours me fait desirer* (ballade No. 19): Cantus.

something of an afterthought. For the cantus in almost the entire first part (from measure 2 on) clearly outlines an inverted arch flowing naturally into the cadence on D found in measure 11 (measure 13 in the second ending). Thus the musical thought seems fairly complete at this point and the turn toward B♭ in the second ending assumes something of the quality of an arbitrary addition. In the second part, on the other hand, this same cadence to D no longer seems a natural outcome of the motion, but rather interrupts its normal flow. For it comes immediately after a rather striking and not quite expected move back up to the high register (measures 24-25), at a time, in other words, when some large-scale easing of tension would seem appropriate. Coming so soon after such an exciting turn of events, the cadence hardly seems strong enough to resolve the tension produced by that dramatic action, so that, quite in contrast to what happened in Part I, the expectation now is that the line will resume its descent and proceed to a more satisfactory resolution. Thus the move to the cadence on Bb at this point fits in with expectations and assumes something of the role of a culmination, instead of suggesting an arbitrary addition to an already closed musical thought.

In *Dame, comment qu'amez de vous ne soie*,[27] on the other hand, it is a question of tonic definition that accounts for the difference in the quality of finality. The definition of Bb as tonic—the point of repose—begins too late in the first part to effect a convincing close by means of a cadence ending on that pitch. Just a few measures before the ending (measures 11-13), the line seems to define first G (although this is actually a double leading-tone cadence to C and then D. In the second part, however, steps are taken early to define Bb as tonic. For each of the descents in this part is followed by a little afterthought that closes off the phrase— almost a question-answer relationship—and both these afterthoughts come to rest on Bb. Still, each of these cadences on Bb seems rather awkwardly achieved, if only because the approaches are so brief and hence so obviously out of balance with the preceding descents. The final descent, which represented such a surprise in the first part, now assumes something of the function of a coda: a more graceful and final-sounding approach to a closing pitch already defined, although somewhat more awkwardly.

The element of surprise in the first part of *Pas de tor* (No. 30) can be traced to the fact that the ending represents one of the few attempts (and the only successful one) to turn the line upward. Otherwise the entire first part is dominated by the descending element: two broad but fairly direct descents with a single countercurrent (measures 7-8). In the second part, on the other hand, although the descending element still dominates, less of a sense of directness attaches to the downward motion. Almost the whole of this part is given over to a very heavily decorated descent in which the general downward direction is suggested only by successively lower peaks (A in measure 32, G in measure 36, F in measure 43, and E in measure 47). This, of course, allows considerable opportunity for internal conflicts between the rising and descending elements to develop between the rather widely spaced notes outlining the descent. So, for instance, two curves that begin as if they were going to pursue descending courses are turned back upward, at least temporarily, to form inverted arches (measures 32-35 and 43-45); another phrase moves directly upward (measures 40-42). The general descent is by no means as unquestioned and as free of resistance as in the first part of the ballade. All of which would make the turn upward at the end seem more a reasonable outcome of the struggle in evidence for some time than the surprising turn of events that it represented at the end of the first part.

In *Se pour ce muir* (No. 36), the first part seems fairly well closed off and is followed by what promises to be a general rise to a climax. Although this climax (measures 29-30) does not appreciably top that presented in Part I, additional tension is generated immediately after it when, instead of the gradual descent expected, an abrupt leap downward takes place. The remainder of the piece can be interpreted as a series of attempts to resolve the tension by returning to the situation from which the surprising event was launched, that is to the climactic pitch G, and effecting a more satisfactory resolution. After some play of forces, this is accomplished with the return of the material from the second ending. The descent that follows, although almost exactly the same as in the second ending, now carries a considerably greater connotation of finality; in addition to resolving the tension generated by a climax, it also releases that produced by the surprise of an abrupt departure from the climactic register.

The three ballades remaining in this category can be dealt with fairly briefly. In *Riches de'amour* (No. 5) and *Se je me pleing* (No. 15), the second parts open with passages obviously designed to create some sense of relief. In the case of the former, a play of forces sets in after the relief, leading to a return to, but not an overshooting of, the pitch that marked the climax in Part I. The descent that follows is considerably less precipitous than the corresponding passage in the first part, and thus seems better able to suggest a resolution of tensions. In *Se je me pleing*, on the other hand, the sense of relief that results from decreased rhythmic activity and a line that seems not to develop much sense of direction (measures

13-16), gives way to an obvious conflict between rising and descending passages (descent in measures 17-18, rise in measures 19-23). The conflict is resolved by the clearly outlined and thus quite striking descent that ends the refrain.

In *De fortune* (No. 23), the first part comes to a close with an inverted arch (measures 7-13) which begins and ends on the same climactic pitch (on A). The return to exactly the same pitch represents something of a surprise—a demonstration of an unsuspected degree of determination—so that the following brief descent does not suggest anything like an adequate resolution. The second part of the ballade is given over to a series of attempts to achieve a more satisfactory release by means of descent. These attempts to descend are cut off by an unexpected leap downward (measure 21) and turned back upward to form inverted arches (measures 23-24 and 27). Each time, however, the descending element seems to gain a little ground, so that the ending descent is seen as the last link in a chain of events placing progressively greater emphasis on the descending element. As a result, it proves far better able to suggest a sense of resolution than did the same passage at the end of the first part.

There are two ballades, finally, in which evidence of careful design of the cantus is not entirely clear-cut: *Dame, ne regardes pas* (No. 9) and *En amer a douce vie* from the *Remède de Fortune*. In both cases, a program that seems in the process of being worked out carefully is undermined by some questionable actions taken toward the end of the piece. In *Dame, ne regardes pas* (Example 28), for instance, a sense of careful design is clear in the first forty-four measures. The program involves several attempts to effect a resolution of tensions by means of a series of descents, only the last of which (measures 34-44) seems entirely successful. It is the very success of this last attempt that undermines the design of the whole. For it is difficult to see what dramatic function can have been fulfilled by the curves presented in the measures that follow (45-65). After so complete a sense of close, one might consider a greater challenge to the resolving tendency an appropriate move; but it is difficult to view what follows as in any way a greater challenge than those that have already been presented. Or, it might seem plausible to interpret what follows as a very minor challenge to the resolving tendency—a brief flare-up before settling into the close. But the material presented does not lend itself to such a judgment either. At least one might expect another leisurely descent to bring the ballade to a close; again, however, this is not

Example 28. *Dame, ne regardes pas* (ballade No. 9): Cantus.

what happens. It is hard to avoid the impression that the last twenty measures introduce a train of thought not really called for by the context and not really assimilated into the dramatic structure. They seem to represent an arbitrarily inserted turn of events rather than one that contributes to a logical unfolding of ideas.

Clearly, however, these are exceptional cases. In all but these two of the forty-one ballades, Machaut's calculations seem sure and true. He was obviously out to fashion a sense of logical narration by organizing the curves of his main melodic line in these compositions.

The Virelais and Rondeaux

The polyphonic virelais and rondeaux offer evidence of much the same kind of concern for organizing individual melodic curves in accord with dramatic programs. True to my promise, however, I shall merely sketch out this evidence, leaving it to the reader to check the accuracy of my assessments by referring to Ludwig's edition.

In the virelais, the programs seem somewhat simpler, probably because of the influence of the repeat form called for by the poetic structure. In these pieces, of course, the opening line of music is heard again within each verse and once more between the verses as a refrain: A b b a A b b a A b b a A. Thus a sense of termination cannot be developed in the leisurely manner found in the ballades, that is, after all of the musical maneuvering contained in the composition has taken place. Rather it must be suggested, at least to some degree, by the end of the first line of music.

Of the eight polyphonic virelais contained in Ludwig's edition, five make use of a climax followed by a resolving descent of one kind or another to create this sense of finality. In No. 27, No. 32, and No. 37, the climax is reached at or before the midpoint of the first section, and is followed by a long, leisurely descent with internal twists and turns which allow ample time for a sense of resolution to take effect. In No. 26 and No. 29, however, the climax falls too late in the first part to allow for the kind of leisurely descent required to suggest resolution adequately. In the case of the former, a rather rapid descent is followed by the addition of a virtually static cadential passage in the register between the extremes of pitch touched by the descent from the climax. The effect is of something like a restoration of equilibrium by the cadence following an unexpected collapse, a quality most appropriate for suggesting termination. In No. 29, on the other hand, the climax and closing descent are preceded by the only appreciable rise contained in the first section. As a result, the impression is of a challenge overcome, with an attendant strengthening of the sense of finality.

In virelai No. 31, the quality of finality is created by means of two very similar inverted arches, only the second of which issues into a satisfactory cadence. The impression is that the failure of the first curve to find an adequate sense of resolution led, very naturally, to another attempt of the same kind, an attempt which was more successful.

In the remaining two virelais, it is the resolution of tension generated by abrupt changes in register that accounts for the sense of finality. While a rather carefully worked out program can be found in No. 38, there does not seem to be the same degree of concern for following out expectations in No. 36. For in No. 36, a rapid move down from an early climax is followed not by any attempt to return to a higher register, but by an additional leap downward into the very low register (measures 9-10)—undoubtedly causing some sense of shock. Since there is no evidence of an attempt to incorporate the sense of surprise generated in this way into a dramatic plan, this seems an awkward spot—a spot to be over-looked and forgotten in the press of subsequent events—rather than an integral part of an unfolding narrative scheme.

The function of the second line of music (the line repre-sented by the symbol "b" in the diagram presented earlier) invari-ably is to offer contrast. In most cases, this is accomplished by means of something like a climactic effect. Thus, in No. 26, No. 27, No. 36, and No. 37, the second part as a whole lies appreciably higher than the first, while in No. 38, the second part contains a descent from a considerably higher pitch than any touched in the first part. In No. 32, on the other hand, the same climactic pitch is reached in both the first and second lines of music, but the approach to this pitch seems more determined in the second part; it is accomplished here by means of the only prolonged rise in the composition. In No. 29 and No. 31, finally, the sense of contrast is created by means of procedures (abrupt changes in register, repetitions of just a few pitches almost to the point of redundancy, frequent confinement within narrow boundaries of pitch) which tend to destroy any quality of directed motion. In these cases, no less than in those described earlier, I would sug-gest that the return to the first line of music clearly represents a relief.

Unlike the poetic forms of virelai and ballade, the rondeau consists of only one stanza which generally contains a two-line refrain and three verses. In Machaut's poems the refrain is pre-sented in its entirety at the beginning and followed by the first verse and then the first line of the refrain. Next come the second and third verses followed by the refrain in its entirety. Since the first two verses invariably are set to the music used with the first line of the refrain, while the third verse is similarly set to the music of the second line of the refrain, the musical repeat scheme can be represented as follows (using capital letters to indicate refrain elements): A B a A a b A B. In No. 5, No. 10, No. 11, and No. 13, this scheme is magnified, so to speak, by the use of internal repeats. Thus, the musical form of the first of these can be represented as A A A B B B a a a A A A a a a b b b A A A B B B, while that of the other three is A A B a a A A a a b A A B.

One of the most striking differences in Machaut's treatment

of the rondeaux, as opposed to the ballades and virelais, is a tendency to bring the piece to a close in what can only be described as a provisional way. That is, so that the tensions generated during the course of the composition are not fully released at the end by means of a resolving descent, but rather give the impression of a question left open. This is the case in the rondelet from the *Remède de Fortune* and in the rondeaux numbered 2, 4, 5, 7, 9, 13, and 20 in Ludwig's edition. For the most part, these "open" endings are carefully prepared, just as was true in the few instances of this kind found in the ballades.

In general, the evidences of care in the arrangement of the sequence of events are quite similar to those already described in connection with the ballades and virelais. Placement of the climax plays some role in eight of the twenty-one compositions in this genre.[28] The climax is introduced in the second line of music (the "b" or "B" in the diagram presented earlier) in all but two of these. In No. 2, No. 4, No. 7, and No. 9, it is introduced as an appropriate reaction either to a prolonged sojourn in a low register or to a fairly long descent, while there is a buildup to it in No. 5 and No. 19. In each case, what follows is a resolving descent of some proportions. There is some slight turning back after the descent, however, in No. 2, No. 5, and No. 9, while in No. 4 and No. 7, the descent is so precipitous as to prepare one to expect a somewhat stronger return to a higher register as a means of restoring the sense of equilibrium. In No. 3 and No. 15, on the other hand, the climax falls near the end of the first line of music, with the second line given over to gradually increasing emphasis on descent.

Another group of rondeaux makes use of other means of suggesting additional challenge to the resolving tendency. In No. 20 and No. 21, the challenge is projected by a sustained rising passage near the beginning of the second part, the only such passage in each of these pieces. A wandering or redundant section—one, at any rate, that develops little sense of direction—accomplishes the same purpose in No. 6, No. 8, No. 10, No. 11, No. 13, and No. 18. When a descent eventually does set in in each of these cases, it gives the impression of resolving the tension and uncertainty engendered by this aimless passage.

In No. 17, the challenge is not to a resolving tendency, but to a circumspect kind of movement. In most of this rondeau, the line moves hesitantly, almost timidly, as though afraid to commit itself to prolonged motion in a given direction. A fairly long sequential descent at the beginning of the second line of music provides a challenge to the prevailing mode of motion that is overcome by a passage incorporating material already presented in the first line; namely, the phrases that brought the first part to a close plus an approach to a cadence found earlier in the piece (measures 5-7). Just how much of a challenge this is, and how clear the sense of restoration that ensues, can be judged from the fact that while this passage occupies some twenty-one beats, elsewhere in the composition the longest motion in any direction takes just seven.

In No. 12, the cantus consists of a series of descents, only the last of which issues directly into a cadence that resolves the tension fully. Other of the descents contribute to the feeling of where the tonic lies (G), but in each case the arrival at this note is by means of a cadential formula tacked on after the completion of the descent—an afterthought rather than a direct result.

Rondeau No. 14, the famed *Ma fin est mon commencement,* offers some problems in interpretation. For one thing, it is the voice labelled tenor that is here provided with text. As Reaney puts it:

> According to the text, the middle part is the tenor, but it may play the part of cantus here, since it is the only voice provided with a text. According to Ludwig the top voice should be interpreted as an instrumental tenor, and this is possible but not altogether certain.[29]

Reaney's instinct in refusing to credit Ludwig's hypothesis completely seems to me to have been quite correct. For we do not really know just what Machaut understood to be the essential characteristics of the melodic lines designated as cantus and tenor, at least in the secular compositions. It may be that he considered the term cantus synonymous with texted voice, or he might thus have designated the main melody of his texture the one that is carefully designed. By the former criterion, of course, Ludwig's suggestion would be valid. If the latter is the correct criterion, however, the designations in the manuscripts would have to be considered accurate. For although the melodies are almost exact retrogrades of each other, it is clear that the cantus makes considerably more sense dramatically than does the tenor. It builds to a climax near the end of Part I (measure 14) and again near the end of Part II (measures 34-37). The latter, furthermore, carries an effect of considerably greater significance; it is approached by means of a stronger rising passage, it is dwelt upon more fully, and it even touches a higher pitch (though fleetingly, to be sure). All of this of course, suggests an amplification of the events presented in the first part during the second, with more tension generated and consequently a greater sense of release at the end. A comparable rationale that would apply to the tenor seems difficult to formulate. Perhaps, then, the designation of the texted voice as tenor was not a mistake, but merely in line with the melodic characteristics then associated with the terms cantus and tenor. At any rate, it would seem a good guess that Machaut lavished most of his attention upon the design of the cantus even though it is not the texted voice.

A second interpretive problem posed by this piece is whether the complexity of either of these lines and the frequent and almost arbitrary slowings of rhythmic activity actually allow any sense of logical progress to come through. The lines do contain a considerable number of twists and turns as well as several abrupt changes from short to long rhythmic values at noncadential points (measures 9-10, 14-15, and 22-23). In addition, slowly moving rhythmic patterns are maintained for some time (measures 15-18 and 23-26). There must be some question, then, of whether the memory can function efficiently enough in the face of these obstacles to permit the kind of continual reduction in the number of impressions retained in mind that is required to effect a sense of continual logical flow. This, it seems to me, is a borderline case— a question for which I can provide no positive answer. Perhaps the answer would vary with the capacity of the individual listener.

A similarly questionable rhythmic procedure can be found in one other of Machaut's rondeaux. In No. 8, a tendency to repeat fairly short rhythmic patterns a number of times—a kind of isorhythm on a small scale—seems to chop the line into fragments, thereby working against the development of the sense of smoothness virtually required to effect a quality of dramatic development. Thus, in spite of a clear program, I would doubt that any sense of unfolding drama would come through.

Two more of Machaut's rondeaux (the first in Ludwig's collection and the rondelet from the *Remède de Fortune*) show little evidence of concern for narrative organization. In the case of the former, it is clearly because Machaut wanted the cantus to participate in a series of imitations that the sense of flow breaks down, for this participation carries the line momentarily into an

alien register—a move that occurs too late in this very short composition to permit a convincing resolution of the tension it generates.

Considered as a whole, then, the rondeaux show slightly
less evidence of narrative orientation than either the ballades or
the virelais. Whether this can be traced to miscalculation, to failure
on my part to comprehend Machaut's design, or to interest in projecting the text in a rather sophisticated poetic repeat scheme, or
even to the conditions imposed by this repeat scheme, would be
difficult to say.

Surveying Machaut's secular polyphonic output as a whole,
however, one must admit that the number of exceptional cases
is so small as to seem almost negligible. Of seventy compositions,
only seven at most do not present clear-cut evidence of narrative
intent. In each of these exceptions, furthermore, the line does not
even come close to exhibiting the kind of loose, haphazard motion
(with considerable redundance and/or many abrupt changes in
register) characteristic of most of the other voices in these works.
The difficulty, indeed, generally can be traced to just one or two
questionable moves or passages. These problematical spots, then,
probably should not be taken to reflect a total lack of design, but
only a questionable decision here and there. It could well be that
these represent miscalculations, or points at which I have been
unable to reach an understanding of Machaut's frame of mind, or
points at which his view of the dramatic course of events may
have differed from mine.

In view of the fact, then, that a clear-cut and obviously
effective dramatic structure can be made out so easily in so overwhelming a majority of Machaut's secular polyphonic works, and
of the fact that the exceptional cases lend themselves to interpretation as the result of just a few questionable decisions, I think we
must conclude that Machaut's basic intention in these works must
have been to forge an essentially narrative style in which the
sense of logical movement is suggested by the organization of a
single melodic line.

This view, of course, is not really new. Scholars have called
attention to the primacy of a single melodic line in these works
for many decades, and have even debated the proper term to be
applied to this phenomenon.[30] Perhaps Besseler's is the best formulation in this respect:

Wherever in such a sense a Lied-melos dominates the structure of polyphonic music, there is a "Liedsatz" (Lied texture). This is just as true for Machaut's ballades as it is for Senfl's tenor-Lieder. . . . The determining factor is simply that an artistic accompaniment is added to the vocal part, and that the structure of the entire work is delineated by means of the vocal part alone.[31]

In a sense, this essay represents an attempt to deal with the substance of the question covered by generalizations such as this one; it attempts to show the mechanics of the processes alluded to by Besseler, Handschin, and others.

In recent years, however, attention has shifted more to Machaut's treatment of the texture, with a technique of motivic relationship asserted to be the main characteristic of his style. This is essentially the view put forward by Perle and Reaney, and apparently accepted by Miss Williams.[32] As Reaney puts it: "Unity is attained through a variety of motives, which are either related to each other or combined with or within each other."[33]

This argument, however, does not seem totally convincing. For if motivic relations were intended to function as a significant force for unification, one would expect that the motives would be defined and presented in so clear-cut a fashion that they would be impressed automatically upon the mind from the outset; they could serve well as the units to which future developments are compared. One might expect some kind of immediate repeat of the motivic figure, or else a consistent articulation between similar fragments, at least at the beginning of the piece, in order to define the basic motive with sufficient clarity to start the listener calculating in terms of such a chain of comparisons.

This, however, does not seem to be the case in Machaut's secular polyphonic works. Only occasionally is a motivic unit clearly outlined in this way, and then it is usually because of some sequential motion occurring well into the piece rather than at the beginning. As a result, no unit is established in memory, so that there is really no point of departure from which a sense of logical progress can take shape. Any sense of progress resulting from the play of motives, then, would seem vaguely defined at best. Judging from this standard, Machaut's style could not be considered narrative at all, indeed, it probably would have to be judged something of an aesthetic failure.

I would go so far as to suggest that the articles by Perle and Reaney in which this motivic interpretation is set forth give evidence of something less than objective standards of scholarship. That Perle is far from a disinterested observer can be judged from the opening sentence of his article: "In order to understand and to justify, if only historically, the integrative devices that Arnold Schoenberg makes use of, we cannot do better than to compare them with those that served the purposes of Guillaume de Machaut." [34]

Although Reaney is not out to bend history to his own aims in this way, one passage makes clear how much he must have labored to maintain his belief in a motivic interpretation:

> Turning to the melismatic works, analysis appears less easy. Motives are visible, but the disguises to which they are submitted often tend to conceal them from view. The variety of these disguises should not surprise the reader who is familiar with the variety of detail in late Gothic miniature work and sculpture. [35]

An easy analogy of this kind cannot dispel the impression that Reaney, like Perle, found motivic relationships not because they were evident, but because he was looking for them.

What is established in the memory in these works—far more clearly than any motivic figure, I would suggest—is motion in a direction or in that combination of directions known as a melodic curve. It is the consistent working out of the implications and expectations introduced by the interaction of these curves, as I have tried to show, that produces the quality of logical flow. Since this entire process is contained within a single voice, I think it is probably reasonable to assert that, although polyphonic in texture, these pieces derive their value primarily from monophonic organization, much as must have been the case for the various repertories of liturgical chant.

THREE

The Early Development of Harmonic Polyphony

NEAR THE BEGINNING of the fifteenth century, a number of developments can be observed which suggest that a new conception of texture was coming into general use. Composers gradually came to think more in terms of textural than of linear effects. Harmonic considerations gradually appear to have shunted into the background the melodic values that dominated much fourteenth-century music. For the first time, in the fifteenth century, we begin to see a harmonically influenced polyphony.

Unfortunately, many of the relevant issues have been clouded by the present-day assumption that harmony is to be identified with one or another of the systems of chord relations and functions formulated during the eighteenth and nineteenth centuries. In Besseler's *Bourdon und Fauxbourdon*[1] and Machabey's *Genèse de la Tonalité Musicale Classique*,[2] for instance, judgments concerning the presence or absence of harmonic influence often seem to hinge upon whether or not the use of tonic-dominant relationships can be observed. Although such a position is easily understandable, particularly in view of the systems of instruction practiced during recent times, it seems a rather questionable basis for objective appraisal of historical developments. For it involves evaluation of past practice in terms of later conceptions; conceptions, it might be added, which are by no means beyond challenge.

In this chapter, I should like to attempt a less prejudiced exploration of the ways in which the texture as a whole ceased to be a more or less accidental byproduct of other constructive processes and became the primary point of appeal, and, further, how it was fashioned into narrative and picturesque means of attracting interest and effecting communication.

Perhaps the first evidence of the new interest in texture is provided by the emergence of what has sometimes been called panconsonant practice—essentially a reduction in the use of dissonances and a change in the conception of consonance, that took place near the beginning of the fifteenth century.[3] In the music of most of the French composers of the fourteenth century, consonances are to be found regularly on what we would today call the "strong" beats (e.g., the first and fourth eighths of a six-eight measure). Between these points, any kind of sonority would be considered proper. And even on the strong beats, appoggiaturas and other less easily explainable clashes often created dissonant effects. The consonances, furthermore, included the octave, fifth and fourth, as well as the third. Only occasionally, then, would one hear the "sweet" sounds of third or triad which today are considered the exemplars of consonance.

What a novelty it must have seemed when composers began thinking of consonance in terms of the triad, as opposed to the "empty" intervals so widely used in the fourteenth century, and began using the new "sweet" consonances, not only on most of the strong beats, but almost everywhere. The music of Dunstable, Dufay, Binchois and other composers who flourished during the early and middle decades of the fifteenth century must have seemed a veritable bath of silver sounds. The sensuous color effect must have been astonishing, seductive. In a way, it hardly seems amiss to compare this development with some from the latter part of the nineteenth century: the unprecedentedly heavy use of the "sweet" intervals may well have had something of the appeal for fifteenth-century audiences that the chromatically altered chords, the major ninth-chords and the quick successions of dominant-sevenths had for those of the nineteenth century.

Composers of the fifteenth century even as early as Dunstable, however, apparently were not content merely to exploit the picturesque possibilities offered by the triad. Very soon evidence can be found of attempts to utilize the new medium of texture (i.e., harmony) to create narrative effects. The trends and the sense of logical progress come to seem the result not so much of melodic organization as of the design of the texture as a whole. Composers gradually found ways of suggesting that the important motion (i.e., the motion upon which a listener should focus attention) was not to be found in individual lines, but in the harmonies which the combinations of those lines produced.

The outlines of this development can be traced in the music of Guillaume Dufay (c. 1400-1474), Johannes Ockeghem (c. 1420 or 1430-1495), and Jacob Obrecht (c. 1450-1505). This is not to assert that these composers were the originators of the techniques they exploited, or even that any straight chronological or influential relationship can be inferred. It merely represents an attempt to piece together the outlines of a development from practices to be observed in the works of some of the major composers of the time.

There are basically three kinds of evidence bearing upon the development of narrative elements in this texturally oriented art: (1) an increasing tendency to design the lowest voice so that it would seem to act as a directing element (toward the cadence) for the rest of the texture; (2) the development of methods for suggesting pressure toward the cadential resolution; and (3) the emergence of a type of practice that can be called "tonal" in the sense that it involves the establishment of a center in memory and the creation of contrasts to that center to furnish appeal and coherence.

In examining many of the chansons of Dufay, one finds little evidence of any intent to design the bass with care. Indeed, the basses in these pieces often seem downright repetitious, in some cases (e.g., *Je me complains piteusement* or *Pour ce que veoir je ne puis*) as a result of a prolonged fluctuation between two notes a fourth or fifth apart—tonic and dominant, in modern terms. These notes appear so often in prominent positions (as turning points, or as beginnings or endings of phrases) that the general effect approaches monotony. In other cases, it is the reiteration of a single note that makes for a monotonous bass (e.g., *Par droit je puis* or *Se la face ay pale*). In the latter, for instance (Example 1 shows the opening), the pitch C and its upper octave form the bass for roughly half the duration of the entire piece. These notes, furthermore, are the goals of all the many cadential motions but one, that one being a fleeting move to G in measure 18.

However it is brought about, the repetitiousness suggests that the shaping of the lowest part was not a primary concern for Dufay—a conclusion supported by the fact that only occasionally can anything like a fluent melodic curve be detected in his bass lines,

Example 1. Dufay, *Se la face ay pale.*

at least in the secular works. These qualities can no doubt be attributed to the fact that all the voices cross freely so that no single voice embodies the bass; it can only be derived by piecing together the lowest notes sounding at each moment. In Example 1, for instance, the first three notes are presented by the contra, the next four by the tenor, then one by the contra, six more by the tenor, etc.

The line which results, furthermore, tends to be shaped or at least influenced by constructive forces having little to do with its own design, as an inspection of the individual voices will demonstrate. In the chansons, at least one line, the discantus, is obviously carefully formed to avoid the stilted quality of the bass and to move smoothly in a variety of curves. A second voice, the tenor, is sometimes also carefully shaped. The third voice, however, often contains some repetitious elements, unexpected leaps, or abrupt shifts in register, all of which seem to indicate that it was added to a previously invented discantus, or to a combination of discantus and tenor, as a harmonic and rhythmic filler. Its primary function, no doubt, was to fill in the triads suggested by the other voices, or to keep the rhythm moving. In this sense the bass tends to become a by-product of other processes rather than an independently organized line. It thus seems likely that Dufay would have considered the shape of certain of his lines to be more important than the flow of harmonies as regulated by the bass.[4]

In the Masses that Dufay apparently wrote during the latter part of his lifetime [5] (which are set for four voices rather than the three found in most of the chansons) the treatment of the bass is quite different. Instead of being a composite entity, it is embodied almost wholly in a single voice, the contratenor bassus. The first *Kyrie* from *Missa Se la face ay pale*, for instance, contains only two places in which the bass note is presented by another voice; the entire Mass contains only about thirty such points; and three of the other four late Masses [6] contain comparable numbers of crossings of the contratenor bassus. It is perhaps significant that only the contratenor bassus is so seldom crossed in these works. The other lines (particularly the "inner" two) still exchange positions freely.

In this late style of Dufay, furthermore, the aimlessness apparent in some of the lines of the chansons (the filler voices) is much less in evidence, perhaps because the addition of a voice had lessened the problems of maintaining rhythmic flow and of reconciling linear and consonantal requirements. This means, of course, that the bass also must have been shaped with some care inasmuch as it is embodied almost wholly in one of these voices. It is this conception of a bass line under the control of its own linear forces that forms the point of departure for the harmonic flowering of the fifteenth century.

The extent to which the designed bass differs from the composite bass typical of the chansons can be judged by inspecting the first *Kyrie* of *Missa Se la face ay pale* (Example 2). It may be noted that there is no longer such emphasis on a single pitch or a set of pitches, that the bass often moves in smooth curves, and that there is a considerably greater variety of cadences (one to D in measure 21, another to G in measure 25, and a third to F at the end of the movement), in addition to several to C. To be sure, there are still a few repetitious places, notably in measures 9-13, where several successive cadences to C unfold within a short time, and in measures 29-33. That these are isolated passages, however, constitutes a remarkable contrast to the basses of the chansons.

Whether the designed bass was a more or less accidental result of the new four-voice texture, or whether it was more in the nature of a conscious achievement (and was perhaps even one of the considerations which led to the adoption of a fourth voice) is difficult to determine. It is interesting to note, in this respect, that the second of the two places in the *Kyrie* just discussed (measures 29-33) contains the only two crossings of the contratenor bassus. Equally interesting is the fact that the single late Mass (*L'homme armé*) in which there is a significantly greater number

Example 2. Dufay, *Missa Se la face ay pale: Kyrie* I.

of crossings of this voice also shows more than a bit of the old redundancy.[7] All of this would tend to support the possibility that the improved design was more a result of textural changes than a conscious innovation. That this was not the whole story, however, is indicated by the fact that one of the Masses with few crossings, *Missa Caput*, still has a repetitious bass. The fact that this has now been established to have been considerably older than any of the other four-voice Masses,[8] suggests the possibility that Dufay at first may have had trouble shaping all of the voices smoothly, but that he later learned to do this. If this was the case, the designed bass may well have been a result of the new conception of texture rather than a conscious goal.

Whether the result of textural changes or of purposeful innovation, it was not long before the designed bass was turned to specifically harmonic ends and before harmonic considerations, notably what has been called the drive to the cadence, began to enter into the shaping of the lowest part. A few instances of this kind can be seen in the Dufay *Kyrie* reproduced in Example 2, specifically around measures 19-21 and 24-25. At both of these points, a skeletal scalewise motion obviously reaches its culmination in the cadential note. During most of this movement, however, there is little to suggest that the cadence exerted much influence on the shaping of the bass. (Note the sense of redundance created by so many similar cadences to C in measures 7-13 and the arbitrary quality of the final cadence in this brief movement.)

A more consistent shaping of the bass to lead directly into a cadence is to be found in the works of Ockeghem, particularly the sacred works. Indeed, one of the most striking and attractive aspects of Ockeghem's sacred music seems to be just the frequency with which the bass drops its wandering and shoots off directly toward a cadence.

An exact description of how this is accomplished is difficult to formulate; there are several variables and many degrees of strength in the approach to the cadence. Yet the shape of Ockeghem's basses seems to reflect quite different principles of organization from those underlying Dufay's late Masses. It is not to the melodic curve that Ockeghem's line owes its sense of direction, but rather to the unmistakable suggestion that certain notes are more significant than others, acting as goals toward which the subordinate notes flow. In the first *Kyrie* from *Missa De plus en plus* (Example 3), for instance, there are obviously four such goals: the G's in measures 7 and 12, and the C's in measures 9 and 15.

The suggestion of varying degrees of significance seems to be accomplished by making use of rhythmic and directional forces. The last two notes of a phrase, of course, are the most important in defining the motion into a cadence, and Ockeghem generally treats them so as to make them seem more significant than anything else in the immediate context. The last note is either the culmination of a scale line or else it is approached by a leap of a fourth or fifth, intervals which somehow have come to be associated with great significance or purpose.

Example 3. Ockeghem, *Missa De plus en plus: Kyrie I.*

The penultimate note of the phrase is brought into relief by
its context: it represents the point at which the bass seems to
regain poise and balance. In many instances, this results from the
fact that the penultimate note is held longer than those immediately
preceding it (Example 4a); the pause seems to hold back the
current of notes and to channel it directly into the cadence. In
other cases, the effect of the pause is made even stronger by virtue
of the fact that the motion preceding has tended to emphasize the
off-beats (Example 4b), so that the penultimate note seems to

Example 4a. Ockeghem, *Missa De plus en plus: Christe*, m. 25-26.

Example 4b. Ockeghem, *Missa De plus en plus: Christe*, m. 20-21.

Example 4c. Ockeghem, *Missa Ecce ancilla Domini: Kyrie*, m. 8-10.

represent a return to the sense of normal rhythmic flow as well as a cessation and channeling of activity. Of course, these factors can be combined and played off against each other in a variety of ways, as the four cadences of Example 3 demonstrate, to create different lengths of phrases and variation in the strength with which the cadence is approached. Perhaps the best general formulation would be that somewhere near the end of a phrase the bass notes are so arranged rhythmically (i.e., through rapid motion and/or emphasis on off-beats) that a certain degree of drive from one note into the next is suggested. This state of imbalance, then, is brought to an end at the penultimate note which thereby seems to focus attention all the more strongly on the following move to the cadential note.

Perhaps the most striking aspect of Ockeghem's style is the frequency with which this procedure is employed. In Example 3, for instance, after the initial phrase, hardly three measures pass without one of these cadential motions. Appreciably longer stretches are but seldom to be found in any of Ockeghem's masses.

In many of Ockeghem's cadences the bass organization alone accounts for qualities of directed motion. This is especially noticeable where the motion culminates in a plagal or a Phrygian progression (Examples 4a and 4c, respectively), as well as in some other passages involving descending scale lines (Example 4b).

In other cases, however, Ockeghem appears to have taken steps to reinforce the bass's drive to the cadence. Attention has been called to one such device, a rhythmic drive to the cadence, by Miss M. L. Clement.[9] Miss Clement's point is that rhythmic activity and independence of voices can often be observed to increase at an approach to the cadence, heightening both the sense of tension and the sense of relief provided by the cadential resolution. Another device, very similar in effect, is more harmonic in nature: the introduction and resolution of tritones.

To the present-day musician, the tritone has a peculiar association of tension. It is a tension, however, involving something more than an implication of a high degree of excitement; for some reason, the excitement it suggests seems fully and satisfactorily released only if certain moves are made. To go from a harmony containing the notes B and F to an E-minor triad, for instance, seems more a disregarding than a release of the tritone's tension. One of the most commonly used methods of suggesting full release of this tension is to move to a triad whose root lies a semitone above one of the tritone notes (for example, from a chord containing B and F to a triad on C or B and E♯ to a triad on F♯). It could well be said, then, that the tritone is associated with certain directional properties in the minds of modern Western musicians. Having heard a B-F combination, one expects to proceed to a C triad (or possibly to an F♯ triad if the tuning is tempered); anything else seems something of a surprise.

While I have seen no documentary evidence that this peculiar sonority carried a connotation of this kind for fifteenth-century composers and theorists, it seems reasonable to suppose that Ockeghem, at least, associated just these directional properties with the tritone. Had this not been the case, it would be difficult to account for the frequency with which tritones are introduced and resolved in the manner described, with the prominence given to these resolutions, and with the way they are coordinated to both rhythmic organization and bass motion to provide a sense of culmination for the drive to the cadence.

Example 3 can again serve as an illustration. As previously noted, there are four cadences in this brief movement: two to C (measures 8-9 and 14-15) and two to G (measures 6-7 and 11-12), each of which is marked as a cadence by the organization of the bass. It may be observed further that each of these cadences is preceded by a passage in which the rhythmic complexity and the independence of the parts are gradually increased.

The approaches to the C cadences (measures 8-9 and 14-15) are obviously reinforced by the directional qualities of the tritone: a B-F combination is heard immediately before each of these resolutions to C. The second G cadence (measures 11-12) probably can be assumed to have involved a tritone also, since the F in the contratenor almost certainly would have been raised,[10] leading to an F♯-C combination resolving to G.

Only the first cadence (measures 6-7), then, does not involve the tritone. Even here, however, its influence does not seem to be altogether absent. For although there is no C to combine with the undoubtedly sharped F [11] in the superious of measure 6, C's have been so often presented beforehand that they must remain active in memory with sufficient force to provide some of the directing quality associated with the tritone.

Indeed, something similar to this can be observed in each of the other cadences as well. One or the other of the two notes forming the tritone is presented well in advance of the cadence. It is then joined by the other note just before the resolution. Thus the directed quality of the bass is reinforced by both an increasing rate of rhythmic activity and an emerging definition of a tritone to make the cadence seem to emerge gradually from the texture, gaining in strength and momentum as the phrase progresses. The result is gentle but continual fluctuation between related centers: in this example, no sooner does the texture move to G than it is on its way to C; immediately after the C is reached, it is on its way back to G.

Just how important the tritone reinforcement of the bass motion was to Ockeghem is difficult to judge. To be sure, there are lengthy passages—even whole movements and compositions [12] —in which cadences of this kind are few and far between. In these, the shaping of the bass into Phrygian and plagal progressions as well as descending scale lines suggests a lesser degree of drive, a gentler flow to the cadence. In other cases, the formation of the tritone would require applications of *musica ficta* which perhaps would not be beyond challenge. There are enough instances, however, in which the presence of the tritone drive seems virtually indisputable, indicating that it must have been an important part of Ockeghem's technique as an expedient to be used in what he considered appropriate situations.

Thus, quite in contrast to Dufay, in whose music the cadence sometimes seems as much an interruption as a goal, the art of Ockeghem is evidently founded upon the idea of frequent cadences, each approached smoothly and logically. Indeed, it does not seem too much to say that a main source of delight in this music is the smoothness and artistry with which the harmony and the rhythm combine to suggest the emergence of a sense of clarity and purpose from what seemed a confused wandering of independent voices early in the phrase.

A further harmonic refinement is to be found in the music of Obrecht. Here it is not the charm of allowing clarity to grow out of confusion that constitutes the point of appeal, but rather a practice similar to that of the late baroque and probably deserving of the designation "tonal" generally applied to the music of the later period. This is tonality not in the sense of major or minor key or in the sense of specific functional operations (such as dominant-tonic), but in the sense of "loyalty to a tonic" as Willi Apel put it.[13] Indeed, it might be well advised to say that it is the use of an implied loyalty to a tonic to achieve structural or aesthetic ends that constitutes tonality. Something of this sort, at any rate, seems to be implied in the definition quoted from D'Indy in this same article by Dr. Apel: ". . . the ensemble of musical phenomena which human understanding is able to appreciate by direct comparison with a constant element—the tonic."

In spite of its advances, Ockeghem's harmony could not well be called tonal by this definition. For it is clear that no center indisputedly takes the role of a tonic—a fundamental center of harmonic repose or reference—for the movement as a whole. In Example 3, for instance, it can be seen that G and C are of almost equal importance. The flow of the music easily could have been shaped so as to make either one sound like the final even at the end of the movement; three measures more and Ockeghem probably would have ended in G rather than in C. While the subsequent *Christe* and second *Kyrie* (neither of which is reproduced in Example 3) make it clear that G was conceived as the center for the *Kyrie-Christe-Kyrie* as a whole, the way this is brought out is so subtle that, even as late as the end of the second *Kyrie,* C easily could be taken to be the tonic.

In contrast to this type of amorphous tonality, Obrecht's practice seems to be predicated upon the assumption that a single center will be retained in memory throughout a movement, even while contrasting harmonic motions are being presented. For at the beginnings of movements and interspersed throughout them are passages which contain, not just the single cadential definition of tonic found in the Ockeghem example, but a whole series of strongly driving approaches to the center. These, then, reinforce the memory of that center as tonic, so that the musical flow is divided into distinct sections, some of which define a basic tonality strongly while the others offer something like a challenge to the memory of that center.

The memory of a tonic, furthermore, is often [14] utilized to suggest a balance between what are usually called the forces of unity and variety, as well as a dramatic program involving the generation and resolution of tensions. That is to say, the excursions from the basic tonality are arranged in a way which creates the impression of a purposeful ebb and flow of the degree of contrast. As the degree of contrast grows greater, of course, more tension is generated, to be released by the return to the remembered tonality. An example perhaps will do more to clarify this conception than would further abstract description; the *Et in terra* from *Missa Fortuna desperata* [15] can serve this purpose.

The first eleven measures of this movement consist of a three-voice canon whose subject defines F major clearly. The multiple cadences to that center which result from the canonic repetitions at successive octaves, of course, implant F major firmly in memory. The following eleven measures offer the first challenge to the impression that this is the tonic, simply by virtue of the fact that no strong cadences to that degree are presented. Indeed, toward the end of this section, there is a move toward a contrasting center—the subdominant B-flat. (Whether or not this has the strength of a modulation will depend upon whether or not one or more of the preceding E's are flatted.[16]) F major is gradually redefined in its role as tonic in the following seven measures (23-39), by means both of a passage (measures 22-25) which contains all the notes of the F-major scale, including the E-B♭ tritone, and of bass motion whose target clearly comes to be F. The decorated set of descending fourths in measures 23-25 (D-A, C-G) suggests that the pitch F is soon to be heard; the pause on the G and the suspension to a leading-tone over this note lend significance to the imminent move to F, thereby reinforcing its tonic function.

Representing the tonic-defining sections as straight lines and the excursions as curves, this much of the movement could be graphed as follows:

Another excursion is to be found in the next eight measures (30-37), this time culminating in a decided and certain modulation to the same subdominant in measure 35. Because the modulation is so decided (using a double approach to B♭, the second one through the very powerful authentic progression with both chords in what would today be called root position), this excursion would seem to offer a greater degree of contrast to the basic F major than the first one, in spite of its slightly lesser length.

Although there are some hints of contrast in the next passages, these seem so negligible, by and large, that the entire eighteen measures (38-55) could well be considered a reinforcement of the F-major tonality. The length of this passage, indeed, makes it a quite powerful reinforcement. The graph now would assume the following shape:

During the next forty measures (55-94), there is not a single strong cadence to F and only two weak ones (measures 63 and 81), both plagal. On the basis of its duration alone, this section undoubtedly offers the greatest challenge so far encountered to the memory that F major is tonic. It could well be compared to a long stretch of desert between the oases which the strong F-major sections represent. The length of this section offers a possible explanation for the strength of definition in the eighteen measures preceding. Obrecht may have reasoned that a tonic had to be planted in memory firmly enough to hold up through these forty measures. The relatively weak plagal cadences of F within the excursion may also have been designed to keep this memory alive without appreciably breaking the sense of contrast.

There is then a brief reaffirmation of tonic (measures 95-97), followed by an equally brief excursion (hardly more than the surprising color produced by a few flatted E's), a gradual but clear return of F via a series of descending thirds in the bass, and finally, four measures of crystallike clarity of tonal definition. The movement as a whole now takes on the following appearance:

Thus the second excursion carries farther the trend (toward tonal contrast) started by the first, the third carries this trend to its zenith, and the fourth represents a tapering off as an approach to the final clarity. Conversely, as a result of this intricate play of the forces of unity and variety, the final return to clarity represents a striking effect, an effect comparable to a clear and beautiful sunset after a day of unsettled weather.

The logic, the planning, and the psychological correctness behind a scheme like this are readily apparent. As the tonality is more strongly impressed on the memory, the challenges grow stronger so that the attentive mind is constantly provided with enough novelty to assimilate to keep it from wandering off on its own tangents. After reaching a point of strain to the memory, it becomes a veritable pleasure to sink back to the original tonality— a pleasure which is much the stronger for the implications of struggle that have preceded.

Patterns similar to this one can be found in others of Obrecht's Mass movements, for example. in the *Et in terra* from *Missa Graecorum* and the entire *Gloria* from *Missa L'homme armé*.[17] In other movements, different but equally clear and rational types of organization can be discerned. The first *Kyrie* from this same *Missa Fortuna desperata,* for instance, divides into three approximately equal sections, the first and last defining F major and the middle one offering contrast—tonally an early instance of an A-B-A design. For another example, the first *Kyrie* from *Missa L'homme armé* contains two excursions, the second unmistakably suggesting a greater degree of contrast, so that the return to the basic tonality carries a greater sense of relief at the end of the movement.

In many movements, however, it is very difficult to discern a rational pattern. In some cases, uncertainties concerning *musica ficta* tend to obscure the presence of any pattern. In other instances, however, one finds simply a number of excursions, some of which perhaps can be ranked, but for a few of which such ranking would seem arbitrary no matter what the decision. The *Patrem omnipotentem* from *Missa Fortuna desperata*, for example, contains essentially four excursions which this writer, at least, would be hard put to arrange according to rank, beyond saying that the last is the weakest, a tapering toward final clarity.

In view of this, it seems best to place the emphasis not on the pattern of challenges, but rather on the returns to basic tonality, while formulating the logic behind Obrecht's practice in general terms. It is probably not the pattern of increasing challenge to an established tonality that is of primary significance, but rather the attempts to reestablish tonal stability in the face of varying types and degrees of challenge. It is the fact that only the last of these attempts seems completely successful that accounts for the striking sense of pleasure and release at the end of a section.

In spite of a considerable variety of practices, only one of the twenty-two Masses [18] contained in the complete edition, *Missa Salve diva parens*,[19] yields little evidence of the type of planning described above. In this Mass, the bass hovers so much about the pitches e and e', and the E-minor triad is so often heard that the result seems rather monotonous. Whether this was a matter of faulty calculation, of intent to bring out a Phrygian flavor, or of a wish to retain the quality of a basic tonality despite the weak cadences available to point up the Phrygian degree, it is difficult to say. It is interesting to note that other settings of Phrygian *cantus firmi* (*Malheur me bat, Maria zart, Sicut spina rosam,* and *L'homme armé*) are not at all of this type, but give evidence of the type of tonal planning already described.

Thus, Obrecht's harmony seems designed primarily for the purpose of creating a sense of cumulation on a large scale, a quality not particularly prominent in Ockeghem's music. Where Ockeghem seems to have conceived harmony largely in terms of the charm of the moment—a continual alternation between drifting and driving qualities—Obrecht appears to have taken a step toward the creation of a logic that operates throughout the length of a movement. He carries the listener from point to point, making him aware that what is happening at any moment has had antecedents and will have further consequences; all of the steps taken are related to the central problem of setting up an eventual return to tonal stability. The varying degrees of challenge and the provisional restorations of tonal influence all seem steps on the way toward the final resolution of this problem.

As a result, there is a tendency for suspense and hence interest to increase as a movement unfolds. In a long movement by Ockeghem, after all, the range of harmonic procedures might eventually become so familiar as to fail to excite further curiosity. Obrecht's variety in the types and degrees of contrast would seem a safeguard against satiety of this kind. This, then, represents an early embodiment of a now-familiar aesthetic principle: the creation of a sense of logical growth by means of the harmony rather than by a series of charming but only loosely related moments.

Obrecht's harmonic practice is implemented by the two factors discussed earlier, the designed bass and the tritone drive to the cadence. In particular, it is the interplay between these two forces that creates the distinctions between definition of and contrast to the basic tonality, as well as the various degrees of strength of definition or contrast required to work out such a program.

As was also true for Ockeghem, the design of the bass is largely a matter of suggesting direct and unmistakable motion into a cadence formula of one kind or another (authentic, deceptive, plagal, or Phrygian). In a great many passages, this is accomplished by means similar to Ockeghem's; namely, by dividing the musical flow into short phrases, each closed by a cadence which is approached by a decorated scale line in the bass. Because this bass motion leads into a cadence just shortly after it has gotten under way, and because the motion is so logical, the impression, in retrospect, is that the aim of the phrase as a whole was just to reach that cadential formula.

In other passages, however, a novel procedure is employed: a more leisurely approach to the cadence by means of a decorated intervallic formula in the bass (e.g., a bass that outlines a set of successively descending thirds or fourths). In Example 5, for instance, a set of three successive descending thirds moves directly into the cadence of measures 105-106. In a way, this type of bass planning seems little more than an extension of Ockeghem's method: the more or less rigid transposition of intervals conveys the impression of purposeful motion toward the cadence in much the same way as Ockeghem's descent along the scale. The long-range similarity to late Baroque procedures is readily apparent.[20]

Example 5. Obrecht, *Missa Fortuna desperata*: *Et in terra*, m. 101-106.

When the bass motion into a cadence is co-ordinated with the pressure of a tritone, either implied (with one of the tones being remembered from the previous context) or actual (with both notes being sounded simultaneously just before the cadence), the result is a strongly driving approach. This is ordinarily the case when the phrase culminates in a VII_6-I, V-I, V-VI, or V-IV_6 progression, to use modern terminology. If, on the other hand, the tritone is little or not at all in evidence (especially in plagal or Phrygian progressions), the drive is, of course, more gentle. As might be expected, the former type of cadence dominates the passages designed to establish or reinforce a basic tonality, while the gentler Phrygian and plagal formulae are more in evidence in the sections devoted to contrast. This is not an invariable rule, however, since contrast sometimes involves a very positive sounding modulation, in which case one of the driving cadences generally would be used.

The establishment or reinforcement of a basic tonality in memory is often accomplished by the simple expedient of a rapid succession of strong cadences to the tonal center. Such is the case, for instance, in the three-voice canon which opens the *Et in terra* from *Missa Fortuna desperata* (Example 6) already discussed. After this series of repeated strong approaches to F major (five in eleven measures), there can be little doubt about the location of what D'Indy called the constant element.[21] In other cases, a similar reinforcement is accomplished by the type of bass motion just described, during the course of which the tritone is implied. Example 7 shows another set of descending thirds.

A combination of multiple cadences and transposition of intervals in the bass can be seen in Example 8, where, in addition

Example 6. Obrecht, *Missa Fortuna desperata*: *Et in terra*, m. 1-11.

Example 7. Obrecht, *Missa Je ne demande*: *Et in terra*, m. 16-20.

Example 8. Obrecht, *Missa Je ne demande*: *Kyrie*, m. 15-23.

to the V-IV$_6$ motion of measures 15-16, the VII-I of measures 17-18, the VII$_6$-I of measures 21-22 and the decorated plagal progression of measures 22-23, there is a decorated set of interlocking descending fourths (D-A, C-G) in measures 19-21—all leading to the same F-major tonality.

The use of a weaker set of cadences during a section which offers contrast to the basic tonality can be seen in Example 9, which contains first a plagal progression to D (measures 66-67) and then a Phrygian cadence to A (70-71).

Example 9. Obrecht, *Missa Fortuna desperata: Et in terra*, m. 65-71.

The key aspects of Obrecht's harmonic practice are the quantitative treatment of harmony and the use of periodic returns to the basic tonality in the course of a movement. In the absence of the latter, of course, there would be no way of separating the flow of harmonies into individual excursions and hence no way of suggesting an ebb and flow of contrast. These returns serve the purposes of reinforcement of memory, and of punctuation, as well as seeming to provide tentative resolutions of the essential problem of restoring tonal stability.

As for the role of quantity, it is obvious that it is the strongest single factor employed. The fact that one of the excursions in the movement described in some detail in this paper lasted more than three times as long as the next largest, far outweighed all other considerations in determining the degree of challenge to the memory of the tonality. On the other hand, duration can be considered a strong influence only if the difference in dimensions is appreciable. The difference in elapsed time between the eleven-measure excursion and the following eight-measure one, for instance, did not seem sufficiently noticeable to offset the influence of the other factors.

Where duration is not a significant factor, an episode that modulates will offer greater contrast than one which simply avoids strong cadences in that a temporary sense of competition will be set up between the new key and the original tonality. Obviously, the greater the proportion of time within an excursion spent implying keys other than the original, the more contrast will be offered.

It is curious that Obrecht's harmony seems, in a way, closer to that of J. S. Bach than do those of such composers as Palestrina, Sweelinck, Buxtehude, perhaps even Monteverdi. This affinity appears even more pronounced when one considers that certain of Bach's fugues (e.g., those in C major and C♯ minor in the *Well-*

Tempered Clavier, Vol. I) contain a series of internal reemphases of their respective basic tonalities which cut the modulations into a series of excursions organized into patterns not too different from those found in Obrecht's works. Many of Bach's chorale harmonizations, furthermore, are similarly organized, taking modest steps toward tonal contrast and returning to the basic tonality several times before moving more decisively away. Even in compositions which do not use excursions so consistently—such as many of the fugues, suites, or concerto movements—one can often find a gradually increasing strain on the memory of the basic tonality with shorter returns to it, before the break toward a new key is made. In view of these considerations, attempts to fit the development of harmonic thought into a simple evolutionary pattern would appear to be not merely oversimplifications, but out-and-out distortions.

One thing seems certain: when a comprehensive general theory of harmony and tonality comes to be written—one that is not merely an attempt to codify the style of a single composer or to force observed practices into a natural-law formulation—the developments of the fifteenth century will have to be taken into account; for they represent an early flowering of this intellectual development that has played so significant a role in the history of Western music.

FOUR

Two "Insignificant" Motets by Josquin des Prez

*I*N ITS ESSENTIALS, the image of Josquin des Prez (c. 1440-1521) commonly accepted to-day is that projected almost a century ago by A. W. Ambros.[1] To be sure, later scholars have gone into more detail concerning aspects of his work and style,[2] and have attempted to fix more precisely some of the ideas only sketched out by Ambros, but they do not seem to have substantially altered or even deepened the picture presented so ably and enthusiastically by this great historian.

Ambros's attention was focused primarily upon what might be termed the constructive aspects of Josquin's music: the treatment of the *cantus firmus*, the use of pervading imitation, canon, ostinato, etc. There are only a few scattered references in his text —and these in the most general of terms—to the psychological effect intended by the compositions, with virtually nothing said about what techniques might have accounted for the appeal.

Ambros attached so much importance to these polyphonic devices that he appears to have judged the chronology of Josquin's works, at least to some extent, by the way they were used. His assumption seems to have been that as Josquin matured, he would have relied upon the technique of pervading imitation more and more and upon all the other constructive devices less and less. In his view, then, as Josquin's style developed, his music must have become simpler, less rigidly bound to a preexistent melody, and more systematic; in a word, it became more nearly like that of composers who flourished later in the sixteenth century.

Ambros seems to have assumed further that the early works were necessarily the inferior ones. As he put it:

> The four-voice motets of the master show the development of his fertile imagination, and although it is impossible to make even approximately a chronological determination of their composition, one can nevertheless distinguish clearly enough the older, still frequently constrained works from the beautifully developed later ones.[3]

Whether he judged value by the presence or absence of certain of these polyphonic devices is not completely clear. The fact remains, however, that value and polyphonic practice of this kind were closely associated in Ambros's mind. And the fact that no other criteria for judging value are specified in his book would seem to suggest that this connection was more than fortuitous.

In this respect, Ambros has been followed almost idea for idea by more recent writers. Antonowytch[4] and Osthoff[5] both have attempted to build chronologies in much the same way, apparently using these same criteria plus the rather loose conception of word-tone relationship, despite the fact that the dangers inherent in this type of style-critical approach were pointed out long ago by Besseler.[6] Only Reese, who was clearly more interested in factual reporting than in erecting speculative structures, seems to avoid this pitfall.[7] Yet Reese also confines his discussions largely to the topics of *cantus-firmus* treatment, ostinato, canon, imitation, etc.

Now this is the type of historiography that was considered standard during much of the nineteenth century and well into the twentieth, when it was believed that the only music worth understanding was that written from the time of Bach on. The aim of these historians, I would suggest, was not so much to determine how men thought and created at various times and in various cultures, but rather how the perfection of the Bach style came into existence. Their primary interest was in finding the roots of the style rather than in evaluating the music and the musical thought of past times in and for itself. Thus any style contributing to the development of the technique of imitation was automatically of importance because it constituted a forerunner of the Bach fugue. Other factors of the style in question were not taken into account particularly; the music of these early composers seemed obviously amateurish and insignificant compared to music created since 1700.

Today, of course, no self-respecting historian would subscribe to such a view. It has come to be generally recognized that there are arts of various times well worth studying for the intrinsic value of the compositions and for the knowledge of the way men thought at different times and under different conditions. We no longer have the supreme confidence in the value of contemporary styles, or even of those of the eighteenth and nineteenth centuries, that would seem to justify ignoring all but selected aspects of earlier arts.

Yet the approach in this field often remains that of the nineteenth-century historian. Attention is still focused primarily upon those particular aspects of musical composition which enjoyed a later development, culminating in a pinnacle of artistic creation such as the Bach fugue or the Beethoven sonata. There is still little attempt to understand the art itself, quite apart from subsequent developments of technical procedures, and what might have made it appealing to an audience of the time.

That this kind of approach, almost necessarily, would result in an incomplete picture of Josquin's art seems undeniable. It is unrealistic to assume that a complex creative personality like Josquin would have been so much valued for, or preoccupied with, simply developing the technique of pervading imitation and suppressing the influence of the *cantus firmus* and other constructive devices, as Ambros and the more recent historians seem to have implied.

To demonstrate just how incomplete the current picture is, I should like to present a study of some specific works. In particular, I have chosen two compositions which have not fared very well at the hands of most writers—insignificant works, from their points of view—the four-voice motets *Virgo prudentissima* and *Victimae paschali laudes* (numbered 25 and 26 in the complete edition [8]). My contention is that these works are so rich in evidence of thoroughly artistic planning—superb planning in terms of psychological effect—that any implication that they are works of lesser importance must be considered a purely arbitrary decision on the part of the historian. If *Victimae paschali laudes* is indeed an early work in a style later abandoned by Josquin, as is generally suggested, it represents a stage of his development the passing of which could as well be deplored as applauded. The supplanting of this style could be taken to reflect a lowering of standards of taste rather than the kind of improvement generally associated with the notion of progress. On the other hand, however, the universal downgrading of this composition may simply show how unreliable the currently used style-critical criteria are for dating works and deciding whether they should be considered significant artistic creations.

The four-voice setting of *Victimae paschali laudes* is one of the few compositions by Josquin that actually called forth a negative evaluation by Ambros. Characteristically, the words of censure are preceded by some rather skeptical remarks concerning *cantus-firmus* treatment:

> It is certain that the motet *Victimae paschali laudes* belongs to the early period of the master. Aside from the fact that for it he takes over whole parts of chansons by Ockeghem und Hayne . . . , *D'ung aultre amer* and *De tous biens*, which moreover must even have a close relation to the ancient sequence by the monk of St. Gall, the entire manner of writing is still very strict, dry, and meager.[9]

Leichtentritt writes in a similar vein:

> It is not without justification that Ambros believes he can place this composition in the first period of the master. In fact, it exhibits many old-fashioned features, not only in the direction indicated above, but also in the fact that various melodic phrases in the various voices are united with one another and that the canonic voice leading and imitation on the whole is allotted but very little space, although the texture is thoroughly polyphonic.[10]

Osthoff agrees exactly with Ambros's formulation, and adds his own words of dispraise:

> In fact the work shows the same imbalance and paucity of expression as the double-anthiphon-motet *Alma Redemptoris mater–Ave regina caelorum,* which likewise possesses an Ockeghem citation and belongs to the earliest works. The constructive elements are not subordinated to an overall conception, but rather they constrict the unfolding of the lines and the few tendencies toward expressiveness.[11]

Although Ambros's treatment of the motet *Virgo prudentissima* is less outspokenly critical, he leaves the inference that his opinion of it is only slightly less negative:

> Among the Marian pieces of Josquin to be mentioned are, above all, the two sensitive, four-voice *Ave Maria* settings . . . to which the *Missus*

est Angelus Gabriel is related. Other Marian pieces are the two *Alma redemptoris* settings, as well as *Gaude virgo mater Christi* and *Virgo prudentissima*. . . .[12]

Osthoff, on the other hand, has a somewhat higher opinion of this work:

> The short setting begins in broad, paired imitation and distinguishes itself through the beautiful flow of the voices. From the middle of the composition onward the relation to the Gregorian melody is abandoned. The treatment of the bass line is still dominated extensively by ostinato tendencies. As in the previously mentioned motet of Isaac's, the concluding words "ut sol" are rendered by solmization.[13]

With this lone exception, then, the weight of critical opinion would seem to indicate that these motets are among the weakest of Josquin's creations and are hardly worth studying. The music itself, however, conveys a quite different impression.

Although these two works are very different in effect, in texture, and in structure, there is an element common to them, and it is an important element: a very clear narrative organization in which direction and shape are suggested, not by melodic curves, nor by harmonic excursions, or even by the organization of any single element, but rather through the coordination of many elements, each of which contributes to the raising or lowering of the sense of excitement. The suggested ebb and flow of intensity creates a series of closed curves (mostly archlike in shape) which are presented in an order suggesting dramatic development.

Virgo prudentissima is divided, after the pattern of the Antiphon on which it is based, into seven sections, in each of which the tenor paraphrases the equivalent phrase of the Antiphon. In the following table, I have used the appropriate portions of the text to identify passages from the Antiphon, and measure numbers to indicate the tenor quotations in the motet:

measures 2–9	*Virgo prudentissima*
measures 16–25	*quo progrederis*
measures 26–43	*quasi aurora valde rutilans?*
measures 44–47	*filia Sion*
measures 49–61	*tota formosa et suavis es:*
measures 62–66	*pulchra ut luna*
measures 68–73	*electa ut sol.*

In the first phrase, Josquin adds but little to the notes of the chant, being content simply to give each a rhythmic value. About midway through the second phrase (measure 19), embellishments and melismas are added, so that the relation to the chant becomes more problematic. The relation of the third phrase to the Antiphon is even more obscure, while the fourth is more clearly derived, and the last three again seem only vaguely related to the chant.

Perhaps one of the reasons for the freedom of the relationship to the Antiphon at times is to be found in the fact that a second type of structure is grafted onto that provided by the *cantus firmus*. This is a structure involving the widespread use of repetitive devices such as imitation, ostinato, canon, etc. Indeed, this composition seems little more than a chain of phrases, each representing one of the most striking repetitive relationships. If one were not aware of the chant paraphrase presented in the tenor, one might well conclude that this represented a sufficient primary means of organization closely related to the points of imitation so widely used later in the sixteenth century.

Thus the first fourteen measures are devoted to two identical canonic duets, the first between superius and tenor, and the other between altus and bassus (Example 1). Measures 15-19 contain

Example 1. *Virgo prudentissima*: m. 1-14.

another canon between superius and tenor surrounded by two free voices, with a free continuation after measure 19 (Example 2). The measures following contain a most interesting and complex play of repetitive devices (Example 3): a repetition a fifth higher of the tenor's phrase of measures 26-30 in the altus of measures 31-35, along with an entry of the beginning of that phrase in the superius of measures 30-32; a sequence around the circle of fifths

Example 2. *Virgo prudentissima*: m. 15-20.

Example 3. *Virgo prudentissima*: m. 26-46.

(starting notes: D, G, C, and F) in the bassus of measures 28-39; an ostinato in the bassus from measure 39 to 45; and a three-voice canon over the ostinato (altus enters in measure 39, superius in measure 40, and tenor in measure 41). In addition, the subject of this last canon is divided into two halves, the second (beginning in measure 42 in the altus), a slightly decorated version of the first.

A brief and slightly free three-voice canon follows (Example 4), but gives way to a close-interval canon in measure 51 (Example 4 again). A few measures later a four-voice canon is presented (Example 5) in which just a few liberties are taken with the lengths of rests. Finally, there is a combination of a canon (with some freedom in the use of rests) between superius and tenor, an ostinato in the bassus, and an extra entry of the canon's beginning in the altus; all are based on the same motive: G-D (Example 6). This obviously is a case of word painting in which the text, *ut sol,*

Example 4. *Virgo prudentissima*: m. 48-56.

Example 5. *Virgo prudentissima*: m. 62-68.

Example 6. *Virgo prudentissima*: m. 68-73.

(luminous) as the sun, is mirrored in the equivalent syllables of the hard hexachord.

It can be seen, then, that there are few points at which some kind of repetitive device is not in evidence.

But these devices do not seem to have been used as ends in themselves. It was probably not fascination with the sounds of the various types of repeat structures that led Josquin to such elaborate organization; chances are it was not even a delight in the play of memory and recognition that this would involve. Rather, it seems to have been the fact that the devices lent themselves easily to manipulation into curves which suggested the ebb and flow of excitement in a variety of ways and to varying degrees that led to their use. At least this would seem a reasonable inference in view of the evidence of care taken to form the ebb and flow of intensity into a dramatic pattern.

The opening canon (see Example 1) suggests a very calm beginning, what with the lengths of the first two notes and the thinness of texture (only one voice is heard at first). As the two voices of this canon begin to be heard together, as the motion goes over from whole notes to half notes, and as the pitch climbs, there is an unmistakable sense of rising intensity, although it is certainly a mild rise. A conflict between the rising and descending forces of intensity sets in around measure 6, as one voice becomes static but the other accelerates to quarter-note and then eighth-note motion. The descent in pitch of this more active voice and its eventual lapse into silence (measure 8) make it clear that this conflict is resolved in favor of the descending forces.

Thus this phrase might be described as a rather shallow arch. It starts from a very low level of excitement, generates a little more intensity as it progresses, and then, after a brief struggle, lapses back to the low level at which it began. The fact that only two voices are heard, and that the rhythmic patterns of these voices are not conspicuously independent, tends to keep the growth rather modest in dimensions.

The exact repeat of this passage an octave lower (measures 8-14) simply serves to establish this particular pattern (first a growing and then an ebbing intensity) more firmly in mind, as well as to set up an expectation that something more exciting will soon happen. To go on much longer at this muted level, after all, would be to tax the patience of an audience that might rightly feel some sort of reaction is overdue. To attempt to design a curve suggesting even lower intensity, the one remaining possibility, would be almost impossible physically; certainly it would not fulfill the role of the expected reaction. The stage is set, then, for some more exciting events.

The fireworks are not long in coming. A four-voice texture is heard for the first time starting in measure 16 (Example 7). In measure 17, also for the first time, each of the four beats in the measure sees at least one voice move. By measure 19, quarter-note motion has wrested control from the predominantly half-note motion preceding. Indeed, the tendency toward generally faster motion is carried even farther in measure 20, to a series of eighth notes. All of these factors tend to suggest that the level of excitement is increasing.

Already in measure 19, however, while the sense of general

Example 7. *Virgo prudentissima*: measures 15-26.

rise in intensity is still in control, the seed of a future descent is planted in the superius. For this line now begins a decorated descent which lasts until measure 25. The other three voices also clearly go into protracted descents beginning in measure 21, giving more impetus to the downward motion. Until measure 23, the rhythmic activity seems strong enough to counterbalance these downward implications and keep the issue in doubt. With the slowing down around measure 24, however (Note that two of the voices go to holding a single note for a full two measures, while the others go momentarily to half-note and dotted half-note motion), it becomes clear that the descending forces are in control. The tapering continues until measure 26, overlapping the beginning of the next rise.

Thus the shape of the intensity curve projected in this phrase resembles that of each of the two preceding phrases: an arch with a leisurely though direct rise, a struggle between rising and descending forces near the top, and a retreat setting in as a resolution of this struggle near the end. This phrase, however, obviously represents something more than a mere repeat of the two opening arches; it seems more an amplification of the course of events presented earlier. The four-voice texture, the much greater emphasis on faster motion which spreads through all four of the voices, as well as the specifically harmonic drives into the two cadences (measures 20-21 and 23-24) unmistakably suggest a much higher level of instensity reached and a much more excited state of mind than anything heard earlier. Thus a trend toward rising excitement is started.

But more excitement is yet to come, building up slowly in the next phrases. Against the imitative repetition of a phrase (tenor of measures 26-30 is repeated a fifth higher by the altus in measures 31-35; see Example 3) is presented a three-voice texture at first moving mostly in quarter notes with just a few eighths sprinkled in. In measures 30-32, the motion slows considerably to suggest that the downward tendency still dominates at this point.

A seed is planted in these measures, however, which eventually will turn the tide upward. This is in the form of the bass sequence which first appears in measures 28-30 (Example 3). The subject for this sequence has a strong quality of rhythmic drive and upward thrust. It is the withdrawal of this sequential subject in measures 30-32 that accounts in large measure for the slowing of rhythmic activity at that point. Because of lesser motion in the other voices, the second statement of this subject (measures 33-34) does not seem to reach the level of excitment attained by the earlier one.

But the seed is doing its work. The sequence subject begins to sound like a rather active and strong external force being applied to prod the texture as a whole into renewed activity. The fact that the bass now goes on to the next links in the sequential chain without pause suggests a more determined effort to raise excitement. When the two voices accompanying this sequence begin to move rapidly (measure 35), it becomes clear that the stimulus is taking effect. Finally (measure 37), as the three voices fall into two strongly independent rhythmic patterns so that a veritable cascade of eighth notes is formed by the combination of voices, a momentary peak of excitement is reached.

But the following retreat (toward half-note motion, measure 39) is only temporary. Perhaps the strongest force in rebuilding the intensity is the bass ostinato which sets in at that point. The monotony of the continual alternation between just two notes creates an expectation of some kind of change. One may well wonder how long this can go on. The composer is bound to break the pattern sooner or later, or else give up all semblance of the rational communication of ideas and impressions. But as three statements of these two notes, then four, then five, then six go by without the expected break, we cannot but begin to sense increasing anxiety about when, or indeed whether, this pattern is going to be broken, which leads to a considerable increase in tension.

Above the ostinato, other factors contribute to the same effect. The three-voice canon quickly gets all four of the voices into play. The canonic subject, furthermore, moves from half-note to quarter-note predominance; a move which is magnified, so to speak, by reflection in the other voices. With the break into eighth notes at the end of measure 44 and the departure from the ostinato pattern immediately following, it becomes apparent that a great deal of energy has been generated and is being channeled into the cadence of measures 45-46. As a result, this cadence seems the most full-blooded effect, the most significant point of the entire composition.

The remaining three intensity curves seem arranged so as to put progressively greater emphasis on descent. A good deal of energy is generated by the close canon of measures 51-55 (Example 8), but the thinner texture and the static quality of the single non-

Example 8. *Virgo prudentissima*: m. 51-61.

canonic voice clearly stamp this as a lesser surge. Further, there is not the kind of strong cadential release which signaled the climax to the curve preceding; the rather surprising cadence to C in measures 60-61 (the expectation is of a V-I cadence to G) obviously comes, not at the apex of intensity, but some time after a descending tendency has made itself felt.

The following four-voice canon (measures 62-68; see Example 5) starts out as though it will generate a great deal of energy, what with entrances at half-note intervals leading quickly to a full texture, quarter-note motion, and a rising line. Very soon, however, the texture thins to two voices (owing to the extra rests in two of the voices) and the lines turn downward in pitch. The shortness of this section (the whole surge and retreat has been accomplished within just six measures) stamps it as of even lesser excitement than the preceding curve.

In addition to the obvious decrease in the level of excitement reached, these last two passages (measures 51-62 and 62-68) introduce a new element into the scheme: increasing emphasis on the descent following the climax. A study of the ratios of the ascending to the descending portions of each of the intensity arches will give some idea of the extent of this shift in emphasis. The pair of duets at the beginning contain roughly five measures of ascent to only two of descent. In the next segment, descent comes clearly to dominance only in the last three or four measures of a twelve-measure phrase. In the passage featuring sequence followed by ostinato in the bass, the ratio moves to roughly nineteen measures of ascent to perhaps four of clear descent. Thereafter the tide begins to turn. The seven measures of rising intensity resulting from the close canon are followed by six measures which begin to point toward an easing of tension. With the four-voice canon of measures 62-68, the balance is almost perfect: three measures of rise to three measures of descent.

In the final phrase, one element seems to carry this trend further. Almost all of the time is spent in a pitch descent following an opening upward leap (see Example 6). For this phrase as a whole, however, it would be difficult to formulate an exact pattern of rising and falling intensity. For the pitch descents in the two moving voices are countered by increasing rhythmic activity and fullness of texture as the phrase unfolds. In fact, a mild drive to the cadence seems to develop. This phrase, then, seems closer to the shape of a plane than of a curve; if there is any rise or fall, it is virtually imperceptible.

Thus, the entire pattern of rising and ebbing intensity can be formulated very simply: the peaks of excitment grow successively higher at first, reach an apex in the sequence-ostinato section (measures 28-49), and then gradually subside to the ending plane. The whole may be represented graphically somewhat as follows:

It is interesting to note that this type of structure places the main emphasis on what would seem a rather insignificant portion of the text. For what can only be regarded as a climactic effect falls on the words *Filia Sion,* daughter of Zion. The poem may be translated as follows:

> Most far-seeing virgin
> Where art thou going
> So like the dawn, very rosy?
> Daughter of Zion
> All sweetness and beauty art thou
> As beautiful as the moon
> As luminous as the sun.

Why Josquin should have chosen to place emphasis just on these words seems something of a mystery. It could have been an attempt to emphasize the virgin's historical connection as the daughter of Zion who would bring forth a savior. Or some personal reference could underlie the musical setting, such as Lowinsky has suggested in connection with some of Gombert's motets.[14] Or it could be that Josquin simply was not thinking in terms of interpreting the text. Perhaps this last is the most plausible explanation, since he actually did go against the sense and punctuation of the poem, coupling the end of one sentence and the beginning of the next (*quasi aurora valde rutilans?* and *Filia Sion*) into a single drive toward climax.

At any rate, Josquin's manipulation of the intensity into curves and the curves into a general pattern of trends is clear and unmistakable. That such a structure could have been achieved by accident seems highly unlikely.

The question still remains, however, of to what extent the idea of the temporal organization of intensity curves influenced Josquin's artistic decisions. The mere presence of trends, even if they fall into very clear patterns, does not necessarily mean that the style is essentially narrative. In order to justify such an assertion, one must first decide whether the pattern would have been perceptible and whether the play of forces has been handled so as to adequately fulfill the expectations aroused.

The first point can be granted out of hand, I would suggest. The differences between the dimensions of the curves are far from subtle. One could hardly help but perceive the general rise in intensity toward the midpoint, and the tapering off that follows. Nor would this perception require an especially acute memory or careful weighing and balancing. The effect is obvious.

As for the question of fulfillment of expectations, there are two critical points: the reversal of general direction following the climax, and the ending. Everywhere else one can sense that a trend is being followed. At all but these two points, something like a sense of inertia—a tendency to continue motion in an already established direction—gives rise to an expectation concerning what the next step should be, and then this expectation is followed out. The question is whether there is evidence of an attempt to modify the expectations at these two critical points, that is, whether something is done to make the reversal of direction and the ending seem to be something more than arbitrary moves.

To take up the change in direction, first of all, we may note that the climactic curve is unique in one respect: It is the only place in this motet where the growth of intensity is channeled directly into a strong cadence. All of the other strong cadences (i.e., those using or implying the pressure of the tritone) set in only after a descending tendency has come into evidence (measures 23-24, 60-61, and 72-73). All of the other intensity arches merely turn around when they reach their peaks and start downward; this one is channeled into a most significant effect. Thus, this is the only place in the composition when the turn downward seems something more than arbitrary. Here it seems a necessity, for it suggests the sense of exhaustion which should follow an accomplishment if it is in any way significant.

It could well be said that each of the earlier rises represented an attempt to build up to a climactic effect which did not reach fruition. Yet each curve left something of an expectation that eventually such a climactic event would come to pass. As one curve, and then another, and then another went by without bringing about such an effect, though carrying implications of increasing intensity, the expectation of climax would become more powerful. When so strong and obvious a climactic effect as the cadence of measures 45-46 came about, it would seem the realization of a goal rather than another step in the rising trend. Thus, one would have come to expect the reversal that sets in directly afterward. It seems clear, then, that Josquin took considerable care to make the turn downward an appropriate result rather than a capricious action.

The ending also seems carefully prepared. In this case, it is not the breaking of the descending pattern that suggests the terminal quality, but rather an unusual way of continuing the trend. The penultimate phrase (measures 62-67), it may be recalled, was adjudged to represent a lesser degree of intensity than the one that preceded it primarily because it was so short (six measures as opposed to approximately thirteen in its predecessor). Qualitatively, however, the beginning of this phrase seems rather strong—perhaps stronger than anything in the preceding phrase—what with its fast motion, the four-voice canon, and the rising subject. Certainly it holds promise of eventually reaching a higher level than can be found in the earlier phrase. That the intensity is so quickly and seemingly so arbitrarily turned downward can only strike one as puzzling.

The net effect is to set up a quality of extreme condensation that is without precedent or preparation in this motet; within a very short time, after all, a rather wide gamut of intensity has been traced out. The fact that there is no preparation for such a turn of events—so promising a rise and so disappointing a descent—lends a quality of surprise. The surprise, in turn, leads to an expectation of reaction or change. It is as though this puzzling passage were inserted purposefully to set the stage for what follows in order to make that seem a return to a relatively normal state of affairs. The reaction takes the form of a plane which seems neither to gain nor to lose much energy. Here the condensation gives way to a free and leisurely unfolding of events pretty much at a single level of intensity. Since this represents a more stable situation, it does indeed suggest return to a more normal state of affairs. Taken together with the novel feeling of tonal stability imparted by the alternation of G and D in the bass, an atmosphere most appropriate for the suggestion of termination is created in a convincing way.

Thus, at this critical point too, there is evidence of care taken to modify our expectations of continuation, suggesting that the change in the course of events (in this case, the ending) represents something more than an arbitrary move. In this entire composition, then, every step seems to flow out of the preceding events, and at the same time to contribute to those yet to come, and to do this most smoothly and convincingly.

The second motet, *Victimae paschali laudes,* presents quite a different picture in several respects. It is much longer, divided into two *partes,* and is built on, not one, but three preexistent melodies. Perhaps most striking, however, is the absence of repetitive devices such as sequence, ostinato, imitation, canon, etc. (There are only two snatches of imitation, these at the beginning of the *secunda pars* in measures 48-51 and in measures 100-103.)

The main preexistent melody is the one from which this motet takes its name and text: the Easter sequence *Victimae paschali laudes*. The Gregorian melody is presented in full (only a few unimportant notes are omitted), even with the verse *Credendum est magis soli Mariae veraci* that has since come to be omitted. For the most part, this melody is presented discreetly elaborated by the tenor, but there are several migrations to other voices: to the altus in measures 10-14, 50-60, 70-78, and 86-90, and to the bassus in measures 14-19. In some of these cases, the migrations lead to an overlapping of chant segments.

The other preexistent melodies are to be found in the superius. During the *prima pars* (measures 1-47), this voice quotes the superius of Ockeghem's chanson *D'un autre amer*, while it presents the superius of Hayne van Ghizeghem's famous chanson *De tous biens plaine* in the *secunda pars*, both with only minor deviations from the versions to be found in, for example, the *Odhecaton*. The titles of these pieces, of course, represent most appropriate commentaries on the text of the Easter sequence which celebrates Christ's self-sacrifice: this was indeed another kind of love from the kind humans are used to and, in Josquin's view, it brought all good things to mankind.

Once again, as in *Virgo prudentissima*, these features come to seem insignificant and only tangentially related to questions of musical value compared to the pattern of the ebb and flow of intensity. The *prima pars* contains four separate curves which form a clear pattern. The first (measures 1-10) is in the shape of an arch, rising in measures 1-6 and falling thereafter (Example 9). The increase in intensity is suggested by successive increases in

Example 9. *Victimae paschali laudes*: m. 1-10.

119

rhythmic activity (from whole notes to halves to quarters and even to a few eighths) and by the addition of two voices in measure 3. The lessening of intensity is marked first by the general descent in each of the voices which sets in at measure 7, then by the cessation of motion in the superius, and finally by the slowing first to quarter notes and then to halves.

The second intensity curve (Example 10) begins with a

Example 10. *Victimae paschali laudes*: m. 10-21.

similar series of increases in rhythmic activity, leading from half-note to quarter-note motion, and then to isolated eighth notes. In measure 17, the quarter-note motion spreads to two of the voices, while the texture is thickened by the entry of the fourth voice in the following measure. Thus the sense of drive extends right to the beginning of measure 19. At that point, three of the voices become static, while the altus, after an initial upward leap, simply moves down the scale in eighth and quarter notes, all suggesting that the energy generated in measures 10-18 is here being dissipated.

Qualitatively it is very clear that this curve does not attain the level of excitement reached by the first. There is much less eighth-note motion; the full four-voice texture is heard only briefly; and, with the possible exception of the altus, the texture seems to lie in a considerably lower register. It does introduce one element, however, that points toward rising intensity: a deemphasis of the descent at the end. Where the descent occupies four of the ten measures of the first curve, it is allotted only two of the eleven measures in this one.

Although the third curve (Example 11) begins as a duet in fairly slow motion, increases in rhythmic activity and the addition of the two other voices quickly bring the intensity up to a fairly

Example 11. *Victimae paschali laudes*: m. 21-33.

high level. All of this bustle is led directly into a rather surprising event, the C-minor triad in measure 30, and from there into a cadence formula in B♭ (measures 32-33). Because of the long passage with full texture, the greater rhythmic activity and the independence of the voices, the striking (because it is unexpected) quality of the C-minor triad, and the strength of the cadence, this curve obviously represents a considerable increase in intensity over the level reached in the second curve.

The trend already noted toward deemphasis of the descent is carried even farther here. By the end of measure 34, after only about one measure of respite, the drive is under way again. The B♭ cadence is just a temporary obstruction to the growing excitement. That such a powerful effect as a strong cadence is so quickly overcome (i.e., without much implication of relapse) testifies to the strength of the force propelling the events on their way to increasing intensity.

The last curve in the *prima pars* (Example 12) uses a full texture throughout. Very quickly the half-note motion is replaced first by quarter notes (measure 35) and then eighth notes. Quarter notes begin to spread into other voices in measure 37, so that by measure 40 three of the voices are in quarters, and by the end of measure 41 all four are in quarter notes. Eighth notes begin to be found in measure 42, with the remainder of the texture still proceeding in quarter notes. No sooner does one voice finish its eighth-note motion, furthermore, than another takes it up, so that the listener is treated to a veritable cascade of eighth notes. With the marked rhythmic independence of the separate voices from measure 43 on, the impression of a great deal of animation is

Example 12. *Victimae paschali laudes*: m. 33-47.

created, and the whole sense of drive and excitement is channeled into a strong cadence formula (measures 44-45).

By all considerations, this represents the highest level of intensity yet reached. The great rhythmic activity and independence in a full texture alone would suggest this. Nowhere have we seen all four of the voices moving so quickly for so long a time. Nowhere have we seen eighth-note passages piled one upon the other, while the other voices moved on their independent courses. Nowhere have we seen so long a drive and so powerful a culmination to it as the cadence of measures 44-45 provides. If the present-day listener can clear his mind of the romantic dimensions of sound to which he has become so accustomed, and place himself in something akin to the frame of mind of someone from this time, he can perhaps get an idea of how thrilling this effect must have seemed.

Such a climax, of course, is perfectly in keeping with the sense of the text, which at this point speaks of the prince of life, who, in dying, lives and reigns. To the devout believer, which Josquin presumably was, what could have been more thrilling!

At the cadential point is to be found one of those strokes of genius, so appropriate and yet so unexpected, that set this great composer apart even from his very able contemporaries. Instead of coming to a close with a perfect authentic cadence, as would be expected, Josquin resolves the dominant to a first inversion of the tonic and then proceeds to root position by way of a weaker plagal cadence. The unmistakable suggestion is of relief, presumably at the positive outcome of the battle between life and death in the text.

The entire *prima pars*, then, might be represented graphically as follows:

After a culmination of this magnitude, there is only one way to go, and that is down. The need is for relief, rest, a surcease from the excitement with which the *prima pars* closed. And the text lends itself to such a condition: for the moment it turns conversational in tone, asking Mary to tell what she saw.

The music that begins the *secunda pars* provides just such a sense of relief. The contrast is so pronounced, indeed, that it seems not just a temporary retreat, but rather a complete reorganization of forces. Not only does this part of the motet start at a very low level of excitement—qualitatively lower than is to be found anywhere in the *prima pars*—but it also requires a good deal of time and effort to prod it out of this low level and start motion toward a climax again. This is not just a mild relief, but a relief of proportions sufficiently heroic to match those of the preceding build-up and climax.

That the opening of the *secunda pars* (Example 13) repre-

Example 13. *Victimae paschali laudes*: m. 48-60.

sents a very low level of intensity can be judged from the slowness of the motion, and particularly from the thinness of the texture: this is the longest passage with less than three voices and it contains the only point in the entire motet where but a single voice is heard. As for the difficulty of rising out of this low level, it need but be noted that there are two attempts to push the intensity upward through the introduction of fuller textures and increased rhythmic activity (measures 60-67 and 76-88; see Examples 14 and 15), but that each of these attempts issues only into a rather prolonged duet which does not have much rhythmic activity. The unmistakable suggestion is that the attempts to rise out of this state of lethargy have not succeeded.

If the individual sections are inspected closely, however, it can be seen that the second attempt to raise the intensity is stronger than the first, and that the restoration of the low level is progressively less emphatic. The first rise (measures 60-67; Example 14), utilizing only three of the voices, turns to some quarter-note motion after three measures, and to the use of quarter notes in the whole measure and in more than one voice only about three measures later. The suggestion of what was probably a Phrygian cadence [15] in measure 67 leads to a very quick collapse of the attempt to rise; only one voice continues briefly in quarter notes before reverting to the halves found in the other voices, and the texture is thinned out to a duet. That so weak a cadence could bring about so rapid

Example 14. *Victimae paschali laudes*: m. 60-74.

a collapse underlines the lack of strength behind the upward thrust and hence the difficulty of arousing energy again.

The second attempt to rise (measures 75-88; Example 15), on the other hand, is appreciably longer (thirteen measures to eight), goes rather quickly to a full texture and to considerable rhythmic activity, and, perhaps most important, exhibits what might be termed a will to live. For the strong move to the E♭ triad in measure 78 probably would have been enough to call a halt to the first rise. And indeed there are signs that something like this is about to happen here—particularly the general pitch descents in

Example 15. *Victimae paschali laudes*: m. 75-93.

each of the voices in measure 79, and the lessening of rhythmic activity and eventual lapse into silence by the tenor. That, in spite of these signs of decay, there is enough rhythmic activity to manage a drive into a cadence (measures 82-83), as well as to bring about a quick return to full texture, testifies to the vitality underlying this surge. Even the eventual tapering off into a duet is accomplished, not gracefully, but protestingly: although superius and tenor subside both in rhythmic activity and in pitch in measures 85-88, the altus and bassus reenter their high registers (measure 86) while the bassus in particular seems reluctant to give up its quarter-note motion. The implication here seems to be that in order to get this thrust to die, one had to beat it down forcibly, quite in contrast to the way the first attempt to rise was so easily brought to a close.

The trend toward added emphasis to the thrusts is matched by a decrease in the importance of the calmer sections. Where the opening section of solo and duet occupies a full twelve measures (Example 13), the duet following the first thrust (measures 68-74; Example 14) has shrunk to seven measures and the last duet (measures 89-92; Example 15) takes up only four.

By now, of course, a break toward a major climax is well expected, what with the dwindling of the duet sections and the expansion of the thrusts. And such a build-up to climax is exactly what follows. It is in three stages, the first cut off by a brief reversion to a three-voice texture in measures 98-99 (Example 16), the

Example 16. *Victimae paschali laudes*: m. 93-100.

second by a cadence to D in measures 105-106 and a slowing of the motion (Example 17), and the third driving directly into the

Example 17. *Victimae paschali laudes*: m. 100-107.

126

climactic cadence which brings the motet to a close (Example 18). Once again the cadence plays a most significant role in building and defining the climax. In the first of these stages (Example 16), the cadence comes after some of the steam has been taken out of the drive by reversion to a three-voice texture (measures 99-100). The next surge (Example 17) drives right into the cadence (measures 105-106) but it is recognizably in the wrong key; so many cadences to G have been heard in the *secunda pars* (measures 54, 60, 74, 93, and 100) that the cadence to D at this point clearly seems an introduction of variety. This feeling, of course, leaves an expectation that G will reassert its influence, so that the cadence on D sounds not so much like the goal of the journey as like an intermediate point. The cadence serves both to close off one stage of the build-up and to lend something of the function of an expected goal to the coming cadence on G. The listener probably feels that it is needed to set the scheme right and to confirm his interpretations throughout the course of the motet.

The final cadence (measures 118-119; Example 18) clearly

Example 18. *Victimae paschali laudes*: m. 108-121.

comes as the culmination of a much longer build-up (eleven measures to five in each of the preceding thrusts), and one in which the activity and rhythmic independence of the voices suggest a great deal more pressure than has been generated heretofore in the *secunda pars*. The increased length and pressure and the goal-like quality now associated with the G cadence combine to make this a most impressive climax and a fitting counterpart to the end of the *prima pars*. As in the *prima pars*, there is a remnant of motion past the cadence (altus), this time introducing an ominous quality.[16]

Once more, expression of the text probably entered into Josquin's thinking. For by use of this structure, emphasis was placed upon the word *Alleluia,* the joyous expression that terminates the Easter sequence. The ominous turn immediately following the final cadence can be taken as a hint of what mankind's condition might have been had the Christian mystery not been acted out. Thus the entire motet emerges as an expression not so much of the dramatic course of events portrayed in the text, as of the intense personal feelings aroused by the events of the liturgical season and by the Christian mystery in general—apprehension giving way to relief and joy.

The pattern of trends is clear. The appropriateness of the various moves seems so readily apparent as to require little comment. In each of the two *partes,* the placement of the climax at the end, and its definition by means of a drive directly into a cadence (a most significant effect because it serves as culmination for the drive), serves to produce a convincing sense of termination. The fact that none of the several build-ups preceding these climaxes has brought about a satisfactory sense of released tension makes the ending culmination seem, not just expected, but welcome.

In both *partes,* furthermore, this feeling is reinforced by a cadence to what is obviously the wrong key (B♭ in the *prima pars* and D in the *secunda pars*) just before the final drive to climax gets under way. Such a venturesome move so near to the end makes the return to the definition of G assume something of the quality of a goal also. The fact that the goals of the culmination of drive and the return to the definition of G are achieved at the same point creates a most powerful and convincing sense of termination.

Easily understandable also are the reaction to the climactic ending of the *prima pars* at the beginning of the *secunda pars* (the long section in which the calmer sentiments seem to have the upper hand), and the pattern of mounting excitement which gradually emerges from this section of lesser vitality and leads toward the climax. If one omits the first curve of the *prima pars* from consideration, the steady growth in intensity leading up to the climactic ending of that portion of the motet also seems reasonable and plausible.

Every step taken, then, is understandable as a narrative move with but one exception: the opening curve of the *prima pars.* Why does this curve reach a higher level of intensity than that of the following curve and perhaps that of the third one as well? This would seem to place it outside the trend pattern of the *prima pars,* which—aside from this—outlines a steady growth in intensity.

While one cannot account for such a move with any certainty, I think there is a possible explanation for it in narrative terms. This explanation has to do with the problem of opening a composition, in particular with establishing a frame of mind at the outset which will be prepared for, and in sympathy with, the forthcoming pattern of trends.

In the motet, *Virgo prudentissima,* Josquin has prepared his audience for the ensuing build-up of forces primarily by maintaining the intensity at a low level for quite a long time (the repeated duets). By the time the building process gets under way, his audience would be anxious to see it come; it would seem a necessary and most welcome reaction to the lengthy passage in muted tones.

In the case *Victimae paschali laudes,* an entirely different approach was used, but the aim may well have been the same. Here there was a quick build-up to a high level of intensity, a fairly lengthy plateau at that high level, and then an unhurried descent. Such a strong sense of excitement so early in the piece sets the stage nicely for a reaction, which is what the second curve represents.

Suppose now that Josquin had simply allowed the low-intensity level brought into play by this reaction to take control and had not presented the gradual rise which follows. I think the reaction of a listener might well have been to question the purpose served by the initial full-blooded curve. "What was all that excitement about?", he might well wonder. It would then seem an effect comparable to the briefly noisy opening of Berlioz' *Roman Carnival,* which never fails to arouse a sense of incongruity, at least to this writer.

The initial curve has led us to expect not only the reaction, but the rise in intensity which issues out of it. In short, it has set the course of events on its way in a manner calculated to predispose the listener to accept the specific line of development that unfolds.

But one question remains: that is, whether one of the climaxes could be considered more intense or more significant than the other. Qualitative tests, I would suggest, would lead to inconclusive results. Neither one sounds noticeably greater in magnitude. There is not enough of an appreciable difference between the rhythmic activity, fullness of texture, etc., to lead to an intuitive judgment in this respect.

There is, however, a considerable difference in the proportions of the two build-ups. The climax of the *prima pars* is reached after forty-four measures, ten of which are devoted to the initial outburst. The trend leading directly to the climax can be said to occupy approximately thirty-five measures. In the *secunda pars*, on the other hand, the climax occurs after seventy-three measures, and, since there is no initial outburst, the trend leading to this climax occupies all of that time. Thus it takes roughly twice as long to build to the ending of the *secunda pars*.

The direct line of ascent in the entire *secunda pars*, furthermore, and the rather complex play of forces which is involved, leave the impression that this climax was reached only after overcoming many more obstacles than in the *prima pars*, and that it therefore reflects a more mature, deliberate and serious effort. The peak in the *prima pars*, by comparison, seems easily reached and hence perhaps more dramatic, but lacking in the stability and broadness appropriate for a convincing ending.

I think it would be a mistake, however, to maintain on this basis that the climax of the *secunda pars* is higher in rank. It makes more sense merely to point out that they are different kinds of climaxes which complement each other: the first suggests an ending that is provisional in nature, calling for a retrenchment rather than effecting a complete termination of the work, while the second suggests the greater sense of finality appropriate for calling the motet as a whole to a halt.

Thus, in this motet no less than in *Virgo prudentissima*, every detail bespeaks a concern for the creation of a convincing sense of narration. The individual effects count for little; it is the sequence of events that forms the main point of appeal. As listeners, we are gradually absorbed into a flow of happenings which, by the arrangement of increases and decreases in intensity, presents a psychologically correct and telling analogy to an easily recognizable pattern of dramatic development.

I think that anyone who takes the trouble to have these two motets performed will probably judge them to be most attractive, interesting, and highly artistic compositions—quite different in quality from what might have been expected from the various historians' pronouncements. At least this has been my experience;

every time my students have come to these works in the course of their studies, they have been most agreeably impressed by the sound of the music and the way the separate events fit together to produce a sense of dramatic continuity. What, then, would account for the largely negative evaluations, particularly of *Victimae paschali laudes,* by Ambros, Leichtentritt, and Osthoff? Did they not hear these works as we do today, or did they see other faults in their construction?

While there can be no certain answers to questions of this nature, there do seem to be some possible explanations. As I have indicated at the beginning of this essay, prejudice against the device of the *cantus firmus* may be responsible for a negative attitude toward *Victimae paschali laudes,* at least in some measure. The continual simultaneous presentation of two preexistent melodies may have seemed so artificial a mode of construction as to have predisposed writers to look for faults in the artistic effect. Then, too, the treatment of dissonance is quite free in this work: there are what today would be called accented passing tones, simultaneous passing tones in different voices, and other types of nonharmonic tones which produce somewhat dissonant effects. Ambros may have reasoned that these are such crude harmonic practices, that they must be taken to reflect an early, undisciplined, and hence not completely successful style.

Perhaps more significant in this respect, however, is the construction of the individual lines. Possibly because of the conditions imposed by the continual presence of two preexistent melodies, as well as by harmonic and textural requirements, the individual lines tend to seem static at times, to wander somewhat, and to develop a sense of leaving commitments unfulfilled. This could be what Osthoff had in mind when he wrote that the constructive elements were not subordinated to a general conception, but rather hindered the unfolding of the lines and the few attempts at expressive writing.[17]

But all of these considerations, I would suggest—if indeed they were behind the low opinion of this work—are more the reflection of a dubious approach to the study of history than of problematical elements in the style. There is really no reason for prejudice against any particular technique of *cantus-firmus* treatment if one considers the *cantus firmus* not as a limiting factor, but as a starting point for the calculation of consonances, harmonic progressions, and the compositional process in general.[18] A more restrained treatment of dissonance, furthermore, does not necessarily imply a more polished or advanced style. It seems dogmatic in the extreme to assume that some absolute value, or at least a value derived from the idea of progress, should be attached to the more conservative dissonance treatment that flourished later in the sixteenth century. I think it makes more sense to guess that a composer like, for example, Palestrina would have adopted a more circumspect approach to the treatment of dissonance, not because it was intrinsically better, but because he saw some advantage to it in terms of his own aims and ideals. Certainly there would seem little justification in projecting this value back onto a style for which it may have had little relevance.

It is the question of melodic construction, however, that brings up the crux of the matter. For I believe that emphasis on this particular aspect of composition is not fully justified. I do not see any real evidence, in other words, to indicate that Josquin's main concern was the construction of attractive melodic lines. Indeed, the examples chosen by Leichtentritt [19] to demonstrate Josquin's skill in this respect are singularly unconvincing. Machaut wrote far more interesting melodic lines than these, as did Dufay and many of the less well-known composers who flourished in the latter part of the fourteenth century and the early part of the fifteenth. If the melodic element were really the focal point of Josquin's style, as Leichtentritt and Osthoff at least seem to imply, there would be little reason for considering him a great composer, or even a moderately successful one.

Thus I would suggest that the general emphasis on melodic value that seems to be at the root of the judgments of at least Leichtentritt and Osthoff (and quite possibly Ambros as well) reflects a failure to observe a fundamental precept of stylistic analysis—the evaluation of style primarily in terms of its strong points. Indeed, I would go so far as to suggest that historians generally have attempted to force the style of Josquin, and of other renaissance composers as well, into a Procrustean bed of harmonic, melodic, and historical conceptions derived from text books but not relevant to the situation as it developed in the fifteenth and sixteenth centuries. The study of these two motets—almost universally deemed insignificant—should make clear just how much distortion an approach of this kind can introduce into the attempt to gain some understanding of Josquin's style. If we are ever to recreate anything more than a fanciful picture of Josquin as a creative personality, we cannot afford to ignore traits or works because they do not conform to our historical preconceptions.

FIVE

J. S Bach:
The Chorale Harmonizations and the Principles of Harmony

PERHAPS NO OTHER ASPECT OF MUSIC has attracted as much attention during this century as harmony. That the problems relating to this musical element— even the problems connected only with so-called traditional usages —are considered to be anything but resolved can be judged from the fact that many of our most distinguished composers and theorists have attempted to codify anew or to sum up the practices of the past, at least of the fairly recent past. They have not been content with the formulations of Goetschius (1853-1943), Riemann (1849-1914), or Rameau (1683-1764), but have obviously felt that something remained unsaid on the subject and that they could improve upon existing methods.

With all due respect, and with appreciation for the many insights contributed by present-day writers on this subject, I would suggest that there is yet some question of how well the so-called traditional harmony is understood. For most of the methods currently in use do not really seek out the sources of judgment and value underlying the harmonic decisions of various composers; they merely present sets of rules-of-thumb derived, more or less adequately, from observation of the works of great composers. Indeed, in some cases, little is done to differentiate the practices of such diverse creative personalities as Bach, Mozart, Beethoven, and Mendelssohn—they are all considered part of "the tradition."

In this essay, I should like to examine the chorale harmonizations of J. S. Bach, a composer who has certainly made great contributions to what is known as the Western harmonic tradition, with a view to determining the bases for his decisions in this respect. The aim is not to catalog the entities or the relationships he used, or the relative frequencies with which they occur, but rather to recreate something like Bach's frame of mind in making particular decisions, and the reasons and reasoning behind his choices.

Although it may seem that a project of this kind would be superfluous in view of the comprehensive study by McHose,[1] I would suggest that there is an assumption underlying McHose's approach that renders his results of dubious value for the purpose at hand. He has assumed from the outset that the virtue in Bach's harmony can be traced to the consistent employment of certain chord progressions. Then, since no simple relations of this kind can be formulated (a tonic, for example, does not invariably proceed to any particular kind of chord in Bach's harmonizations), McHose adopted the expedient of classifying chords, presumably according to some kind of function, and then studying this functional behavior statistically. In this way, he derived various sets of model progressions—progressions such as Bach used at least a good deal of the time.

But how do we know that chord progression is entirely, or even primarily, responsible for the harmonic logic so readily apparent in Bach's chorale settings? And how do we know that the classifications devised by McHose bear any resemblance to Bach's own conceptions, or that they really represent meaningful and significant entities in his practice? It seems open to debate, for instance, whether the motion from a II to a V, or from a VI to a IV must be granted exactly the same kind and degree of significance in this style as the motion from a V to a I. Perhaps, after all, it was only the latter progression that was important to Bach, with the approach to the dominant more or less a matter of indifference.

Indeed, the whole statistical approach does not seem well advised. For there are so many problems of diagnosing and labeling chords, even in the chorales, that any set of figures must be considered somewhat unreliable. One is constantly forced to make decisions concerning whether a passing-tone or neighbor-note actually forms a new chord, or whether it is merely a contrapuntal decoration; whether a group of passing-tones and neighbor-notes between two positions of the same chord should itself be considered an intervening chord; or whether a particular formation should be interpreted as a seventh chord or as a triad with an accented passing-tone. Because of these problems, and because basic assumptions of questionable validity necessarily underlie any method of gathering figures, statistics probably should be considered of only limited applicability. They are useful, perhaps, in support of an hypothesis, but certainly should not be employed as a means of formulating first assumptions about Bach's intentions.

In order to find a better procedure, it seems essential to derive the general approach not from chance observation or preconceived theories, but from a consideration of the most fundamental question bearing upon the subject. The most fundamental question here is obviously one more concerned with value than with chord progressions or natural law. It is generally taken for granted, I think, that Bach's harmony has some special merit, a merit above and beyond that to be observed in the works of most, if not all, other composers. But what is the source of this merit? What practices account for it? These are the questions that should be of concern in this kind of study, and these are the questions that are ignored in most present-day approaches to Bach's harmony.

When the problem is phrased in this way, it becomes a matter of no great difficulty to find a starting point on which there would be general agreement. For undoubtedly the merit is connected in some way with the ability to suggest a sense of direction to the harmonic motion. Compared to Bach's treatment, most earlier composers' harmonies seem either to wander more or less aimlessly, or else to proceed mechanically from point to point.[2] Even the styles of great contemporaries such as Corelli, Vivaldi, and Handel— men rightly noted for their harmonic inventiveness and polish—do not seem so highly developed in this respect, so powerful, as Bach's. After this time, of course, the general slowing of the harmonic rhythm and, later, the increased use of the rich sonorities obtained by chromatic alteration tended to weaken this sense of harmonically suggested direction.

The essential questions, then, are how the sense of direction was created, and how it was used to evoke the powerful psychological responses that would account for Bach's acknowledged preeminence in this respect.

From Bach's own point of view, the problem would have been to create a quality of drive by the choice of harmonies and to induce the feeling in a listener that a particular series of harmonic events should have such and such an outcome. Indeed, the sense of commitment to just that type of outcome would have to grow stronger as the phrase progressed. In other words, the series of harmonies which forms the phrase gradually would have to give rise to certain expectations, expectations which would become more and more definite as the phrase unfolded. These expectations, then, either would be fulfilled fairly soon, or else modified by subsequent events. Eventually, however, the chain of expectations and modifications would have to find some kind of fulfillment. It would be the gradually mounting sense of suspense to see if the expectations are fulfilled, or else to see in what manner they would be modified —the impatience, if you will, to perceive the ground plan underlying the various separate events—that would create the psychological impression of the harmonies' driving somewhere, and that would make the harmonic motion seem directed rather than haphazard. The question is, then, just how Bach might have gone about influencing the expectations of his audience by means of the harmony.

One of the strongest and best recognized methods of influencing harmonic expectations in Bach's time, as well as in our own, undoubtedly was what might be termed the commitment of the dominant. The dominant obviously must have carried a connotation of tension, tension which seems completely resolved only by a move to tonic. Something of the same kind of commitment, furthermore, is suggested by the diminished and diminished-seventh chords built on the leading-tone of the scale. These also generate a sense of tension that seems completely resolved only by a resolution to tonic. This, of course, has been recognized by many theorists, who view the diminished and diminished-seventh chords as forms of incomplete dominant sevenths or dominant ninths—forms in which the root is omitted.[3] Although this may be considered an artificial position, it does suggest something of the similarity of commitment which is the focus of study here. Hence, in the following discussions, it will be assumed that the conception of the dominant includes these two chord types. What holds for the dominant will hold also for the diminished and diminished-seventh chords, provided only that they resolve appropriately; that is, in a way that makes it clear that they were functioning as substitutes for the dominant.

Thus, whenever it is sensed that a particular chord is a dominant (or one of these substitutes), a listener familiar with the style would come to expect a resolution to tonic. Needless to say, this expectation would not always be fulfilled. The resolution might be to the submediant or to the very similar-sounding subdominant in first inversion, injecting an element of surprise. But this is a conventional kind of unexpected turn of events—one which seems half expected in retrospect—and itself induces a class of expectations for the subsequent flow of events. One cannot be certain whether the next move will be another approach to the dominant, this time with the "correct" resolution, or whether it represents the first step in a move to depart from the key. In other words, the deceptive cadence represents a modification of expectations in that it prepares one for a very specific set of alternatives; indeed, it makes one anxious to find out which of the alternative courses will be followed out.

Another type of modification of expectation would be brought about by motion from a dominant to another dominant a degree higher (V to V of II, for example), or to the dominant of the submediant (V to V of VI). In these cases, the sense of tension (i.e., of need for resolution) associated with the original dominant is not only preserved, but heightened. The tension, after all, has not been resolved, but merely turned in a new direction: the entity suggesting resolution has been changed. These particular kinds of changes, furthermore, carry an unmistakable connotation of raised excitement. On the other hand, a move from the dominant to the dominant of the subdominant (V to V of IV) carries something of the sense of resolution of tension associated with the move to tonic (the degree on which the dominant of the subdominant is erected) but also sets in motion another drive toward resolution, namely toward the subdominant.

In this way, then, using the various types of dominant resolution, Bach could well have fashioned a flow of harmonies which would have raised expectations, modified them, and eventually brought the whole process to a sense of fulfillment.

If this was the case—if Bach actually was thinking along these lines—one would expect to find, above all, very frequent dominant resolutions in his chorale harmonizations. For unless a dominant followed by one of its proper resolutions is heard very frequently, the play of expectations, modifications, and culminations hardly would seem tight enough to suggest the directed quality so obviously at the root of Bach's harmonic practice. If dominants were not heard frequently, the impression might be of a kind of harmonic drifting issuing occasionally into a brief drive toward some chord or other—an impression not much different from that imparted by much of Ockeghem's music.[4] Perhaps, then, every third or fourth chord should be a dominant if the chain of commitments is to progress without a noticeable break. If the rate of incidence were to get much beyond every fifth or sixth chord, the contrast between harmonic drift and drive might well set in. Thus, on the average, two of every three or four chords should be a dominant and its resolution—that is, if we are to judge that this factor played any major role in developing the sense of harmonic direction.

On the other hand, however, it is entirely conceivable that a program of this type could involve considerable variation in the incidence of dominants. Indeed, this variation would itself provide a means of influencing expectations, as well as the strength of expectations. For, assuming that a norm of a high incidence of dominants was established, a listener would be predisposed to expect a steady flow of dominants and their resolutions. He might then interpret any prolonged absence of such relations as something rather unusual, and begin to look for the dominant commitment with an increasing sense of urgency: he would know that it was coming because of his familiarity with the normally high rate of incidence. The longer it is avoided—within limits, of course—the stronger the expectation would grow, and the stronger would be the sense of tension to see if the expectation is realized.

Thus, there are two conditions that we should expect to find fulfilled if we are to judge that dominant relations played any considerable role in Bach's harmonic thinking: a very frequent use of dominants, and some variation in the rate of incidence.

Something of the frequency of the dominant relationships can be judged from a few examples. In the following illustrations, each of the separate chords [5] is marked with an Arabic numeral. Whenever the chord is a dominant, an asterisk is added to the right of its number, while the chord that resolves the dominant is similarly provided with a cross. In Example 1, all but twelve of the total of forty-nine chords are dominants or their resolutions—an average of just under four of every five chords. In the opening phrase, for instance, only the first and sixth chords do not participate in a dominant resolution. Only twice in the entire chorale are there as many as two consecutive chords which are not dominants or standard resolutions of dominants (numbers 11-12 and 18-19). On the other hand, at one point a chain of dominants and resolutions extends through seven consecutive chords (numbers 40-46); at two others, such a chain runs through six chords in a row (20-25

Example 1. Bach: *Lass, o Herr, dein Ohr sich neigen* (No. 218).

and 27-32), and in two additional places it extends through four chords (2-5 and 7-10).

To be sure, this chorale has one of the higher incidences of dominants to be found in Bach's collection. It does not by any means represent an exceptional case, however. For eighty of the 348 chorale harmonizations [6] are roughly comparable to this one in this respect.[7] That is, in each of these harmonizations, approximately four of every five chords, on the average, participate in dominant resolutions. In ten of these, indeed, the incidence is closer to nine of every ten chords.[8]

In another group of chorales, the incidence is somewhat lower, but the difference is hardly appreciable. In Example 2, for instance, only thirteen of the forty-six different chords are not dominants or resolutions of dominants. These thirteen chords, however, still seem lost in the forest of dominants and resolutions. They certainly can do but little more than interrupt the chain of dominant commitments briefly, in spite of the fact that the incidence has

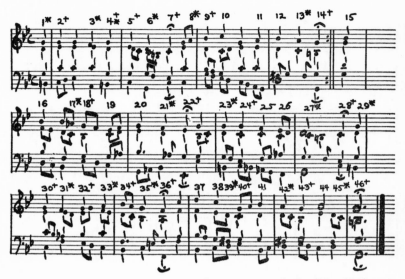

Example 2. *Durch Adams Fall ist ganz verderbt* (No. 100).

here fallen to just over three and one-half of every five chords. Sixty-nine more of the chorales have comparable rates of incidence.[9]

Thus, in well over one-third of Bach's chorale harmonizations (149 of 348), the dominant appears so frequently that it certainly must have played a major role in the generation of expectations. There would be no chance at all for a sense of harmonic drift to develop, inasmuch as all but an occasional chord would be either defining the need for a specific kind of resolution, modifying this expectation, or else providing a fulfillment of it.

But what of the remaining chorales? Example 3 shows a harmonization in which the dominant resolution is heard somewhat less frequently than in the cases treated above. Here only thirty-two of the fifty-two chords are dominants or their resolutions—approximately three of five.

Assuming that this average reflected something like a homogeneous distribution—that is, that this ratio would hold true for most of the phrases contained in the chorale—a frequency of three of five chords still would preclude any possibility of harmonic drift. A typical phrase made up of ten chords, for instance, would contain only four chords which did not participate in a dominant resolution. A possible distribution of these four chords might involve one at the beginning of the phrase, another after the first dominant

Example 3. *Ein' feste Burg* (No. 250).

resolution, and two more between the second and third resolutions. Using the asterisk, cross, and arabic numerals as in the musical examples, such a phrase might be represented as follows: 1 2* 3+ 4 5* 6+ 7 8 9* 10+. Clearly the four chords in an arrangement of this kind would not be sufficient to blur the impression of a chain of dominant commitments and resolutions. At most, they might suggest a slight delay of the next expected dominant.

Only if these four notes were grouped together, perhaps between the second and third dominant resolutions (i.e., 1* 2+ 3* 4+ 5 6 7 8 9* 10+), would there be any possibility of disruption of the chainlike impression. In this case, however, the grouping of the four noncadential chords would produce the effect of a deviation from an established norm, a norm of very frequent dominant resolutions. The sympathetic listener, then, would tend to look for a return to the "normal" state of affairs (i.e., another dominant) with an increasing sense of urgency. Thus when the dominant commitment finally came to be heard, it would carry a greater sense of accrued tension, and hence a greater potentiality for suggesting resolution because it has been so long awaited and so actively anticipated. This, of course, does not represent evidence of a turn away from the use of dominant commitments, but rather seems to be merely another means of manipulating them to produce a modification in expectations, particularly in the strength of the expectations.

A similar consideration is applicable on a larger scale as well. For it may be noted that, in Example 3, the assumption about homogeneous distribution of dominant resolutions simply is not valid: the ratio of three of five chords does not hold for all phrases. For considerable stretches, the frequency of dominant resolutions is quite high—comparable, perhaps, to that found in Example 1. In the first phrase, for instance, only three of the nine chords do not participate in dominant resolutions; in the third phrase (chords 17-24) the ratio is down to two of eight; and in the last phrase (chords 43-52) to two of ten. On the other hand, the second phrase (chords 10-16) has but a single dominant-tonic resolution in seven chords, while the fourth phrase (chords 25-29) likewise contains only one resolution in five chords. Here, too, then —on this larger scale—Bach may well have been establishing a norm of frequent dominant resolutions, then introducing deviations to that norm to heighten the quality of suspense. At least it seems likely that a cultivated and sympathetic listener of the time would have interpreted the organization in this way.

Whether the distribution is homogeneous, or whether it represents a series of deviations from an established normal incidence, the ratio of three chords of five would seem more than adequate to keep alive the suggestion of a chain of dominants and their resolutions and to preclude the emergence of any considerable sense of harmonic drift. Comparable ratios (indeed, often a little better) are to be found in 173 harmonizations.[10]

This leaves only twenty-six harmonizations to be considered. The incidence in nine of these [11] is illustrated in Example 4. Here eighteen of the thirty-five separate chords—slightly over half the total—do not participate in dominant resolutions. Twice there are four consecutive chords without a dominant resolution (numbers 1-4 and 30-33), and three times there are three such chords in a row (14-16, 19-21, and 25-27). Whether dominants occur frequently enough to suggest, with any sense of certainty, that these passages are deviations from a norm is open to question. To be conservative, at any rate, it seems advisable to consider that the dominants do not occur frequently enough to serve this purpose. In these chorales,

Example 4. *O Haupt voll Blut und Wunden* (No. 98).

then, the evidence is not strong enough to permit the inference that dominant resolutions played a very important role in the generation of expectations.

As for the remaining seventeen chorales,[12] each of them has an incidence lying somewhere between those of Example 3 and Example 4. To be on the conservative side once again, let us assume that they do not present conclusive evidence of planning in terms of dominant commitments.

Thus, in all but a handful of chorales, dominants and their resolutions occur so frequently that they must play a most significant role in the generation of expectations. Before one can recover fully from the sense of tension resolved or rechanneled that is suggested by the resolution of a dominant, one would become aware of another commitment posed by the introduction of another dominant. Those cases where the dominant commitment is not felt for some time, furthermore, almost certainly would be interpreted, intuitively, as delays of the expected, delays tending to heighten the strength of the resolution when the expected dominant finally is presented and resolved. All but a few of the chorales, then, consist of a veritable chain of commitments, modifications of those commitments, and resolutions—all generated by the dominant and its implicit need for resolution.

This obviously is not the whole story of Bach's harmonic

technique. If it were, instruction in so-called traditional harmony would be a simple matter indeed: one would only have to urge students to use a great many dominants, and to resolve them in one of the standard ways.

That this will not work can be demonstrated by a simple experiment: by attempting to convert some harmonizations that obviously do not sound like Bach into a reasonable counterfeit of his style merely by an increased use of dominant resolutions. Bukofzer offers a convenient point of departure for this experiment: a reproduction of harmonizations of the first two phrases of *Ein' feste Burg* by Schütz, Schein, Scheidt, and König, alongside the corresponding passage by Bach.[13] All of these versions are presented in Example 5.

Example 5. *Ein' feste Burg.*

The difference between Bach and all of the others is readily apparent. Even Scheidt's quite elaborate contrapuntal setting seems bare, forced, and angular compared with the richness and smoothness of Bach's harmonic motion.

In part, Bach's superiority may be traced to the use of dominants as suggested above. For Bach's version does indeed contain an appreciably higher incidence of dominant resolutions than is to be found in any of the other examples except König's: in the Schütz harmonization, roughly one of five chords engages in a dominant resolution, in the Schein one of two, in the Scheidt two of five, and in the König and Bach roughly three of five. It is interesting to note that the version by König bears considerable resemblance to Bach's—much more so than in the case of the other composers—all of which lends some support to the view that the frequent use of dominant resolutions is a distinctive feature of Bach's style. A natural question to ask, then, is whether a recasting of any or of all of the other versions so as to make greater use of dominants would, by itself, bring them any closer to the superb sense of smooth, directed motion characteristic of the Bach excerpt.

Example 6a represents an attempt to do just this to the Schütz harmonization. The result sounds but little closer to the

Example 6a.

quality of Bach, despite a much increased use of dominants. Perhaps the principle is sound, it might be argued, but the execution faulty, inasmuch as all but three of the seven dominants resolved not to tonics, but to submediants—the so-called deceptive cadence. A better ratio can be achieved by revising the König version in another way (Example 6b).

But this version still does not seem to offer any noticeable improvement. If anything, it seems farther removed from Bach's power and smoothness—particularly at the ends of the phrases—than König's original setting, again despite the increased use of dominants.

One may well wonder, then, whether the frequent use of

Example 6b.

dominants really does contribute so much to the virtue of Bach's harmony. Yet, if Bach's own version of these two phrases is recast, changing only a few notes to avoid some of the dominants (Example 6c), much of its sense of power is lost, although the Bach

Example 6c.

stamp remains recognizable. The dominant commitment obviously plays a considerable role in the style, but it certainly cannot be considered the sole means Bach used to create a sense of harmonic direction.

What other kinds of changes, then, would be required to convert one of these versions to something resembling a Bach harmonization? The answer, I would suggest, is a careful design of the bass, a design which, by itself, would suggest a sense of directed motion toward the cadence.

The mechanics of such a bass organization are fairly easy to formulate. This clearly would be a matter of shaping the bass so as to suggest that a phrase consisted of not just a series of individual notes, or even of isolated clusters of related notes, but rather that it embodied an intuitively perceptible pattern of trends—a pattern which would culminate in the cadence. Only by the employment of trends could one even conceive of a line generating the qualities of commitment, progress, and fulfillment that are necessary to suggest a sense of direction. As the trend developed and the listener got a firmer grasp of the pattern of motion, he would come to be more and more certain of the steps to follow. Having heard two notes of the pattern, he could only guess at the third; having heard three, his guess would become less tentative; having heard five or six, it may have ceased to be so much a guess and become more of a certainty.

As the trend grows ripe, of course, the expectation is gradually weighted more and more in favor of a culmination, a quality which will be supplied by the cadence ending the phrase. In this way, then, it would have been possible to suggest a quality of momentum as well as a general direction to the motion—the commitment to a culmination will have grown stronger and stronger as the pattern unfolded.

Obviously the harmonizations by Schütz, Schein, and Scheidt (see Examples 5a-c above) do not develop much of a sense that the bass is organized into trends, largely because there are so many skips which cannot easily be incorporated into a larger pattern (a sequence, for instance). As a result, one tends to hear either isolated notes, or, at best, isolated groups of two or three notes. Even where there is an obvious attempt to develop a trend (for example, in the first three measures of Scheidt's harmonization), the motion is so filled with quick changes in direction and abrupt leaps of considerable compass that it becomes a question of whether the primary perception is of the underlying rise or whether it is of each of the small units whose totality goes to make up the ascending trend. Is one, after all, more clearly aware of the general direction, or of the shapes of the individual units closed off by the major leaps?

The first phrase of the König version (Example 5d), on the other hand, is organized into a smooth and very easily perceptible pattern of trends: an arch whose last note (C) represents the beginning of a IV-V-I cadence. The curve so formed seems so modest, however—particularly in view of the threefold repetition of C that opens the phrase—that only a moderate degree of momentum is generated.

The bass in each of the phrases of the Bach version (Example 5e) consists of what might well be considered the simplest and most easily perceived of trend-forming patterns: the scale line—descending in the first, ascending in the second. Both of these scale lines, furthermore, run through a complete octave before issuing into the cadence, quite in contrast to the rather timid curve that opens the König harmonization. The improvement in the sense of direction and in the sense of momentum is quite marked.

Another series of experiments may help demonstrate just how large a role the bass trends play in creating the drive to the cadence.

Suppose, first of all, that König's version is redone to create a stronger sense of trend in each of the phrases (Example 7a), yet

Example 7a.

in a way that would use chord progressions different than Bach's. The gain in sense of direction is readily apparent. That this gain can not be traced to the chord progression can be judged from Example 7b, in which the chords are the same as in Example 7a

Example 7b.

but are all in root position. Quite obviously, much of the improvement noted in Example 7a has been lost. Especially noticeable is the static quality resulting from the successive cadences to G in measures 2-4, and also the sense of redundance created by having the bass move from D to G in three of four successive cadences (measures 1-4). And this arbitrarily introduced revision has not even succeeded in making the bass into a really "bad" line (that is, one that has little sense of purpose); for the motion around the circle of fifths in each phrase does succeed in injecting some sense of direction for considerable stretches of time—probably more of a sense of direction than is to be found in the settings by Schütz, Schein, Scheidt, or even König.

The importance of the bass is made even more readily apparent if the Bach setting is revised so as to change the shape of its bass (Example 7c). Even more strikingly than in the König version, the quality of the harmonization—the Bach stamp—has deteriorated. Compared to Bach's own harmonization, this one sounds stilted and static, hovering about the notes C, F, and G to the point of redundance.

Example 7c.

These rather informal experiments are intended merely to indicate the possibility that the bass is a factor contributing to the sense of harmonic directedness in Bach's chorale harmonizations. In order to evaluate the validity of this guess, of course, it is necessary to determine just how consistently Bach shaped his bass in such a way that it would suggest a quality of drive toward the cadence by itself. To some extent, this is a matter of considerable difficulty. It is, after all, no easy matter to judge whether certain types of linear arrangements would or would not generate a drive. Then there is the question of length: what minimum number of notes in the bass would be required to establish a sense of direction? There are so many cases, however, where the answers to these questions are so readily apparent that at least a rough estimate of Bach's intentions can be formulated.

As mentioned previously, the simplest type of linear arrangement to suggest a trend is motion along a scale line. Very quickly, as the listener becomes aware of the pattern underlying the various changes of pitch (i.e., of the scale), the element of prediction, hence of commitment, comes into play. The surer the listener becomes of what the next step will be, the more he is inclined to look for a culmination to the trend. Familiarity with late-baroque procedures, then, probably could be counted upon to make him expect the culmination to take the form of one of the standard cadences of his time (V-I, V-VI, IV-V-I, II-V-I, II$_6$-V-I, VI-IV-V-I, V-I-V, etc.). Thus, something in the nature of an illusion would be created in the mind of the listener, an illusion that the bass was generating energy, or momentum, as it progressed up or down the scale, and that this energy was used up in bringing about the cadential resolution.

It would be essential, of course, that the energy generated by the bass should seem to flow smoothly into the cadence. For if any appreciable disruption of the scale-line trend should occur just before it issued into the cadence, there would be a tendency to concentrate on the surprising turn of events, and hence to drop from memory much of the sense of momentum generated earlier. In other words, the inference might be that the energy previously generated had been used up, at least partially, in bringing about the unexpected deviation from the trend, with little left over to drive forward into the ensuing cadence. Thus, in order to suggest drive to the cadence, the bass would have to flow directly (that is, by conjunct motion) into one of the well-known cadence formulae of the time, since a leap of any size at this point would tend to lessen the sense of momentum.

At the beginning of a phrase, on the other hand, an isolated leap or one or two notes which did not fit into the scale line would not preclude the emergence of a drive to the cadence. For if, as the phrase progressed, four or five notes should move along the scale and flow smoothly into the cadence, the chances are that earlier events which did not fit into this pattern of motion will be quite forgotten. They could be interpreted, intuitively, as having been designed to set the stage from which the drive gets under way. The question, after all, is not whether every note in a phrase is part of a scale line, but whether a scale eventually comes to dominate the phrase to the extent that it generates the sense of drive to the cadence.

Some illustrations might be in order. In Example 8a, a de-

Example 8a. *Freuet euch, Ihr Christen alle* (No. 8).

scending scale terminates on the subdominant degree (although the harmony in this case is an inversion of a supertonic-seventh chord). This degree, then, represents both the end of the descent and the beginning of motion into the familiar II_6-V-I cadence. A very similar instance is shown in Example 8b, the only difference

Example 8b. *Herzlich tut mich verlangen* (No. 21).

being that the descent terminates upon the leading-tone to the dominant instead of on the uninflected subdominant degree, producing a V_6^5 of V-V$_7$-I cadence. A descent terminates upon the supertonic degree in Example 8c, leading to a II-V-I cadence. Of

Example 8c. *Meinen Jesum lass ich nicht* (No. 348).

course the scale might lead directly into the dominant itself, giving rise either to a half cadence (Example 8d), or to an authentic as in Example 8e.

Example 8d. *Vater unser Im Himmelreich* (No. 267).

Example 8e. *Herr Jesu Christ, du höchstes Gut* (No. 266).

Similar considerations obviously are applicable to ascending scales. A scale line moving upward until it reaches the dominant would suggest a channeling of energy just as surely as would a descent. The motion from the dominant to the tonic, then, would resolve that energy. In Example 9a, the scale line itself brings

Example 9a. *Herzlich tut mich verlangen* (No. 21).

about a II_6^5-V-I cadence; in Example 9b the cadence is V_6^5 of

Example 9b. *Ermuntre dich, mein schwacher geist* (No. 9).

Example 9c. *Befiehl du deine Wege* (No. 367).

V-V-I; and in Example 9c the motion does not bring about any standard approach to the dominant, but merely moves through the subdominant degree as a passing-tone. A similar rationale will apply to scales culminating on supertonic (Example 9d), or on submediant as in Example 9e. Of course, the resolution to tonic

Example 9d. *An Wasserflüssen Babylon* (No. 5).

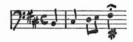

Example 9e. *Freu' dich sehr, o meine Seele* (No. 64).

may be deferred in any of these cases, resulting in a half cadence as in Examples 9f and 9g.[14]

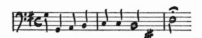

Example 9f. *Wir Christenleut'* (No. 55).

Example 9g. *Zeuch ein zu deinem Toren* (No. 23).

All of these cadences may be said to center about the dominant. That is, they either come to rest on that degree (half cadence) or else they utilize it (and the sense of commitment it carries) to approach the tonic. The approach to the dominant, in turn, is either by direct scalar motion or else by way of a chord which will create one of the standard cadential formulae of Bach's time, with the note that begins the cadential motion at the same time forming the terminal point for the scale.

Suppose, however, that a descent terminates, not at a chord which serves as the start of a standard cadence, but at the tonic itself (Examples 10a and 10b), or at the leading-tone which then resolves to the tonic (Example 10c). Could such a bass phrase still be said to generate a drive to the cadence?

Example 10a. *Allein zu dir, Herr Jesu Christ* (No. 13).

Example 10b. *Ermuntre dich, mein Schwacher Geist* (No. 9).

Example 10c. *Eins ist not! ach Herr, dies Eine* (No. 280).

While a hard and fast answer, applicable in all cases, would be difficult to formulate, there are at least two sets of circumstances under which judgments can be made with some degree of certainty. The first of these involves arrival at the tonic, not by way of a single dominant, but by way of two dominants a degree apart, each in first inversion (see Example 10a above). The commitment to resolution obviously has been so much intensified by the successive dominants, that the arrival at tonic probably carries enough of a sense of released tension to use up the energy generated.

The other set of circumstances involves an additional cadence in the same key following the arrival at the tonic. In this case, the impression is that a tentative resolution—one that used up only a little of the energy generated by the scale line—was followed by a more definite move to resolve the accumulated tension. Thus, the intuitive judgment would be that the scale line, far from being fashioned idly, was formed for the purpose of suggesting the same kind of drive found in the scale passages leading directly to the dominant. Only the means of resolving the tension are a little different; the sense of purpose and direction is equally evident in these tonic-centered scales. Example 10b (above) shows a case of this kind in which the arrival at the tonic is followed by a II_6-V-I cadence; in Example 10c the additional cadence consists simply of a V-I progression; and in Example 10d it takes the form of an additional dominant, a half cadence. Even where the first approach to the tonic was not by way of a dominant (Example 10e), the subsequent cadence undoubtedly would have seemed a reinforcement, and hence part of a program to generate and resolve tensions.

Example 10d. *Ach Gott, vom Himmel sieh darein* (No. 253).

Example 10e. *Es ist gewisslich an der Zeit* (No. 260).

Indeed, even if the scale were to lead into the dominant whose resolution to tonic was followed by an additional cadence (Example 10f), the use of the additional cadence probably would

Example 10f. *Ach Gott und Herr* (No. 40).

be construed as a reinforcement of this kind, and hence as contributing to the resolution of tension.

In some circumstances, even the presence of a skip of a third does not obscure the sense of drive to the cadence generated by a scale line. This obviously would be the case if the skip came right at the beginning of the phrase and were followed by at least four notes outlining a scalar ascent or descent (Example 11a). For

Example 11a. *Werde munter, mein Gemüte* (No. 233).

the early leap would tend to be forgotten as the scale unfolded. If, on the other hand, a scalar descent reached the leading-tone and then skipped to the dominant degree before resolving to tonic (Example 11b), the effect would be merely to reinforce the commitment to resolve the energy that was generated by the scalar

Example 11b. *Valet will ich dir geben* (No. 108).

motion by means of an authentic cadence. Thus, a skip of this kind would not really break the quality of drive toward the cadence. Similarly, a descent to the subdominant degree followed by a skip to supertonic just before an authentic cadence (Example 11c)

Example 11c. *Nun lieget alles unter dir* (No. 343).

would not damage the sense of drive. The skip to the supertonic, after all, would come to seem an integral part of a standard cadential formula of the time (IV-II-V-I). Even an isolated internal skip of a third, as shown in Example 11d, does not really obscure the scale-line drive.

Example 11d. *Helft mir Gott's Güte preisen* (No. 99).

A second type of linear arrangement that would create a quality of drive toward the cadence would be some variety of arch shape which contained only conjunct motion, or else the few kinds of exceptional leaps of thirds just enumerated. Here the initial motion up the scale would lead the listener to predict subsequent events with increasing certainty. The easier the prediction, the more the listener would tend to look for either a culmination or a change of some kind. In this case, the expectation would be fulfilled by a change in the form of a reversal of direction, rather than by a culmination. Without question, such a move would seem as reasonable a continuation, in retrospect, as a direct flow into the cadence. As the descending portion unfolded, furthermore, the same psychological processes would make a culmination seem increasingly appropriate.

Identical considerations will apply to what might be termed the inverted arch: a figure formed by first a descending and then a rising scale.

Since both the arch and the inverted arch are made up of two scales, the problems and possibilities of connecting them with the cadence are exactly the same as those already discussed. There is, however, some difference in effect. Other things being equal, a fairly symmetrical arch or inverted arch (i.e., one in which the ascending and descending portions are roughly equal in dimensions) will carry the connotation of a somewhat gentler drive to the cadence than a scale of the same size. For, since the descent (or ascent) at the end would take only half as long as it would in a scale of equivalent size, there simply would not be time to develop a comparable degree of momentum and strength of commitment to culmination. Where an opening ascent is much smaller than the following descent, on the other hand, the impression may be that the initial rise was intended to get up enough momentum to get the drive toward the cadence under way—a wind-up, it might be called. This would bring about a considerably stronger drive than a comparable symmetrical arch, but probably not as strong a one as would be produced by a straight scale. In the remaining case, where the change in direction sets in near the end of the phrase, the turnabout probably would give the impression of using up energy so that there would not be as much left over for the cadential resolution—again creating a gentler flow into the cadence.

The simple configurations of scale, arch, and inverted arch can be found in the basses of well over one-quarter of the total number of phrases in Bach's chorale harmonizations: six hundred of 2138 phrases.[15] A list of these phrases may be found in Appendix A.

It is perhaps worth noting that this is really a conservative figure inasmuch as any phrase whose scale does not extend over at least four notes is not included, while any arch or inverted arch containing fewer than five notes also has been omitted. Any phrases with irregularities in the cadence, furthermore (such as an authentic ending in which either the dominant or the tonic is inverted, an inversion of the last chord in a half cadence, or an ending which does not contain a dominant, have been left out of this category.

A great many other phrases contain basses which deviate only slightly from these fundamental shapes of scale, arch, and inverted arch. In some cases, the deviation takes the form of a brief internal change in direction—a twist, it might be called. This momentary turn of the line, of course, must be small enough not to obscure the underlying sense of direction; it must be only a delay of the motion toward the cadence rather than an independent move in a new direction. In Example 12a, for instance, the bass obviously outlines a descending scale moving toward the Phrygian cadence which ends the phrase—this in spite of the detour following the first B. In this example and those following, the notes that do not

Example 12a. *Ich ruf' zu dir, Herr Jesu Christ* (No. 71).

conform to the arch or scale shape are enclosed in brackets. In
Example 12b, it is an inverted arch that is interrupted in this way.

Example 12b. *Ach Gott, wie manches Herzeleid* (No. 156).

Even a whole series of twists sometimes does not obscure the
basic sense of directed motion along the scale or arch (Example
12c).

Example 12c. *Komm, Heiliger Geist, Herre Gott* (No. 69).

In a number of phrases, the departure from the scalar or archlike pattern seems somewhat more radical inasmuch as leaps are
involved rather than mere bends in the line. Often, however, these
do not really obscure the basic shapes. In Example 12d, for instance,

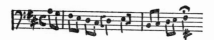

Example 12d. *Herzlich lieb hab' ich dich, o Herr* (No. 58).

it is clear that the fundamental shape is of an inverted arch, but
with a premature change in direction. In Example 12e, the isolated

Example 12e. *Allein zu dir, Herr Jesu Christ* (No. 359).

downward skip of a third certainly does not obscure the essential
qualities of an ascending scale. The same is true even in as brief
a phrase as is shown in Example 12f. Indeed, the insertion of one

Example 12f. *O Ewigkeit, du Donnerwort* (No. 26).

or two notes (or even three if the phrase is fairly long and the duration of these three notes is short) in virtually any way probably would serve only to interrupt, rather than to obscure an underlying scalar or archlike motion (Examples 12g–12l).

Example 12g. *Gott der Vater wohn' uns bei* (No. 135).

Example 12h. *Erstanden ist der heil'ge Christ* (No. 176).

Example 12i. *Es spricht der Unweisen Mund* (No. 27).

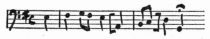

Example 12j. *Nun freut euch, lieben Christen* (No. 183).

Example 12k. *Ich bin ja, Herr, in deiner Macht* (No. 251).

Example 12l. *O Ewigkeit, du Donnerwort* (No. 274).

The question of whether an underlying scale or arch shape is recognizable becomes somewhat more problematic when the

motion along the original pattern resumes at a note a third beyond
the point at which the interruption occurred, rather than at that
point, or at the note adjacent to it. In order to obtain conservative
results, I have not included most instances of this kind in the
category of minor deviations. In just a few cases, however, the
underlying shape seemed so clearly outlined, despite the leap, that
exclusion of the phrase would seem to run counter to all canons
of perception (Example 12m).

Example 12m. *Aus meines Herzens Grunde* (No. 1).

The question of decoration brings up another problematic
area. When the additions are as modest as in Examples 12n and
12o, there can be no doubt but that the scale or arch shape would

Example 12n. *Was willst du dich, o meine Seele* (No. 241).

Example 12o. *Nun danket alle Gott* (No. 330).

be clearly enough perceived to influence the course of expectations.
Even in cases such as those shown in Examples 12p and 12q, the
skeletal scales (the notes of which are indicated with crosses)
would almost certainly be recognized since they are marked out,

Example 12p. *Aus meines Herzens Grunde* (No. 1).

Example 12q. *Jesu, meine Freude* (No. 96).

respectively, by the lower and upper turning points in the line. Anything going beyond these degrees of decoration, however, was excluded from this category.

Finally, in the case of scales only, I have assumed that an octave leap was tantamount to a repetition of a single note, and have therefore counted basses which outlined scales except for a leap of this kind as minor deviants (Example 12r). Even if this

Example 12r. *Aus tiefer Not schrei ich zu dir* (No. 10).

assumption seems questionable, it might be noted that the predominance of scalar motion in the same direction (only a single leap, after all) would itself produce some development of expectations leading toward a sense of drive to the cadence. In the case of arches, on the other hand, I have assumed that an octave leap introduces a degree of complexity that might well obscure the shape.

On the basis of calculations such as these, the basses in 343 additional phrases can be added to the list of those producing a sense of drive to the cadence, making a total of 943. These phrases are listed in Appendix B.

Very closely related to the scalar drives to the cadence are those basses which consist of two or three separate scale lines moving in the same direction, with the later ones going over some of the same pitches covered by the earlier ones. In a case like Example 13a, undoubtedly there would be an impression of a drive

Example 13a. *Ist Gott mein Schild und Helfersmann* (No. 122).

to the cadence inasmuch as the second descending scale moves to a pitch appreciably lower than that reached by the first. Thus the drive developed by the first scale would not seem wasted; rather, it probably would be interpreted as preparing the way for the more far-reaching motion of the second scale. In retrospect, the impression might be that the first scale represented an attempt to channel the growing momentum into a cadential resolution—an attempt that failed. The second descent, then, would come to seem another and more successful effort to reach a point from which a cadential formula could begin to unfold. Thus it would seem to fulfill the commitment generated by the first scale, rather than to lead a completely independent existence. In other words, the breaking off of the first descent might seem little more than an interruption of the drive toward the cadence—a regrouping of forces for a more serious attempt.

Very similar considerations would apply when the second scale does not extend as far as the first one (Example 13b). In this

Example 13b. *Wenn mein Stündlein vorhanden ist* (No. 52).

case, the first approach might be interpreted as having overshot the cadence, whereas the second flowed directly into it.

In both of the above examples (13a and 13b), it may be noted that other features of organization tend to reinforce these interpretations. In Example 13a, the second descent contains five notes in conjunct motion, whereas the first had only four, with a leap of a third between the last two. The presence of an additional note obviously would lend more momentum to the second drive. The absence of a leap, furthermore, would tend to suggest the same thing, since even a leap of a third would not carry the quality of smooth continuation (hence of generation of momentum) as strongly as strictly conjunct motion.

In Example 13b, on the other hand, the second scale makes use both of more notes and of slower motion. The effect is of a much more protracted and deliberate motion toward the cadence. By comparison, the first ascent embodies the kind of rashly dramatic gesture that might well overshoot its goal.

In some cases, just such features of organization as these seem to be the main contributors to the quality of drive. In Example 13c, for instance, the most noticeable difference between the two ascents

Example 13c. *Gott hat das Evangelium* (No. 181).

161

is not that they culminate on different pitches, but rather that the second is so much shorter than the first. The impression left by such a passage might be formulated as a greater sense of concentration: a rambling first attempt to find a cadential resolution, followed by a more concise and direct approach. In a similar vein, in Example 13d, it may be noted that although the two scales go over exactly

Example 13d. *Befiehl du deine Wege* (No. 286).

the same notes, the more rapid motion of the second one serves to increase the quality of drive. In these cases also, the second scale serves to fulfill expectations generated by the first, so that the whole of each phrase develops a quality of drive toward the cadence.

In some passages, a sense of amplification is suggested by a series of three successive scales. In Example 13e, for instance, the

Example 13e. *Hilf, Gott, dass mir's gelinge* (No. 199).

second descent is roughly twice as long as the first, while the third is equal to the second in number of notes traversed, but proceeds at a much more leisurely pace. Here too, then, the last descent fulfills the commitment of cadential resolution generated, with increasing strength, by the two earlier ones. Exactly the opposite case is shown in Example 13f, where the ascents become shorter and faster.

Example 13f. *Jesus Christus, unser Heiland* (No. 30).

On the basis of judgments such as these, forty more phrases can be added to the list of basses which produce a sense of drive toward the cadence, bringing the total to 983. A listing of these may be found in Appendix C.

An element of predictability, and hence of an increasing sense of commitment to the cadential resolution, also makes itself felt in many sequentially organized basses. The repetition of the same figure obviously would produce an ever more strongly felt expectation of culmination,[16] while adherence to an interval or a pattern of transposition would serve to impart a sense of directedness to the motion. The presence of these two qualities, then, could well give rise to a sense of growing momentum leading toward the cadence.

There are some difficulties in judgment, however. The first has to do with length. It is clear that the whole effect of directedness in this case requires a focusing of the listener's attention on the progress of the bass. If he should ever become convinced that there is little point in following the unfoldment of the bass, there would be no way of impressing a sense of drive on his mind. If a sequential passage becomes very long, a point will be reached, sooner or later, at which the new transpositions of the figure will not carry enough information to retain the listener's interest and attention: they will be too easily predictable. In all but one [17] of the sequential basses in the chorales, however, this limit obviously is not approached. For, with this lone exception, the sequential motion is restricted to just one or two transpositions of the original figure—sometimes a single transposition of only the beginning of the figure—clearly far from any conceivable point of satiety.

The other problem has to do with the connection to the cadence. As in the cases of the scale and arch shapes, I have counted only those phrases where the bass flows smoothly into the cadence. In this case, of course, smooth connection with the cadence would require the avoidance of any seemingly arbitrary interruption of the sequential figure. Hence I have limited this category to phrases where the sequential motion either brings about a move to the dominant that then resolves in a standard manner (Example 14a), or to the tonic whose resolving effect is then reinforced by

Example 14a. *Straf' mich nicht in deinem Zorn* (No. 38).

an additional cadence (Example 14b); or else to phrases where the sequence terminates on, or is interrupted at, a note (such as

Example 14b. *O Haupt voll Blut und Wunden* (No. 89).

subdominant or supertonic) marking the beginning of a cadential formula (Examples 14c and 14d, respectively). In addition, I have

Example 14c. *Wo soll ich fliehen hin* (No. 25).

Example 14d. *Wachet auf, ruft uns die Stimme* (No. 179).

included phrases where the sequential figure gives rise to an easily recognizable variant which then makes its way to the cadence (Example 14e).

Example 14e. *Freuet euch, ihr Christen* (No. 8).

As in the case of scales and arches, I have assumed that minor deviants, such as a small change in the interval of transposition, a slight modification of the sequential figure, or even a brief interruption of the sequential pattern (Examples 14f, 14g and 14h, respectively), would not completely obscure the general sense of

Example 14f. *Ach Gott, vom Himmel sieh darein* (No. 253).

Example 14g. *Wär Gott nicht mit uns diese Zeit* (No. 285).

Example 14h. *Warum betrübst du dich, mein Herz* (No. 94).

directedness. Even the presence of some light decoration would not seem to disqualify a sequential passage (Example 14i).

Example 14i. *Es wird schier der letzte Tag* (No. 238).

Finally, I have included two patterns in this category which, while not strictly sequential, are nevertheless rather closely related to sequence in effect: motion along the circle of fifths (Example 14j), even with some decoration (Example 14k), and lines whose

Example 14j. *Gott sei gelobet und gebenedeiet* (No. 70).

Example 14k. *Meine Augen schliess' ich jetzt* (No. 258).

turning points outline ascents or descents by successive thirds (Example 14l).

Example 14l. *Weg, mein Herz, mit den Gedanken* (No. 254).

On the basis of these judgments, another 104 phrases can be added, bringing the total to 1087. A list of these phrases may be found in Appendix D.

Although a great many more phrases might be added to this total, they would require a series of more elaborate and more individual discussions ranging well beyond the scope of an essay.

The mere fact, however, that this figure can be brought so easily to the half-way mark indicates that Bach's shaping of the bass was not an occasional thing; it could not easily have been a matter of chance.

On the other hand, there are some 245 phrases in which the characteristics of the bass are such as to virtually preclude the emergence of any sense of drive toward the cadence. In some cases the lack of drive can be traced to the shortness of the phrase (Example 15a). In others, the phrase seems little more than a cadence (Example 15b) or a series of cadences with characteristic bass leaps (Example 15c). In both of these phrases, there

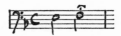

Example 15a. *Wie schön leuchtet der Morgenstern* (No. 323).

Example 15b. *Was bist du doch, o Seele, so betrübet* (No. 193).

Example 15c. *Als der gütige Gott* (No. 159).

simply is not enough room for any drive to get under way.

An element of redundance can be found in a number of other phrases. In Example 15d, for instance, the pitch G is so often heard

Example 15d. *Hilf, Herr Jesu, lass gelingen* (No. 155).

and so long held that there is hardly any sense of directed motion. In Example 15e, the static quality results from the fact that four of

Example 15e. *Als der gütige Gott* (No. 159).

the five bass notes are allotted to the dominant and tonic degrees, while in Example 15f, the line merely fluctuates between the

Example 15f. *O Herzensangst* (No. 173).

pitches D and E♭—hardly more than a slow, slightly embellished trill. The presence of several leaps accounts for the lack of directedness in still other phrases (Example 15g). In cases of this kind, of

Example 15g. *Warum betrübst du dich, mein Herz* (No. 94).

course, it is not just the presence of leaps, but the fact that they do not come to seem part of an easily recognized pattern (e.g., a sequence or a general descent) that prevents the development of a drive.

Finally, there are some phrases in which the bass seems to wander up and down for so long a time that it loses all sense of directedness (Example 15h), and others where the bass is split by

Example 15h. *Christum wir sollen loben schön* (No. 56).

leaps into segments which seem somehow disconnected (Example 15i).

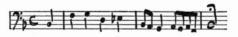

Example 15i. *Heut ist, o Mensch, ein grosser Trauertag* (No. 168).

The 245 phrases in which the bass does not develop much sense of direction are listed in Appendix E.

It is clear, then, that Bach uses two types of harmonic construction to influence expectations: the commitment of the dominant, and the shape of the bass. In some phrases, dominant relationships are few and far between, but a considerable amount of drive is generated by the bass alone. Example 16a, for instance,

Example 16a. *Herzlich lieb hab' ich dich, o Herr* (No. 277).

contains but two dominant relations (each marked by a bracket), but the bass obviously consists of a decorated scalar ascent. Just the opposite is true in Example 16b, where dominants and their

Example 16b. *An Wasserflüssen Babylon* (No. 5).

resolutions are heard quite often, but the bass is redundant. Neither force seems particularly strong in phrases like that shown in Example 16c: only the last three chords suggest dominant rela-

Example 16c. *Es Woll' uns Gott genädig sein* (No. 16).

tions, while the bass seems rather disconnected because of the abrupt shift in register brought on by the octave leap. Example 16d, on the other hand, contains both a profusion of dominant relations and a driving bass. In cases like this last one, the dominants within the phrase provide some added impetus to the bass

Example 16d. *Wenn mein Stündlein vorhanden ist* (No. 351).

in its motion toward the cadence—an extra shove in the direction it is pursuing—thereby intensifying the quality of drive.

By coordinating these two forces, Bach could achieve a considerable variety in the degrees of drive generated by the various phrases. A phrase containing a clearly shaped bass with a great many dominant relations obviously would make a much stronger impression than either one with a directed bass but few dominants, or one with a great many dominants but a redundant bass. Nevertheless, any one of the latter two would seem much stronger than a phrase containing but few dominants and little sense of bass direction. And, of course, each of the bass shapes and every variant in dimensions or in decoration would produce differences in the degree of drive. All in all, this seems an approach allowing for the utmost flexibility, richness, and variety.

The question now is what factors may have influenced the choice of type and degree of drive. Was Bach's aim merely to make each phrase as striking an entity as he could by means of the harmonic decoration of a melody which he assumed would be well known to his audience? Was his harmonic planning kept within the confines of the individual phrase? Or was he trying to produce a constantly refreshing sense of novelty by this means, attempting to renew interest from time to time by, for example, setting a strong drive in motion after a series of weaker ones? Or does his practice seem to reflect a more systematic approach?

The preponderance of evidence suggests that the last is the correct view. For, in all but a very few of his harmonizations Bach, appears to have been concerned not only with the structure within the individual phrase, but also with the suggestion of relations between the several phrases that make up a chorale. That is to say that he apparently applied his harmonic technique in order to make the chorale into something like a drama in miniature, with points at which the sense of tension would increase, other points where relief would be offered, and still other points where resolution would be effected.

The use of so varied a palette of types and degrees of drives, then, becomes perfectly understandable, for this breadth of resources is needed to effect the smoothness of flow that is virtually required to suggest dramatic unfoldment convincingly. As pointed out previously, the least sign of stiffness or artificiality in the succession of events is enough to destroy all sense of dramatic continuity—a tenuous illusion at best. This means that the composer cannot be content to fit events together roughly, or with any quality of inappropriateness, but must tailor them to each other so that they seem invented precisely to suit the conditions imposed by the context. The more varied the palette, of course, the better the chances of finding an effect that would convey just such an impression.

While the dramatic programs vary considerably in detail, they can be reduced to just a few general types. Perhaps the simplest involves an initial set of two or three phrases in which the harmony does not venture out of the home key. The phrases following, then, contain one or more modulations before there is a return to the original tonality. A case of this kind is shown in Example 17, where the only two modulations (to supertonic and dominant)

Example 17. *Straf' mich nicht in deinem Zorn* (No. 38).

are found shortly after the double bar (measures 6-8). After so straightforward a beginning, the modulations seem to introduce an element of complexity. To use a well-known, if melodramatic, phrase: the plot thickens. The return to the original key, of course, carries the suggestion of difficulties overcome; in spite of the complications, all has turned out well.

Even the way the complexities are presented seems designed to enhance the effect of the eventual return to the home key. For although the first modulation represents a very strong gesture, what with the chromatic rise of the bass, it is so abrupt and so quickly brought to its cadence that it cannot have demonstrated much staying power. This is not much of a complication, and hence restoration of the original tonality at this point would not have constituted a very strong dramatic effect. The second modulation, however, settles into its new key (dominant) quite decidedly, by means of a fairly extended bass-cadence combination which develops a considerable sense of momentum and release (an inverted arch culminating in a deceptive cadence followed by an authentic: II_6-V-I). This seems to imply that the complicating element was not something very easily overcome, but rather an impulse of considerable vitality. It resulted not just in an obviously temporary move away, but in what amounts to an actual attempt to settle in a new region. The return, then, seems all the stronger because of the magnitude of the challenge overcome.

This is not to say that just such a scheme is to be found in every one of the chorales of this type. In the simpler ones, in particular—the ones that sound most like the hymns of the more fundamentalist protestant denominations—Bach is content with just one modulation (see, for instance No. 42). On the other hand, there are other cases where the modulations that set in in the later phrases are more numerous, lengthy, and complex than in the example described above (see No. 5). But, however the details are worked out, there must have been some kind of thinking in terms of making the end seem to contain the point of the chorale. It is not necessarily the most highly charged passage—what might be termed the climax. Indeed, in many cases it is distinctly anti-climactic in quality, the climax in these instances merely setting the stage for a dramatic return of a subdued mood-color and demonstrating how powerful that subdued mood is by the degree of contrast overcome. The last phrase, then, represents a quality toward which everything else has been working. It is the key needed to convert all the individual phrases heard earlier into a generalized, meaningful statement.

A second general type of program is actually very similar to the first, except that, instead of having no modulations at all in the early phrases, it has relatively brief or conservative ones. In the later phrases, the range of modulations is expanded and the moves are made in a more decided fashion. Such is the case, for instance, in Example 18, where the first two phrases contain a move to the dominant and back, while the later ones have modulations to supertonic (measures 6–7 and 12–13), subdominant (measure 8), and relative minor (measures 10–12), before the return to

Example 18. *Freu' dich sehr, o meine Seele* (No. 76).

tonic. Once again, it seems that the plot thickens after the double bar, with the tension mounting and ebbing as it becomes apparent that a struggle is taking place to reestablish the sense of stability associated with the original tonality. Because this struggle is consistently steered away from an anticipated resolution to the home key until the very last phrase, the return seems all the more significant an event.

In many cases, the early phrases develop so strong a character or so great a sense of momentum that what follows is not a thickening of the plot, but a relief. In Example 19, for instance, the consistently somber qualities of the minor harmonization in the first two phrases, and the chromatically descending bass in the second, combine to make the third phrase in particular seem distinctly milder in character. The avoidance of chromatic motion in the bass makes this passage seem much less complicated; the fact that it is directed toward the key of the relative major until near the very end of the phrase lends it a more positive feeling-tone. The move toward major is carried a step farther in the fourth phrase, with an actual cadence in a major key—the only one in

Example 19. *Herr Jesu Christ, du höchstes Gut* (No. 73).

the chorale. Once again, the stage is set nicely for a contrasting return to the original tonality, and the somber qualities associated with it, about half-way through the last phrase. Indeed, the whole program seems to have been designed with the effect of this last phrase in mind. So strong is the somber mood that even the introduction of more positive evocations cannot dispel it; this feeling, in turn, makes the major ending a more impressive effect for being set against so serious a background.

The return, in this case, itself introduces an element of novelty. For it is obvious that the bass is far more active in the last phrase than it was in either of the first two. Partly as a result of this, it describes a curve of far broader dimensions (a kind of sequential motion which actually decorates a descending scale)—a curve whose contour generates a good deal more momentum than was the case in either of the first two phrases, and whose cadence therefore seems a stronger resolution. Thus, from the point of view of bass construction, the return seems far richer than the quality originally established. On the other hand, there is nothing to match the intensity generated by the chromatic motion in the bass of the second phrase. It would seem likely, then, that Bach wished to fashion a fairly complex ending to this chorale, but without the implications of high drama and instability inherent in chromatic progressions. The more rapidly moving bass which also generates more momentum may well have served to implement this program.

Exactly the opposite type of ending must have been in Bach's mind when he worked on the chorale in Example 20. Here it is the

Example 20. *Wie bist du, Seele, in mir so gar betrübt* (No. 242).

last phrase that is climactic, largely because of the associations of force and determination attached to a chromatically rising bass. The program that culminates in the steeply dramatic ending can be described as follows: The first two phrases establish a rather somber atmosphere and a relatively conservative key treatment; only an approach, via its own dominant, to the dominant in an authentic cadence (measure 3) poses any threat to break away from the key. The third and fourth phrases offer relief, through a shift toward the relative major, after which the complexity begins to build up again to lead into the climactic ending. The build-up is suggested first by the active bass of the penultimate phrase, a bass which outlines a very large curve and hence generates considerable energy. The energy is not really resolved with any finality, however, since the phrase ends in a half cadence. The chromatically rising bass in the last phrase, then, although itself a most powerful effect, also seems to carry the energy left unresolved at the end of the phrase preceding, channeling it all into an extremely strong cadence. The impression left is clearly not of a return to a more subdued or more settled mood, but rather of a highly exciting, almost melodramatic, ending.

Another type of program makes use of the kinds of excursions away from a basic tonality discussed in connection with Obrecht.[18] Such a case can be seen in Example 21, where the F-minor tonality

Example 21. *Freuet euch, ihr Christen.*

is challenged in the second phrase, the fourth and fifth together, and the seventh, eighth, and ninth together. Between these challenges, of course, are returns to the basic tonality and the somber mood connected with it. The interesting thing is that the scope of the challenge is allowed to grow as excursion follows excursion. Where the second phrase moved quickly into the relative major, the fourth took more time to make the move and proceeded by way of another key, the subdominant (measure 7). The introduction of sequential motion in the bass, furthermore, raises some feelings of uncertainty as to where the tonic really is, these all may be well and good as temporary modulations, but where the phrase is going to settle finally becomes a matter for conjecture. With the uncertainty, of course, a degree of tension is generated. The next phrase, instead of returning to the original tonality, continues both the series of modulations (coming to rest in subdominant) and the sequential motion (measures 9-10). The final excursion does roughly the same sort of thing, but on a larger scale; indeed, it is approximately twice as long as the second one. In this case, it is clear that the tension generated both by the growth in the scope of the challenges and by the uncertainties surrounding the use of sequential motion is utilized to build a climactic ending.

The one question remaining concerns the twenty-four chorales which do not give evidence of planning of this kind. How can these exceptions be accounted for if we are to hypothesize that Bach's aim was essentially dramatic?

Perhaps the first thing to note is that three of these chorales probably should be eliminated from consideration—two (No. 228 and No. 320) because they are too short (only two phrases) to permit any sense of dramatic unfoldment to develop, and the third (No. 205) because it apparently was conceived as a string of somewhat independent movements, some of which are repeated as many as six times.

Of the remaining twenty-one chorales, fourteen lose the sense of dramatic organization because of what might be termed a surprise ending—in most cases, a turn to what seems the wrong key or the wrong kind of cadence to call the chorale to a halt. The close is on a half cadence in No. 127, No. 187, and No. 208, while there is a sudden move to what can only be interpreted as the key of the dominant at the end of No. 82, No. 227, No. 262, and No. 284. Even more unsettling are closing moves to supertonic (No. 162 and No. 314) and to the subdominant (No. 200). In the last case, the chorale actually closes on the chord (C major) that served to open it, so that the final cadence might seem to satisfy theoretical requirements for a tonic. It does not satisfy practical requirements, however, inasmuch as C major is never firmly enough established to remain in memory as an element of reference; indeed, the feeling probably would be that G major assumes something like the function of a tonic. The return to C major at the end, at any rate, is effected so abruptly that it certainly can give no impression of bringing the chorale to a close adequately. A similar case may be found in No. 230, where B♭ major seems to usurp the tonic function originally claimed by G minor. The G-minor ending, then, carries little sense of return, and hence does not really serve to close off the dramatic structure.

The endings also fall on cadences that might be judged tonics on the basis of key signature and opening chord in No. 279 and No. 358. In the case of the latter, however, the final chord has changed function and come to be heard as a dominant in the last measures, so that the ending presents a completely unexpected move to the subdominant key. In No. 279, on the other hand, although the signature suggests that B♭ major is the tonic, the structure makes it clear that F major actually takes this function, so that the B♭ ending once again seems a move to the subdominant. This close, furthermore, comes at the end of a long, driving, tonally unstable phrase, and is not approached by means of some standard cadential formula such as might suggest release of tension. As a result, there is little feeling that the processes set in motion during the course of this chorale have been brought to a close at all convincingly.

In No. 288, finally, no tonic is ever really established adequately: one is never sure whether D major or A major should be so interpreted. The ending reflects something of the same ambiguity, for although the close is on an A-major triad, this chord is given something of the function of a dominant in D major.

Some idea of how unsatisfactorily these various surprising moves fulfill the function of suggesting termination can be judged from Example 22, where the chorale last discussed is reproduced.

Example 22. *Gelobet seist du, Jesu Christ* (No. 288).

I think it is hard to avoid the impression that the last phrase represents something in the nature of a postscript; it is not really related to what is presented in the body of the chorale.

The lack of evidence of dramatic planning in three more of the chorales can be traced to a perhaps overly simple scheme. Thus, the four phrases of No. 192 merely present a continual fluctuation between the keys of B♭ major and F major, without any appreciable sign of increase or decrease of tension in one way or another. In

No. 235 and No. 239, on the other hand, the structure clearly involves excursions from an established tonality, but there is little to suggest that one excursion creates anything like a stronger effect than the other.

It is an element of complication that works against any quality of dramatic development in the remaining four chorales. Thus, No. 56, No. 214, and No. 277 are long and rambling, to the point where the sense of orientation—to a tonic or to a degree of tonal stability —becomes lost, while the same effect results from rather free and frequent changes of key in No. 222.

Perhaps it should be emphasized once more that the chorales in which evidence of dramatic organization is lacking constitute a very small minority in the total bulk of Bach's harmonizations: only 21 of 345,[19] or approximately six percent. As small as the number of these exceptions is, however, I think that they cannot be ignored in attempting to put together a picture of Bach's assumptions.

The temptation, of course, is to relegate these to the ranks of early works, or at least of works produced under some kind of pressure, and hence perhaps carelessly fashioned. And there may be some justification for a view of this kind. Bach's chronology is not firmly enough established [20] to rule out the possibility that some of these may have been early efforts, and, of course, physical and mental conditions at certain times may have caused a lowering of his usual critical standards. Everyone has a bad day now and then, after all. Certainly the number of exceptional cases is sufficiently small to be accounted for plausibly by either or both of these hypotheses.

But these are really far too conjectural hypotheses to serve the purposes of objective evaluation. I think I could be accused, justifiably, of attempting to bend facts to fit a preconceived interpretation if I ignored the exceptional cases. At any rate, I think it is not necessary to fall back upon an escape mechanism of this kind in attempting to piece together a picture of Bach's mind at work. For I would suggest that it is not the fact that there are exceptional cases that is remarkable, but the fact that they are so few in number in view of the circumstances surrounding the procedure of harmonizing a chorale melody.

Bach, after all, could have felt quite confident that his audience would be able to orient itself to the musical flow by means of the chorale tune alone. These melodies would have been so familiar to those for whom he wrote that, to some extent, he could have well afforded to ignore the problem of creating directional implications by means of his harmonic settings. All that really would have been expected of him was a decoration of the known melody, perhaps through the addition of interesting sonorities—touches of color, they might be called—or possibly through the grafting of various degrees of drive onto the line of development defined by the melody alone.

The conceptions of decoration and of dramatic development, of course, are really quite separate and distinct; indeed, they are often considered somewhat antithetical. A decorative art ordinarily involves an addition of devices intended to lend some ornamental quality—shadings of what might be termed color—to a preexistent design. One thinks of "fleshing out" a skeletal sketch, of embellishing an already complete structure, of merely adding cosmetic touches.

All of these things, it may be noted, are accomplished very well in the twenty-one harmonizations that have been termed exceptional—those which show little evidence of dramatic organization. These fulfill the requirements of decoration more than adequately. Bach could well have fashioned all of his harmonizations along lines such as these—indeed, that is what might have been expected, given the nature of the problem involved. The fact that Bach was not content to do this (except in a handful of cases), the fact that he saw fit to imbue what could well have been a purely decorative process with dramatic function, the fact that this not completely natural wedding of decorative and dramatic elements is to be found in all but six percent of his harmonizations—all this suggests how important the conception of dramatic development must have been to him. Certainly it must have been one of the fundamental conceptions governing his compositional practice. Even when Bach was attempting merely to decorate, after all, he almost invariably resorted to dramatic construction and the kind of intensification that it is capable of bringing about.

I would suggest, then, that it makes little sense to posit some value system based on an all-embracing conception of functional relationships—such as is implied, after all, by the general neglect of all factors but harmonic progression—when one can so easily account for Bach's harmonic practice in terms of readily understandable human behavior: an attempt to communicate, to influence the state of mind of a listener, largely by creating an impression of dramatic development. If this hypothesis is accepted, the dominant commitment and the bass drive toward the cadence can be viewed as expedients designed to produce the variety of impressions required to differentiate the qualities of the separate phrases so that a sense of dramatic unfoldment can be built up. The whole technique seems best described, not as an embodiment of a metaphysical principle, but as a product of human ingenuity.

In saying this, I do not mean to belittle Bach's achievement, or to minimize the element of artistry in his work—what is often considered an irrational or semidivine and hence inscrutable, inspiration. I do not wish to suggest, in other words, that his whole art can be equated with his technique, or that he was just a musician who happened to stumble upon a most effective method of procedure and exploited it to the full. Quite the contrary, I think there is a very powerful conception behind Bach's technique. There is an imagination at work that lifts his creations far beyond the realm of mere craftsmanship—an imagination capable of grasping and making tangible a very meaningful, rich, and deep conception of the human condition, with its contradictions, its precariousness, its excitement, its delicate balance between the urge toward powerful assertion and the longing for peace and concord. All of these qualities, I think, can be read quite legitimately even from such modest works as the chorale harmonizations. Thus, it hardly seems surprising that romantic composers, who were also very keenly aware of the contradictory and overpowering elements in the human condition, should have seen so much in Bach's music.

The realization of so complex a vision, however, could only have been effected by a technical apparatus at the same time highly rational and highly realistic—a technique, in other words, based upon psychological calculations, since its aim clearly was to produce psychological effects. It is for this reason that I have felt it worthwhile to attempt to reconstruct the rationale underlying Bach's harmonic practice from essentially psychological principles, rather than from a broader field of observations. I hope this type of formulation brings us closer to a genuine understanding of Bach's harmonic art.

SIX

The Exuberant Bach

MANY PERFORMANCES of Bach's instrumental music today seem to assume the quality of acts of devotion. The performers apparently realize that they are dealing with the work of a great composer—possibly because they are familiar with some of the deeply moving and imaginative choral compositions—but their execution does little to suggest that the pieces in hand have any particular aesthetic worth. In some cases, notably in instrumental ensemble music, Bach comes to seem a rather dull fellow, slavishly devoted to the glorification of an unyielding, plodding beat-pattern: heavily accented on the first beat, more lightly on the third (if the meter involves four beats), etc. The beat-pattern, in these so-called purist performances, appears to be an end-in-itself; the play of melodic lines, the harmonies, the textural manipulations all are lost to the ear—obscured by the steady succession of heavy and light beats. The tempo, furthermore, generally is slow enough, in performances of this kind, to prevent the succession of beats from developing any sense of excitement. As a result, the punctuating quality of the beat-pattern virtually precludes any sense of flow.

In other cases, particularly in music transcribed for full orchestra or performed by soloists, Bach is treated as a protoromantic composer. Nuances, shadings, rubati, diminuendi are introduced in profusion. The performer obviously goes to great pains to focus his audience's attention on one melodic line or another, freely sacrificing the nuances of harmony and texture so carefully built into the piece by Bach. And he often shapes the phrases in a typically romantic way: building to a climax somewhere between the middle and the end of the phrase, and then gliding down toward the cadence. A brief downward turn in the line, furthermore, usually will call forth a noticeable diminuendo, often a slowing of tempo as well. The arrival at the cadence will be gentle; there may even be some lingering on the final chord. All of which guarantees that individual phrases would be nicely separated with little momentum carrying over from one to the next—something like the tenuously related character sketches which form the substance of so many of Schumann's piano works. Truly a poetic Bach!

Either of these interpretations—the plodding or the poetic—obviously makes Bach into a second-rate composer. Any composer, after all, who allowed his music to become so far removed from the realm of human experience as to concentrate on the glorification of a simple-minded beat-pattern could hardly be credited with a supreme creative intellect. Somehow the idea of associating value with a phenomenon of this kind seems little short of ridiculous when put into words; yet this is the implication underlying many performances that have come to be quite respected.

The poetic approach, on the other hand, runs into the difficulty that Bach simply was not a particularly good romantic composer. Schubert, Schumann, Brahms—all could communicate romantic sentiments, phrasing and nuances far more delicately, powerfully, and richly. A single stroke of harmony, or of execution (fortissimo, piano, staccato, etc.) under the hands of these composers could be much more tellingly evocative of sentiment than could an entire five-minute movement by Bach. Bach might then be considered a figure of some historical interest—a composer who had a vague premonition of romantic thought a century early—but on these terms he would have to be considered an aesthetic failure.

Both of these rather negative evaluations, I would suggest, can be traced not to deficiencies in the style, but rather to many performers' failure to recognize Bach's approach to his art, and their consequent inability to adjust their performances to the limitations imposed by his assumptions. In this essay, then, I should like to go into the question of the assumptions underlying Bach's instrumental music, particularly as they would affect standards of performance. I should like to draw evidence bearing on this question from the music itself, specifically from the structure of the phrases and of whole movements.

The first thing to note, perhaps, is that the Bach phrase is defined primarily by means of the harmony. The phrase reaches its conclusion, not when the melody reaches some kind of goal, or even when all the voices come to a stop (this does not happen too often), but when the harmonic motion leads into a recognizable cadence formula, usually dominant to tonic with both chords in root position. When this happens, no matter what is going on in other voices—and there is often quite a bit going on—a sense of culmination can be felt, a sense that a particular train of thought has come to an end, and, perhaps, that a new one is about to be taken up. The harmonic release of tension suggests a caesura, even when, as often happens, a considerable amount of activity carries over the cadence.

This much is common knowledge and the generally accepted viewpoint. Indeed, it is obviously true not only for Bach, but also for most of the composers of the so-called period of common practice. In the music of Beethoven, Berlioz, Schumann, Verdi, Dvorak, to name but a few, it is the arrival at the cadence that generally marks off phrases, although in these cases the melodic lines usually reinforce the impression of caesura instead of blurring it.

What is not so generally recognized, however, is that the harmony is also the primary source of direction within the Bach phrase. For the melodic lines often contain so many changes in direction, with so little to mark off units from each other, that one would be hard put to find any general sense of shape to the line of the phrase as a whole. Even where a direction seems quite readily apparent, the motion is often considerably slower than that of the harmony. In Example 1, for instance, in which the top line obviously describes a much decorated descent, the moves down the scale (marked with crosses above the top line) occur roughly half as often as the changes in harmony (marked with asterisks below the bass). The line, furthermore, has neither the clarity of profile nor the marked repetition of fairly large rhythmic units that would serve to impress it on the mind as a self-attractive entity. Rather, this seems a somewhat amorphous kind of melodic shaping—a technique which could be adapted easily to prior conditions (in this case the harmony) so as to contribute to the feeling that there is a sense of direction, but without attracting enough attention to itself, by virtue of its contour, to provide the primary source of momentum.

The harmony, on the other hand, is exceedingly clear-cut,

Example 1. French Suite No. I, *Allemande:* m. 1-5.

fast-moving, and rich with directional implications—both because of the bass shape and the play of dominant commitments. One might well follow the unfolding of the harmonies with considerable anticipation and pleasure even in the absence of any melodic figuration.

It might be said, then, that, where the harmonies are in the nature of supports for the melodic lines of the classic and romantic composers, the lines are in the nature of embellishments of a harmonic progression for Bach. It is the harmony that provides the fundamental source of direction, the drive; the lines probably were adapted to meet its requirements.

The primacy of the harmonic element has one important consequence: it makes it most difficult to suggest a diminuendo effect convincingly. About all one could do would be to attempt something like what Hindemith prescribes, namely, reducing the level of dissonance as one nears the cadence, or else slowing the harmonic rhythm toward the end of the phrase. Given Bach's harmonic vocabulary, neither of these alternatives seems to offer much possibility for exploitation: the range of dissonances hardly seems wide enough to facilitate the former approach, while the slackening of the harmonic rate of change probably would lead also to a lessening of interest. At any rate, Bach's music does not show much evidence that either of these possibilities was explored.

Quite the contrary, there seems to be some tendency to increase both the harmonic rate of change and the level of dissonance as the end of a phrase is approached.

Some idea of how far a tapering phrase must have been from Bach's conception can be gained by reading through Example 1, with a diminuendo, and possibly a gradual ritard as well, setting in where the top line begins to move more slowly (end of the third full measure).[1] No matter how hard one tries, one can hardly help but feel the drive set in motion by the harmonic progressions as the cadence is approached. A reading that tries to subdue this energy sounds not really poetic, but artificial.

A composition by Bach, then, I would suggest, consists of a series of phrases, each of which embodies a drive to the cadence—a kind of crescendo effect, or a cumulative generation of energy which is discharged only upon arrival at the cadence. After the release, another build-up must start almost immediately, by the nature of Bach's harmonic idiom. This build-up may proceed more slowly or more rapidly than the one preceding; it may move to a cadence that seems qualitatively higher or lower in forcefulness or climactic value. But the important thing to note is that there can be very little in the nature of a respite—one can hardly pause to catch one's breath—before the harmonic motion begins to assume direction, and speculation about its goal brings on a growing degree of curiosity and tension. This process could be represented graphically somewhat as follows (the sharp descents in the line represent the discharges of energy at the cadences):

A procedure of this kind, quite apart from any other factor, would produce what might be called a sense of pressure. The direction is always toward increasing intensity. The cadences merely punctuate the drive, holding it back momentarily from time to time, but never able to contain it or call it to a halt, even temporarily, until the end of the movement. The cadences, indeed, might be thought of as obstacles in the way of the drive—obstacles whose inability to stem the tide serves to suggest how strong a pressure lies behind it.

On the basis of these considerations alone, we might guess that a style of interpretation which obscures the sense of pressure in one way or another (for example, by the use of a great many diminuendi or rubati, or by establishment of a tempo so slow that little drive is felt) is no more being true to Bach's intentions than one which changes some of the notes or adds doublings of one kind or another. Such a performance would be more a projection of the executant's own personality than a faithful reflection of Bach's. The chances of a happy result would seem rather small.

But this is not all of the evidence indicating that a sense of pressure underlay Bach's style. For, in many movements, particularly those of considerable length and of dramatic character, there are other procedures designed to suggest a growth in the degree of intensity as the movement unfolds. One can hardly escape the feeling that the stakes grow higher as the hand is played out. One of the most widely used procedures involves the suggestion of a dialogue between sections that seem relatively stable harmonically and others that are less stable—a dialogue in which the element of instability is allowed to grow in magnitude as the movement progresses. The first movement of the fourth Brandenburg Concerto offers an example of this type of organization.

This movement contains two distinctly different types of harmonic treatment. Some sections consist entirely of alternations between tonics and dominants in the same key, with both chords in root position.[2] Such is the case wherever the main theme—the so-called ritornello—is presented (Example 2). This is a very stable harmonic arrangement, of course, in which there is no evidence of

Example 2. *Brandenburg Concerto* No. IV, First Movement: m. 1-13.

a will to break away from the tonic key, or even to explore any but the most familiar areas of it. All the drives are created by the dominant commitment and are consequently very short-lived. With the resolution to tonic every second or third chord, the tension generated by the dominant seems fully released. The bass obviously contributes nothing at all in this respect. These ritornello sections clearly are designed to be enjoyed, not for what they promise for the future—but for their own lyrical qualities. They do not engender a sense of restlessness or even of directed motion, but rather one of relaxation and pleasurable enjoyment of the moment.

In those portions of the movement not concerned with the presentation of the ritornello, this entire organization is reversed. Here the dominant commitment often plays a negligible role, but the bass proceeds in such ways as to suggest a sense of directedness and of the accumulation of momentum at virtually all times. That is to say that the bass proceeds predominantly, indeed almost exclusively, along one or another of those rigid patterns of motion (sequence, circle of fifths, descent by thirds, etc.) so widely used by late-baroque composers.[3] Unlike many of the composers of the early seventeenth century, however, Bach is quite successful in imbuing these formulas with life. For, instead of exploiting a single bare sequential pattern for a long time, as Sweelinck or Scheidt had done, he generally either introduces an element of variation in the way the figure is presented, or else he moves smoothly and easily from one such pattern to another. The brief passage shown in Example 3a, for instance, contains two distinct formulas (marked

Example 3a. *Brandenburg Concerto* No. IV, First Movement:
Bass m. 13-23.

with numbered brackets), the second derived from the first merely by the addition of faster repetitions of the notes forming the succession of thirds that is so essential a part of the earlier figure. The longer passage shown in Example 3b contains four separate formulas, all clearly related to each other. The second figure, after all, merely outlines the descending triad, shorn of repeated notes,

Example 3b. *Brandenburg Concerto* No. IV, First Movement:
Bass m. 35-57.

which ended the first; the third makes use of the interval of the descending third found at the beginning of the second pattern, as well as of the rhythm in which it was presented, but reverses the direction of the last leap; and the fourth represents a return to the fast, repeated-note version of the descending triad outlined by the second figure. A different formula is shown in Example 3c,

Example 3c. *Brandenburg Concerto* No. IV, First Movement:
Bass m. 161-185.

where the bass proceeds twice around the circle of fifths, with ingenious and ever-changing figural variation the first time (the important notes are marked), before entering into a decorated rising scale.

To one degree or another, these passages suggest a state of becoming. One could hardly claim to appreciate them for their own evocative qualities. They do not show anything of the lyricism so characteristic of the ritornello, nor indeed do they seem to exhibit any other kind of self-attractive quality.

In addition, the rigidly patterned motion of the bass—motion which permits a considerable degree of prediction—gives an unmistakable impression of proceeding in a specific direction. The direction may change at times, but the feeling of directedness remains: the change seems to be according to plan rather than a matter of chance. Where there is a sense of directed motion of course, an expectation of culmination is bound to arise. The result again is to focus attention on what is to come—the culmination—rather than to absorb it in the pleasurable sensations offered at the moment. The main characteristic of these sections could be termed a sense of restlessness, of drive, of accrual of tension. Their whole function seems to be to prepare a favorable climate for the emergence of a significant and pleasurable situation.

Thus this movement can be said to consist of two antithetical types of passages: one which is sensuously pleasing but develops little drive, and another which develops a considerable drive but offers little in the way of immediate appeal. In the former, the harmony is exceedingly stable inasmuch as it hardly ventures away from the tonic; in the latter, it seems to introduce an element of adventure not only by virtue of modulations, but also because the arrival at any tonic is avoided often for considerable lengths of time—indeed, one is frequently not too sure what the tonic is at a given moment.

At first glance, the organization of the movement seems most uncomplicated: merely a continual alternation between the two types of sections. The feeling of restlessness resulting from the driving passages gives way several times to more self-attractive ritornelli. By contrast with the unsettled quality that has preceded, the ritornelli seem all the more enjoyable. The time, we might judge in each case, has grown ripe for a return to the pleasurable lyrical atmosphere with which the movement began. With each return of the stable ritornello, the attractiveness of the material presented is enhanced by a sense of relief.

A closer examination, however, discloses something more to the organization. For it is quite clear that various degrees of drive, hence of tension, are generated in the different sections, and also that the degree to which resolution of these tensions is suggested is far from uniform. The varying degrees of tension and resolution, furthermore, seem to follow a clear pattern which reflects an obvious aesthetic scheme.

The opening and closing sections (measures 1-83 and 345-427) consist of three ritornelli (first and last in G major and the middle one in D major), separated by two episodes (measures 13-23 and 35-57 in the opening and 357-367 and 379-401 in the closing section).[4] Following the third ritornello are two rather brief episodes, each culminating in a very strong approach to a cadence in G major (measures 69-74 and 74-83; Example 4). Although the number of measures allotted to each section would seem to favor the unstable element slightly (it occupies forty-five

Example 4. *Brandenburg Concerto* No. IV, First Movement: m. 69-83.

of these eighty-two measures), the self-attractiveness of the ritornelli makes them so much more striking effects—effects whose essential qualities are so much more easily impressed upon and retained in the memory—that I think the whole section must be counted as fairly heavily weighted in favor of stability. I would venture to assert that the episodes would be interpreted as challenges to that state of stability, rather than as the normal state of affairs or a predominant current. The overcoming of these challenges serves only to enhance the power and pleasure associated with the return of the ritornelli. It might be noted in passing that the second challenge is somewhat more substantial than the first— hence the return seems more welcome—largely because it endures more than twice as long.

I would suggest that a similar function is served by the two episodes which end this section (measures 69-74 and 74-83 shown in Example 4). The fact that there are such quick and powerful returns to a key already firmly implanted in memory makes these passages seem little more than futile attempts to break away from the sense of stability and enter into more significant harmonic adventures. The overcoming of the venturesome tendencies— especially the fact that they are so emphatically overcome twice in so short a span of time—serves to strengthen the grip of the tonic and hence to reinforce the impression of stability.

Thus, every attempt to break away from the safety and pleasure of stability in these first and last eighty-two measures has failed; every uprising has been quelled. The episodes have assumed the function of contrasts obviously designed either to enhance the pleasure of the return or to test the resolve to retain the stable atmosphere.

Between the opening and closing sections, however, the suggestions of stability are relatively few and far between. There are only ritornelli, in some cases with concluding excursions, in E minor (measures 137-160), A minor (185-197), C major (209-235), and B minor (323-343)—a total of but eighty-five of 263 measures. In view of this preponderance of the unstable element, one could no longer consider stability the dominant feature, nor could one even consider the two forces to be in a state of balance; one could not well maintain that the energy generated during a drive is completely used up by the ritornello into which it flows. The memory of the drive is bound to be so strong that the drive following must seem a resumption of activity after a respite, rather than a completely fresh effort. The predominant impression left by the interior portion of the movement, then, would be of a driving, restless quality. The ritornelli would be interpreted, automatically, as obstacles set in the way of the drive, and overcome by it. Even during the longest ritornello, one could hardly lose the feeling of a pressure propelling events along their course.

As time goes by, of course, the sense of tension generated by this pressure is bound to increase, if only because the lack of adequate resolution at each ritornello leaves a residue of tension to which the succeeding drives make further contributions. In addition, the threat of disorientation becomes more acute with the passage of time. We begin to wonder how this will end, when it will end, where it will end.

Thus it would seem that the degree of tension would reach its maximum at the end of the interior portion of the movement, at the point where the reprise is about to begin. That something like this must have been Bach's intent can be confirmed by a study of the pattern formed by the alternation of ritornelli and episodes.

Of the four ritornelli, only two, the ones in E minor (measures 137-160) and C major (209-235), seem strong enough in quality or persistent enough in the definition of a key to call a halt, even temporarily, to the drive leading up to them. The E-minor ritornello is able to fulfill this function because, although the statement of the ritornello itself is abbreviated, it is followed, as at the end of the earlier G-major section (measures 69-83), by a series of passages threatening the state of stability, but each brought to a close with a strong cadence to this temporary tonic (measures 143-148, 148-157, and 157-160). The same is true for the C-major ritornello, which is not at all abbreviated.

The other two ritornelli seem only partially able to arrest the drive. In the case of the one in A minor (measures 185-197), the sense of repose is weakened somewhat by the use of persistent thirty-second note passages in the *violino principale* (the only place in the movement where such rapid motion is to be found). The absence of any closing episodes threatening the new tonic but not quite able to break away, hardly seems designed to suggest the kind of tenacious holding to a key that might reinforce the impression of stability. As a result, the quality of restlessness persists throughout the presentation of this ritornello, making it clear that it was not so much a goal of the drive as an obviously momentary interruption of it.

As for the B-minor ritornello (measures 323-343), it should be noted that the ritornello proper is quite short (323-329), that it follows an exceedingly long and complex episode, and that its goallike quality and sense of stability are somewhat compromised by the use of a tonic organ point which brings about a number of harmonic conflicts. In addition, it obviously has the wrong color— a minor cast quite different from the expected return to a sunny atmosphere. Thus, even though it ends with two episodes cadencing to B minor (measures 329-334 and 334-343), it probably must be considered only a provisional resolution of the energy generated by the preceding episode. The final resolution awaits the return to G major which occurs within just two measures of the end of the last cadence in B minor.

Thus, there are only three points where there is even a short-lived suggestion of a culmination to the drive, rather than merely of an interruption of it: the E-minor and C-major ritornelli, and the reprise. The interior portion of the movement, then, can be said to be divided into three separate drives leading up to these points. The last of the drives obviously develops a good deal more of a feeling of tension than either of the others, simply by virtue of its greater length (roughly 110 measures to forty-nine in the second and fifty-four in the first). In addition, it may be noted that most of the material presented in the first two of these large episodes is to be found in the third as well. Hence there can be no question that either of the earlier ones were qualitatively more intense than the third.

As for the other two large episodes, it may be noted that, although the first is somewhat longer (fifty-four measures to forty-nine), it is qualitatively the more conservative. For the most part, the harmonic rhythm is rather slow and the harmony is unadventurous. A simple progression (I-V of IV-IV-V-I) is spread over seven full measures (83-89; Example 5a), repeated once in the

Example 5a. *Brandenburg Concerto* No. IV, First Movement, m. 83-92.

same key, with slightly varied figuration (measures 91-97), and twice more in the dominant key (measures 105-111 and 113-119). Separating these sluggishly moving sections, furthermore, are hints of the opening of the ritornello (measures 89-91 as shown in

Example 5a, 103-105 and 111-113). From measure 125 on, the harmonic rhythm is slowed even more to one change of chord every four measures, although the addition of instruments and thickening of the texture do contribute to some heightening of the drive (Example 5b).

Example 5b. *Brandenburg Concerto* No. IV, First Movement, m. 125-137.

Since these rather timid steps toward adventure occupy forty-four of the fifty-four measures contained in this section, it is clear that only a mild drive develops here. The growth of tension can be traced more to prolonged failure to settle decisively into a key than to positive suggestions of force or drive inherent in the motion of the bass.

Although the second drive (measures 161-209) also has some conservative elements (notably the weak A-minor ritornello), it nevertheless seems to generate a good deal more tension, at least at times. For, in the first half of it (measures 161-185), the harmonic rhythm is much faster, and the tie to a key or series of keys seems more nebulous. The bass describes the two motions around the circle of fifths shown in Example 3c, the first carrying two and one-half times and the second once around the entire cycle. Within these twenty-four measures, furthermore, are either quick key changes (measures 161-164, 171-180), or else fairly prolonged definition of a tonic, but without any settling into it by means of a strong cadence (measures 165-170). All in all, a restless atmosphere is established, far more restless than in the first episode. Even the A-minor ritornello that follows might be considered evidence of intent to make this drive seem stronger than the first. For the fact that the sense of restlessness persists during this ritornello (largely because of the thirty-second note passages), as well as the fact that the allegiance to this tonic is so easily broken, suggests, as I pointed out earlier, that this was not so much a goal of the drive preceding and hence a point of respite, as an unsuccessful attempt to arrest its progress. The failure of this attempt, of course, merely serves to underline the strength of the current sweep toward the C-major ritornello that follows.

Thus, there can be little question that the second drive develops a considerably greater degree of tension than the first. This means that the three major episodes attain successively higher levels of intensity. The first represents a rather tentative step toward adventure, the second a bolder one, and the third the climactic one. In retrospect, at least, it seems that each has prepared the way for the next one. The second episode represents a logical continuation to the context established by the first, while the third seems virtually required, sooner or later, by the trend set in motion by the first two.

In this way—the way he has organized the alternation of ritornelli and episodes—Bach has indicated an intent to reach the maximum degree of tension just before the beginning of the reprise. The result is that a great sense of pleasure and relief attaches to the reprise, with its return to harmonic stability and to the presentation of predominantly lyrical and attractive thematic material. It is no longer just a pleasant lyrical section, as it was at the beginning; it is now a return to a long-expected quality after a considerable amount of conflict, restlessness—almost discomfort. Anyone who has ever been deprived of seemingly insignificant pleasures for a considerable span of time—perhaps because of a period of service in the armed forces, for instance—will recognize how potent an aesthetic effect this is. For such things as the sight of familiar faces, the observance of familiar customs, even just keeping comfortably warm and dry—things usually taken for granted—become charged with emotion and pleasure after a period of deprivation. And the longer the deprivation and the more problematic the question of return, the more intense will be the pleasure when the return is effected. In just this way, I would suggest, the lyrical, sunny qualities of the ritornello-dominated last section carry connotations of stronger emotion and greater pleasure than had been associated with them earlier in the composition. Thus, it might well be said that Bach's aim in writing this movement was not just the delineation of the emotion which he considered to reside in his ritornello material, but an intensification of that emotion.

A similar type of organization, though on a far smaller scale, can be found in many of Bach's dance movements. The *Allemande* from the first *French Suite* (D minor) can serve as illustration. Here, of course, the design is created not by the play of ritornelli and episodes, but rather by the alternation between passages establishing or reinforcing the basic tonality on the one hand, and excursions from that tonality on the other.

This *Allemande* is arranged in the fashion customary for dance movements during the seventeenth and eighteenth centuries, with a division into two sections, each repeated; the first ending on the dominant, presumably to facilitate the repeat. There are six excursions from D minor, four in the first part and two in the second.

The first two excursions are exceedingly brief: an implication of a move toward F major (though no resolution to that key) in measure 2 (Example 6a), and a short-lived move to G minor at

Example 6a. *French Suite* No. I, *Allemande*: m. 2-3.

the end of measure 3 (Example 6b). With but these exceptions—totaling approximately three beats—the whole of the first four and

Example 6b. *French Suite* No. I, *Allemande*: m. 3-4.

three-quarter measures is devoted to the definition of the tonic D minor. The third excursion (Example 6c) begins with an implication of F major at the end of the fifth measure; the resolution,

Example 6c. *French Suite* No. I, *Allemande*: m. 5-7.

however, is to a dominant-seventh on F, followed by its resolution to B♭ major. The remainder of this excursion is taken up with a fairly deliberate motion to G minor terminating on the third beat of measure 7.

Clearly a trend is in evidence here, a trend toward more ambitious attempts to break away from the tonic. Where the first excursion, after all, consisted merely of an implication of a key change, the second actually defined another new key by means of something resembling an authentic cadence, and the third defined a series of new keys and remained away from tonic for a considerably longer period of time.

At first glance, the following excursion (Example 6d) seems to interrupt the tendency toward broader and more significant

Example 6d. *French Suite* No. I, *Allemande*: m. 9-12.

adventures: it lasts only from the middle of measure 9 to the middle of measure 10 and contains only an implication of a move toward F major. In one respect, however, it does represent another step in the sequence established. It ends not with a strong return to tonic, but with a half-cadence where the significance of the ending dominant chord is enhanced through being approached by way of its own dominant. Thus this excursion has dared to do what none of the others did: to end away from home. If it does not itself go farther away, it at least serves to further weaken the ties to the home key. In this sense, then, it contributes to the trend that is developing.

Following the double bar, there is another return to the D minor tonic—quite in contradiction to the usual textbook observations. Undoubtedly it was designed to reinforce the memory of the tonic—a memory which is to be threatened severely by the next excursion (measures 15-18; Example 6e). This represents a far greater threat to D minor than is to be found anywhere else in the movement. It lasts considerably longer than any of the others;

Example 6e. *French Suite* No. I, *Allemande*: m. 15-19.

it runs through the sequence of keys found in the third, and until now the most extensive, excursion (F major, B♭ major, G minor) and adds a second move to F major after all of these; and it contains very strongly defined cadences to both G minor and F major (measures 17 and 18). The last excursion (measures 21-22; Example 6f) is once again short, and touches only the keys B♭ major, F major, and G minor.

Example 6f. *French Suite* No. I, *Allemande*: m. 21-23.

Thus there is very clear evidence of intent to increase the challenge to D minor with each passing excursion, with the exception of the last one. Along with this, I would suggest, goes an implication of progressively increasing tension, as the questions of how, when, or even if the excursions are to be brought to a close become more and more problematical. After the fifth excursion, furthermore, we cannot but begin to wonder whether the reversion to D minor actually represents a return to tonic or just a move to another key in a series of modulations. The memory of just where tonic lay must have dimmed somewhat by this time and a threat of disorientation set in, adding to the sense of increased tension.

It is precisely this consideration that accounts for the lesser dimensions of the last excursion. For, at this point, Bach would have faced the problem of restoring the feeling that D minor actually represented the tonic. What better way, he might have reasoned, than to offer a challenge that would be overcome, making the futility of the attempt to escape testify to the strength and staying power of the D-minor tonality. But if the just reestablished definition of D minor as tonic is allowed to fade from memory again, any subsequent move toward it would tend to be interpreted, not as a return, but merely as an exploration of another new key. Hence, if the framing function of this tonality is to be reestablished, the return to it must be made relatively soon, before its memory is obliterated. And thus the final excursion fulfills quite a different function from that fulfilled by the earlier ones: its purpose is not to suggest another step in the growth of adventurousness, but rather to provide that small amount of challenge whose overcoming makes possible the reestablishment of D minor as the tonic for the entire piece.

Along with this scheme goes something of the same sense of virtually continuous pressure noted in the interior portion of the concerto movement discussed earlier. The basses develop a good deal of drive within phrases (note how often they outline decorated descending scales, as in Example 6g), while the arrival at the cadence obviously is the signal for, not a respite, but the beginning of another drive almost immediately, much as is the case in the fourth measure of Example 6g.

Thus both the continual pressure and the pattern of excursions suggest a clear aesthetic plan: something in the nature of a climax at or near the end of the movement. The fact that there is so little let-up in the drive is bound to raise the level of tension as the movement nears its end. And the return to D minor at the close seems something hard won after a considerable struggle between what might be termed centrifugal and centripetal forces (i.e., those

Example 6g. *French Suite* No. I, *Allemande*: m. 2-6.

forces tending to break the sense of allegiance to D minor and those tending to retain and restore the influence of this key)—a struggle that has become more and more intense as the movement unfolded. The implication, once again, is not just of the delineation of an emotion, but of the intensification of it.

It is in the fugues, however, that this kind of aesthetic planning is most easily observed. So many other constructive factors are brought into play in these compositions that both the quality of pressure and the program of intensification hardly can be overlooked. Thus the sense of growing pressure within a phrase results not just from the directedness of the bass, but from the addition of voice, the increase of rhythmic activity, the spread of such increases into more of the voices, and, in some cases, from the increased use of dissonance. The same factors make it possible to suggest considerable qualitative differences between the levels of intensity achieved in various sections, and thus to create an obvious ranking of climaxes by means other than the relative lengths of episodes or excursions. Not that the quantitative element is completely without influence in this respect, or even that its importance necessarily is significantly reduced. But it is now only one of several factors contributing to the process of intensification, although its influence is still often decisive.

The first fugue in the *Well Tempered Clavier* [5] offers a good starting point for discussion; it is organized along lines not radically different from those found in the *Allemande*. As we saw also in the Obrecht examples described in Chapter 3, returns to the tonic throughout the course of the movement cut it into a series of excursions suggesting a pattern of intensification.

Even the pattern formed by the various excursions is similar

to that found in the *Allemande:* successively greater challenges to
the memory of the basic tonality, but closed off with a more conservative one. In the first six measures—the so-called exposition—
the challenges are minor: two brief modulations to G major and one
to F major, the three together occupying a total of only seven of
twenty-five beats (Example 7a). In the following seven measures,

Example 7a. *Well Tempered Clavier, Fugue* No. I: m. 1-7.

these proportions are almost exactly reversed, as only nine of
twenty-eight beats define the tonic of the piece, C major (Example
7b). In addition, there is an almost shocking, hence quite powerful, move to A minor (measure 11), followed by a fairly long

Example 7b. *Well Tempered Clavier, Fugue* No. I: m. 7-14.

passage in this key, and even a strong cadence in it (measure 14) which succeeds in calling the drive to a momentary halt. On the other hand, until the move to A minor, the range of modulations is rather conservative: aside from a single move to D minor (measure 8), the texture is restricted to an alternation between the keys of C major and G major.

In the opening of the next excursion (end of measure 15 to measure 18; Example 7c), the range of modulations is extended

Example 7c. *Well Tempered Clavier, Fugue* No. I: m. 15-19.

considerably (G major, A minor, F major, C major, G major, D minor, C major, F major, and D minor) and the speed with which keys are exchanged is stepped up: these nine key changes take place within just eleven beats. Here the threat of disorientation acts to raise the level of tension well beyond what was experienced during the early part of the preceding excursion. As in this earlier excursion, the highly modulatory section is followed by something like an attempt to restore the sense of stability by settling into a particular key (beginning in measure 19). In this case, however, the attempt is not so immediately successful, as the texture runs through D minor, G major, C major, and F major before settling into C major with a strong cadence (Example 7d). The fact that the settling into a key takes so long and is so round about only serves to affirm the impression that the earlier series of rapid modulations did indeed pose a far more serious threat to the memory of the original key and to the whole sense of tonal stability than did the equivalent passage of the preceding excursion (measures 7-11; see Example 7b)—a threat from which it is more difficult to recover.

The last excursion consists only of a single modulation to the subdominant in measures 24-26 (Example 7e). It would seem to

Example 7d. *Well Tempered Clavier, Fugue* No. I: m. 19-24.

Example 7e. *Well Tempered Clavier, Fugue* No. I: m. 24-27.

have the same function as the final excursion in the *Allemande:* providing a challenge that can be overcome easily to restore the sense of stability in general, and the feeling that C major represents the framing tonality for the whole fugue in particular.

Thus, the arrangement of the excursions quite clearly reflects an intent to intensify as the movement nears its end. When, in addition, it is noted that the full four-voice texture is heard only rarely in the early part of the fugue (only in measures 5–6, 9, and 12–13; a total of only about fourteen of fifty-eight beats), but is virtually always present from measure 15 on (the beginning of the strongest excursion), something like climactic intent can hardly be doubted. Once again, then, Bach's aim must have been to intensify the emotion residing in his theme rather than merely to delineate it.

All of this, however, is merely a way of presenting evidence. If a meaningful picture of Bach's thought processes is to be reconstructed, it is necessary to coordinate this gross evidence of intensification with the more subtle manifestations of drive or, as I have termed it, pressure.

In the exposition of this fugue (see Example 7a), the development of a considerable drive is clearly perceptible, partly because of the addition of voices and the general increase in rhythmic independence and activity, and partly because of the growing need for a culmination of some kind. This drive is cut off at the beginning of measure 7 by the simple expedient of dropping two of the voices from the texture after a rather provisional cadence (V_2-I_6; see Example 7b). What follows is not an interlude designed to restore the sense of equilibrium—to rest up after the exertions of the drive— but an immediate resumption of the drive by means of the stretto entrances in measure 7. This time the drive is given additional impetus first by the sense of greater tonal instability fostered by the lesser amount of time allotted to C major, and then by the power of the almost shocking move to A minor (end of measure 11). The strong A-minor cadence at the beginning of measure 14 (see Example 7b) now assumes the function of a culmination of major proportions, thereby calling the drive to a halt. It is clear, then, that this second drive was far more serious than the first and generated a good deal more momentum. Yet it is still capable of being braked, though only by a powerful cadential formula.

Again what follows is not a respite designed to restore a sense of equilibrium, but another quick build-up, once more through stretto entrances. This drive, furthermore, generates still more of a feeling of excitement than did the preceding one, largely because of the threat of disorientation brought about by the rapid modulations in measures 15-18, the subsequent difficulty in restoring any sense of tonal stability, and the fact that all four voices are active almost all of the time (see Examples 7c and 7d). So powerful is this drive, indeed, that even the very strong cadence of measures 23–24 does not suffice to call it to a halt. No voices are dropped from the texture after this cadence; there is only a temporary slowing of rhythmic activity, a slowing more than compensated by the continued fast harmonic rhythm (Example 7e). It takes a full four measures following this cadence for the energy to run down sufficiently to permit an ending.

This should not be interpreted to mean that a diminuendo is intended in these last measures. Such an effect would seem completely incongruous after the prolonged emphasis on rising intensity. It would be equivalent to trying to bring a fast-moving locomotive to a stop within a short time merely by cutting the pressure in its boiler. When so much momentum has been generated, the application of considerable force is required to bring the motion to a halt. This, I would suggest, is the only reasonable approach to bringing a fugue of this kind to a close; it must be made clear that the close is the result of a growth in resistance to the impetus, rather than merely of a tapering of pressure.

In a way, the closing section could be considered the equivalent of a cadence extended in time. For the function is very similar to that of the cadence; namely, to use up energy rather than to generate it. Where the cadence accomplishes this almost immediately, the final section takes some measures to do it, thereby suggesting how strong the drive has become at the end.

This whole fugue, then, can be viewed as consisting of a single drive toward a climactic ending, with serious interruptions at only two points. The climax takes the form not of a single peak, but of a broad plateau. The effect of the fugue could be likened to an incoming tide, in which individual waves are halted in their progress by such obstacles as reefs and breakwaters, but in which the underlying surge eventually proves strong enough to overcome these obstacles and propel the rising waters to the shore.

The sense of pressure leading toward a climactic ending is equally in evidence in the second fugue from the *Well Tempered Clavier.* Indeed, in this work it is rather difficult to find points at which the drive is really stopped, even momentarily—so continuous is the motion. A consideration of the structure, however, provides some clues to how the climax was prepared.

Unlike the first fugue, in which an entrance of the subject can be heard virtually at all times (only about eighteen of 108 beats are completely free of an entry, and eight of these are in the toccatalike ending), this movement divides into two types of sections: one in which entrances of the subject are prominently displayed, and another—the so-called episode—in which a portion of the theme or of the counter-subject to it is developed by means of sequential repetitions or imitations. Since the profile of the subject itself tends to define a tonality very strongly (so much of its time is spent emphasizing the tonic and its leading-tone, after all), the entrances of the subject invariably lead to a fairly stable settling into the tonic so defined. The sequential nature of the episodes, on the other hand, serves to impart something more of an impression of tonal instability.

Obviously, this is a scheme of contrasts not too different from that found in the concerto movement discussed earlier. In this case, however, the similarity of the thematic material used in the two types of sections, as well as the way the episodes seem to merge almost imperceptibly into the entries, suggests that the entries assume the function not so much of relief as of summation. The episodes generate energy; the subsequent entries sum up the posture achieved by means of this energy, thereby using it up. Thus the ending of an entry can be thought of as the terminus of the drive generated by the episode preceding it.

It is at this point that Bach may have had the choice of introducing a respite, or even a gradual descent, designed to restore the sense of equilibrium. Needless to say, at no point is there evidence that he chose either of these alternatives; indeed, it is clear that his choice in all cases was an immediate resumption of the drive by means of another episode and the tonal instability it would bring on.

In the main body of the fugue,[6] then, a drive can be considered to be cut off at the beginning of measures 9, 13, 17, and 22. And a pattern of growth in the intensity suggested by each of these drives is easily discernible.

Although the first three sections formed in this way occupy the same amount of time (two measures of episode balanced by two measures of entry), the textural arrangement suggests progressively greater levels of tension. In the first episode (measures 5–6; Example 8a), even though the sequence rises by step, the

Example 8a. *Well Tempered Clavier, Fugue* No. II: m. 5-7.

texture is so thin and in so relatively high a register that only a limited amount of energy is generated. The fuller texture and wider spread of the voices in the second episode (measures 9–10; Example 8b) make for an implication of greater intensity, or at least of a more significant attempt to build, despite the fact that the sequential motion now leads downward. The third episode (measures 13–14; Example 8c) combines an even fuller texture in which all voices are active all of the time, with an emphasis again on the rising element.

Example 8b. *Well Tempered Clavier, Fugue* No. II: m. 9-11.

Example 8c. *Well Tempered Clavier, Fugue* No. II: m. 13-15.

In the next passage, for the first time, the balance between the episode and the following entry is shifted in favor of the former: three measures of episode (measures 17-19; Example 8d) to the

Example 8d. *Well Tempered Clavier, Fugue* No. II: m. 17-21.

usual two measures occupied by the entry. Combined with this are a full texture and a rising sequence—all suggesting a somewhat greater degree of drive. Even more momentum is developed during the last episode (measures 22–26; Example 8e), however, primarily by virtue of its length (a full four and one-half measures, more than twice as long as the following entry). This next entry furthermore, does not really succeed in giving the impression of having used up the energy so generated. The entry proper comes to an end this time with a less final sounding cadence (V_2-I_6; Example 8f, measure

Example 8e. *Well Tempered Clavier, Fugue* No. II: m. 22-26.

Example 8f. *Well Tempered Clavier, Fugue* No. II: m. 26-31.

28) followed by a general pause and another, more powerful and more protracted cadence (Example 8f, measures 28–29). This cadence, in turn, is the signal for an even fuller presentation (i.e., with four- and five-note chords, although this is nominally a three-voice fugue) of the subject. As in the first fugue, the implication is that a great deal of effort is required to overcome all of the momentum generated by now, and bring the motion to a halt.

In a somewhat different way than the first fugue, this fugue also is divided into a number of drives, each reaching a greater peak of intensity. Or, to put it another way, it could be said to consist of a single drive interrupted at several points, with the interruptions progressively less capable of suggesting that the impetus has been stopped, even momentarily. In either case it is clear that the entire play of forces is designed to facilitate a climactic ending, almost certainly with the connotation that the basic emotion has been intensified.

A third scheme can be seen in the sixth fugue from the *Well*

Tempered Clavier. Here the drive is split into just two parts; only the cadence in measures 20–21 seems strong enough an event to hold back the momentum even momentarily. The two parts, moreover, are very similar. The second part is only four measures longer than the first; there are rough correspondences between measures 21–29 and 1–8; and there are quite exact relations between measures 30–36 and 9–15.

One could take the position, of course, that the mere fact that the drive is longer would generate a greater quality of intensity by the end of the fugue than that found at any place within it. For this reason alone, the ending would seem to have a more climactic effect than the cadence near the middle of the piece.

In this case, however, Bach has provided a striking reinforcement for this impression. He has expanded what was a highly dramatic but isolated turn of events in the first section (beginning of measure 16; Example 9a) into an equally striking but much more

Example 9a. *Well Tempered Clavier, Fugue* No. VI: m. 15-17.

extended passage near the end of the fugue (measures 36–38; Example 9b). The sense of increased intensity is unmistakable.

Example 9b. *Well Tempered Clavier, Fugue* No. VI: m. 36-39.

Each of these three fugues gives evidence, beyond that offered by the ever-present drive, of having been carefully arranged to produce an effective intensification as it progressed to a climactic ending. The arrangements, however, are clearly quite different in each work. And, indeed, individual differences of this kind are so often found in the various fugues of the *Well Tempered Clavier* that it becomes most difficult to speak in terms of general procedure without considerable qualification. Yet I would venture to assert that there is not a single fugue in this collection, or in the so-called Volume II of the *Well Tempered Clavier*, that does not contain clear and distinct evidence of arrangements such as these. I think there can be little doubt that the idea of building a climactic ending and hence an emotional intensification was an essential, if not the main essential, of Bach's conception of the fugue—at least of his mature conception of the fugue.

Similarly, the programs described in connection with the *Allemande* and the concerto movement are far from being unrepresentative. The various movements of the French and English Suites, for example, as well as of the six *Brandenburg Concerti* and the four Orchestral Suites, give evidence of one or another of the kinds of organization described in this chapter, or of an organization that can be related to one of these types without undue difficulty.

If the interpretations offered in this essay are in any way close to being correct, I believe we are in a position to attempt to reconstruct the outlines of Bach's thought processes. His first aim must have been not just to delineate, but to intensify an emotional expression. The emotion itself would have been considered defined by the rhythmic and melodic contour, as well as by the harmonic implications, of the thematic material whose spinning out generated the entire movement. Thus a fugue subject with a great deal of fast motion and many repeated notes probably would have reflected something like humorous intent, while a slow subject with much chromatic motion would have been considered more serious in character. Bach must have reasoned that the intensification of the emotion so defined could be brought about either by achieving a heightening of the sense of relief, as in the concerto movement described above, or else by a climactic ending—an ending in which the motion, defined somewhat matter-of-factly at the beginning, would be trumpeted forth to the heavens in mighty tones.

With the instruments and ensembles available at that time, however, the stentorian accents needed to suggest a climactic ending convincingly, or even a heightening of relief, must have seemed most difficult to achieve. Bach knew of no romantic-size orchestra, after all—an ensemble that could overpower a listener with the sheer volume of sound produced. The stringed keyboard instruments, furthermore, had only limited powers in this respect: the loudest sounds of harpsichord, clavichord, or even pianoforte of that time hardly could have been calculated to shake the foundations of a building. Only some of the winds and the organ had some capability in this respect, although the winds could not offer the flexibility and sureness of strings, and the organ undoubtedly was not the overpowering instrument it has become today. Additional limitations inherent in the organ, however, seem to work against the achievement of a climactic effect by sheer volume in this instrument as well: its inability to suggest a crescendo would make it most difficult to create a natural-sounding approach to the climactic summation.

Whether as a result of considerations such as these or of conceptual limitations, Bach apparently was led to attempt to deceive his audience into the belief that they were hearing a mighty ending to the piece, even though the sheer number of decibels put out at that point was not greatly different from what was heard in the main body of the composition. The illusion was created by employing procedures designed to suggest what today would be called a gradual crescendo, but which might be better characterized as a gradual increase in intensity. Such a crescendo, if I may use the term in this way, would plant the impression that the accumulation of so much momentum as is generated in the course of a movement must have been arranged with a view to a significant outcome. To return to a figure I have used before, if the mountain should have labored and brought forth a mouse, one could hardly help but feel some sense of disappointment. Thus, any phenomenon that could succeed in arresting the increase in momentum, and even suggesting that the energy was being used up, automatically would be invested with greater significance than it otherwise might have. The sense of heightened significance lends a feeling-tone closely related to an evocation of power, and thus would make possible an ending that might seem truly climactic.

The problem, then, was to effect the quality of a gradual crescendo without any appreciable increase in volume. To accomplish this, Bach had several expedients at his disposal: he could add to the number of voices and to the independence of their rhythmic patterns; he could introduce increases in the rhythmic activity, allowing the faster motions to spread into more and more of the voices; he could fashion a general rise in pitch either in a prominent voice, in several voices, or in the entire texture; he could increase the harmonic rhythm, the incidence and sharpness of dissonance, and even the rate of change of keys; finally, he could count on the emergence of a sense of harmonic drive as the phrase grew riper and the need for the clarification offered by a cadence became more and more acute. The one resource not available to him was the direct crescendo—the appreciable raising of the number of decibels put out.

Each of these expedients, however, can be applied in only a limited way. A rise in pitch eventually must give way to a descent, or else it must exceed the range of audible frequencies. Long before that point, however, a sense of monotony probably would have set in. The addition of voices, if carried beyond a certain point, would exceed digital possibilities on the keyboard instruments, and, in any case, would eventually reach a point where additions would no longer be perceived. The same would be true of the increases in rhythmic activity: eventually they would exceed even the best performer's capabilities, as well as the threshold of discrimination. Even the drive to the cadence has a point of diminishing returns. For if it should remain unsatisfied for too long a time, the listener probably would judge that he was wrong in expecting a cadential resolution, and would simply cease to follow the harmonic patterns.

Thus Bach would have been virtually forced to bring his crescendo to a halt every so often, simply because he lacked the means to sustain it much longer. If he was to maintain anything like the over-all sense of drive needed to lead into the climactic ending, however, he could not often afford the luxury of a respite or descent; for either of these might allow the listener to forget the quality of drive, to the point where all sense of gradual intensification would be lost. He must have felt impelled to start up another drive immediately, so that a residue of tension would remain from the preceding one, and so that all that would be left in a listener's memory would be an impression of an ever-present drive, with just a few momentary interruptions. The interruptions would come to seem merely obstacles placed in the way of the drive—obstacles, however, that did not really succeed in breaking its impetus.

Finally, Bach may have been concerned with reinforcing the impression created by the constant upward pressure by an arrangement of the separate drives, an arrangement designed to suggest increasing tension as the movement nears its close. Thus he would have applied quantitative and qualitative expedients to make the separate drives reach successively higher peaks of intensity before being cut off, with the last one actually not cut off by the cadence, but rather grinding to a halt slowly.

This reconstruction of Bach's approach to composition—if it has any validity at all—calls into question the commonly accepted view of emotional treatment in the baroque. For it is generally held that composers of this time were not particularly interested in intensifying an emotion, but only in depicting or imitating it. As Bukofzer put it:

> This term [*expressio verborum*] does not have the modern, emotional connotation of "expressive music" and can more accurately be rendered as "musical representation of the word." The means of verbal representation in baroque music were not direct, psychological, and emotional, but indirect, that is, intellectual and pictorial. The modern psychology of dynamic emotions did not yet exist in the baroque era. Feelings were classified and stereotyped in a set of so-called affections, each representing a mental state which was in itself static. It was the business of the composer to make the affection of the music correspond to that of the words. According to the lucid rationalism of the time, the composer had at his disposal a set of musical figures which were pigeonholed like the affections themselves and were designed to represent these affections in music.[7]

This is a formulation that might apply well enough to the second rank of baroque composers, but it certainly could not be considered valid for some of the acknowledged creative giants such as Bach or Monteverdi. That Bukofzer's formulation represents something of an exaggeration has already been pointed out by Dr. Haydon.[8]

I should like to enter a plea, then, for a conception of Bach as neither effete poet nor dull pedant, but rather as an *exuberant* creative personality—a man whose music is filled with vitality and drive. The sense of energy is so great, indeed, that it survives almost all obstacles in its pursuit of emotional intensification. Thus to perform this music with beautifully tapered phrases distinctly separated one from another by pauses or holds, or with exaggerated nuances and attention to detail, or with long-enduring soft passages offering a good deal of relief, is to betray its very nature. The same would be true of performances at which either a slow speed or an exaggerated differentiation between stressed and unstressed portions of the measure bring the beat pattern too much to the foreground of attention. The basic rule of performance, I would suggest, should be to do everything possible to bring out the sense of ever-present drive, while at the same time making clear the degree of challenge to this drive posed by the various (largely cadential) obstacles placed in its way. If this is done, I would venture to assert that the structure of the piece as a whole would probably take care of itself. For Bach has built the various gradations of intensity achieved by the separate drives directly into the music. Attempts to heighten the effects of any or all of these drives might well run the risk of exaggeration and hence of caricature.

Interpretations of this kind, I believe, would end the tendency to consider Bach's instrumental music in the category of interesting museum pieces—quaint testimony to an outmoded way of thinking and feeling. These works no longer would serve primarily as program openers to warm up the fingers and mind of a keyboard artist, or as not quite understood or understandable vehicles for showing off the sound and virtuosity of unusual groups of instrumentalists. Rather, I think they would speak to us of human problems, aspirations, and situations as vital, meaningful, and moving today as they were in Bach's time. I speak, then, for a living Bach, an exciting Bach, a Bach whose accents retain their force and meaning despite the passage of time and the many changes in fashion—all this made possible by the conception of an exuberant Bach.

SEVEN

Intensity and the
Classical Sonata Allegro

*A*LTHOUGH THE TERMS CLASSICISM and romanticism are among the most widely used in
musical criticism, their applications are somewhat ambiguous: they
are taken to signify both sets of stylistic characteristics and bodies
of music written by specific groups of composers. Musical classicism generally is associated with qualities of elegance, restraint,
formality and objectivity, and with the works of certain composers
active during the latter part of the eighteenth century and early
part of the nineteenth—specifically, Joseph Haydn (1732-1809),
Wolfgang Mozart (1756-1791), and, usually, Ludwig van Beethoven [1] (1770-1827). Romanticism, on the other hand, is commonly
associated with such characteristics as freedom, imagination, subjectivity, emotionality, and expressiveness, as well as with the works
of the major composers (usually excepting Beethoven) of the
nineteenth century.

The most natural assumption might well be that there is an
affinity between the two uses of each term, that the two sets of
traits accurately reflect the practices found in each of these bodies
of compositions. Any familiarity with the works in question, however, makes it apparent that this is not the case. Beethoven, Mozart,
and Haydn are often patently expressive and emotional; the G-
minor symphonies of Mozart, the *Sturm und Drang* works of
Haydn, and almost any of the major works of Beethoven would
be unintelligible if one did not understand that the composer's aim

was a strong emotional evocation. Furthermore, questions of free-dom and imagination—supposedly the strong points of romantic composers—seem specious. It certainly would be difficult to pin down the aspects of the classic composers' styles which could be interpreted as limitations on free choice, or as reflections of lack of imagination. Elegance and objectivity, finally, seem far removed from the rough-cut humor as well as the pathos so often found in both Haydn and Beethoven, while the demonic aspects of Mozart's art have been appreciated at least since the time of E. T. A. Hoffmann.

The question arises, then, whether there are reasonable grounds for distinguishing between classic and romantic musical arts—the former embodied in the works of Haydn, Mozart, and Beethoven, and the latter in the works of the major nineteenth-century composers. Perhaps it would be more accurate to consider the two bodies of music to reflect essentially the same ideas and viewpoints, perhaps with some minor shift in emphasis much as Blume suggests.[2]

This is more than a question of terminology or a nice distinc-tion. Standards of performance as well as an understanding of intellectual developments will depend, to a large degree, on answers to this type of question. An interpreter, after all, is trying to repro-duce not just the notes of a composition, but the spirit—the view of the human situation and of human experience—embodied in those notes. If he cannot grasp the assumptions under which a composition was brought into being, he has little chance of captur-ing that spirit. The historian, similarly, does not wish merely to compile more and more facts. At some point, he must attempt to convert factual information into a reasonable picture of human activity, beliefs, and motivations, all of which requires a study of assumptions.

A study of the two bodies of music indicates that a major change in viewpoint did occur sometime during the early decades of the nineteenth century. The key to this fundamental change in outlook is to be found in the treatment of climax and of the rise and fall of intensity in general. In this chapter and the following one, I should like to present evidence bearing on this change, and some inferences I have drawn from the evidence.

Although the extent of the difference in the treatment of intensity can be seen most easily in the works of the more radically romantic composers (such as Berlioz, Liszt, Wagner, Mahler, Hugo Wolf, etc.), the compositions of these artists contain so many departures from classic procedures (chromaticism, form, texture, programs, etc.) that one would be hard put to determine just how significant the novel treatment of intensity is amid all these stylistic innovations. A truer and deeper picture of any underlying conceptual changes can be gained by drawing comparisons between the classic works and those of the more moderate romantics, such as Schubert, Mendelssohn, Schumann, and Brahms—composers who did not attempt to break so radically with the past.

In particular, the differences in the treatment of the intensity can be seen to good advantage in the way the various composers handled what has since come to be known as the sonata-allegro form. It is this type of movement, then, that is the focus of study in the present essay and the one following.

The sonata-allegro usually is thought of as a form or mold—a geographical outline—into which composers cast their ideas and materials. While this conception is of dubious validity, especially for the classic composers, the terminology developed in connection with it is most useful in a discussion of this kind, and hence worth outlining briefly.

As generally formulated, a sonata-allegro movement can be divided into three main sections: exposition, development, and recapitulation. The exposition consists of three main subdivisions, usually called first theme, second theme, and closing section, the latter two subdivisions being in a different key (often the dominant or relative major) from the first. The change in key is effected during what is called the bridge—a passage which separates the first and second themes. The whole of the exposition is repeated in many cases. The recapitulation, the third of the main sections, follows the plan of the exposition except that the second theme and closing section generally are presented in the original key. The development, which lies between the exposition and recapitulation, is a free, unstable, even restless section. Tonal allegiances are shifted rapidly and continuously in this section; the thematic materials presented in the exposition are torn apart, recast, and recombined at the discretion of the composer. The recapitulation that follows ordinarily gives an impression of some restoration of order and stability. In many cases, the movement comes to a close with another section, sometimes fairly long, called a coda.

In the classic sonata-allegro movements, the ebb and flow of intensity seem most carefully designed. In a great many of these movements, for instance, the entire exposition contains just two main climaxes, one at or near the end of the bridge and the other at or near the end of the exposition.[3] In some cases, what appears to be an additional climax after the second theme turns out to be the natural result of a brief interruption; with the resumption of the upward drive very quickly thereafter, its subordinate or preparatory function becomes clearly defined. The same relation of intensities is, of course, found in the recapitulation.

The second theme in movements of this kind, furthermore, is generally of a more relaxed character, and is usually rather short and not too significant or even attractive in itself. As a result, it assumes something of the quality of a respite from the previous building up of forces apparent in the bridge and often in the first theme as well. This respite, in turn, makes the build-up to the second climax (the one near the end of the exposition) seem a resumption of activity rather than an initiation of a new thought—an impression sometimes strengthened by references to the first theme in the closing section. Thus the exposition gives evidence of having been very neatly organized, because of the rise and fall of intensity, in such a way that the tonal flow seems natural from beginning to end: one big rise of forces with just a few detours like the second theme.

Another scheme, used particularly in fairly short movements by Haydn,[4] entirely omits the respite offered by the second theme. After the initial theme, a bridgelike section begins (i.e., one that modulates and builds toward a climax), but both the climax and the arrival in the new key are delayed until just before the end of the exposition. Here the close consists of just a few measures during which the energy generated in the course of the exposition is allowed to run down. This scheme, of course, represents even a simpler, more direct pattern of intensity flux in that there are no detours of any significance on the road toward the climax. Certainly it represents a highly controlled, carefully regulated play of intensity.

A few other arrangements of the sonata-allegro exposition can be found in the classic literature. None, however, offers evidence of anything resembling a haphazard rise and fall of intensity.

While a considerable variety of schemes can be found in development sections of classical compositions, the practice still seems far from a real freedom in the sense of proceeding without much regard for consequences or antecedents. It is clear that the rises and falls in intensity are calculated to lead into what might be called a dramatic reentry at the recapitulation. If the reentering theme is to be soft, one can almost count on the appearance of a climax just before the beginning of the recapitulation. A forceful reentry, on the other hand, often will take place at a point clearly recognizable as the climax of the whole development. This point of climax, furthermore, often will be preceded by a section in which the intensity is held down almost artificially, so that the subsequent rise seems a reaction—a welcome relief. So regularly are devices of this kind employed that one could almost formulate a psychological equivalent to Newton's third law: Every significant event tends to be a reaction to an appropriate and opposite action.

More evidence of regularity can be observed, however, than the mere placement of climax in a position appropriate to the character of the reentry. For a development section often contains not just one climax, but a series of them, interspersed with periods of ebbing intensity and with suggestions of very low energy. In the works of Haydn (after his very early efforts), Mozart, and Beethoven, these climaxes are arranged in an order undoubtedly designed to make the final climax seem a logical outgrowth of *all* of the events in the development, not just of the immediately preceding climax or anticlimax. It is apparent, in these works, that this last climax has been in the making since the very beginning of the development. In some cases, the earlier part of the development consists of a series of build-ups, none of which manages to bring about an event significant enough to use up much of the energy generated during the preceding drive. The peak of the last build-up, then, is defined as a climax partly because it does issue into a significant event—a change of key, a cadence, or a very forceful statement of important thematic material—that seems to fulfill the by now strongly felt commitment to culmination. On the other hand, the unsuccessful attempts to achieve culmination lend a sense of plausibility to the final move into the climax; the failure of previous attempts to accomplish something specific makes it seem most natural to try again, harder. In other cases, the main climax is preceded by a series of lesser peaks, each one stronger than any of its predecessors. In this way a suggestion of a rising trend, or of an ever-broadening opposition of forces, is created, again making it seem that the main climax is not brought about entirely without preparation. Whatever the scheme, there is no mistaking the clear intent to organize the ebb and flow of energy into easily perceived and logical patterns.

Some idea of the procedures used to bend the development to the purpose of creating a dramatic reentry—and hence a heightening of emotional effect—can be gained by studying a number of specific examples. In the first movement of Haydn's Symphony No. 104, the development begins with an alternation between soft passages (measures 108-120 and 129-138) and quite forceful ones (measures 121-129 and from measure 139 on), an alternation that seems to set the stage well for a build-up in intensity. For although the forces seem to be in balance, it is clearly a precarious equilibrium: the sharpness of the opposition tells us that the two elements cannot long continue to exist side by side without one becoming subordinated to the other. In this case, it is the strong element that wins out—there is no reversion to soft passages from measure 139 to 176. Quite to the contrary, all of these thirty-seven measures show a considerable and quite direct build-up in pressure, with the last half at a fortissimo dynamic level—a rather strong indication for Haydn to use for so long a time.

The drive is brought to an end by a rest (with fermata), but only after reaching a most exciting series of repeated dominant-seventh chords. The peculiarly unstable quality of this sonority suggests that the enormous amount of energy built up has not been resolved—and it never is resolved, at least not for some fifty measures or more. Nevertheless, the recapitulation begins immediately after the rest. What has happened to all that energy? How does the intensity pattern of the development serve to make the reentry seem a significant event?

The answer to these questions is to be found in the character of the reentry, and indeed of the movement as a whole, namely, its sense of humor. It becomes clear that what Haydn has been doing is joking with his listeners—leading them to expect some grandiose resolution of forces, when in fact all he had in mind was forging a climate from which the reentry would emerge as so grotesque an understatement as to seem almost ludicrous. Haydn was "putting us on," as the slang saying goes.

And when we think back on it, there was something strange, but perfectly consistent with this jocular intent, about the way the conflict between loud and soft passages was resolved at the beginning of the development. The usual classic practice is to decide the issue at first in favor of the softer element, but then to build from this low level of intensity to a grand climax. In this way, the feeling grows that the intensifying forces have prevailed against great opposition. Haydn's procedure of working upward from the heights instead of the depths, on the other hand, suggests that perhaps there isn't really much opposition to be overcome. Under these circumstances, the very strong quality of drive to climax which Haydn musters seems somehow out of place. It seems equivalent to gathering together an army of men with sledge hammers to drive in a single thumb tack—all of which contributes nicely to the humorous effect of the understated reentry.

When we add to these considerations the implications of heroic conflict in agitato passages such as measures 137-140 and 155-159 (Examples 1a and 1b), and the "dark" qualities of the

Example 1a.

Example 1b.

minor keys which dominate much of this development—all quite uncalled for by the nonheroic context established by the exposition —it becomes clear that Haydn was fashioning a joke on us. The whole build-up was nothing but a paper tiger, far from evidence of a heroic frame of mind. But that this also represents a neat and effective use of intensity patterns simply cannot be doubted. To put it another way, the humorous effect could not have become so powerful without the clear and efficient organization of this element; what started out as a mildly pleasant situation has turned into an uproarious joke.

In some developments, classic composers seem to pave the way for the drive not by an implied opposition of equal forces, such as was found in this movement, but rather by introducing one or more outbursts into a basically relaxed, nondriving atmosphere. An example of this kind can be found in the first movement of Haydn's well-known Symphony No. 94 ("Surprise"), in which the outburst of measures 111-112 forecasts the build-up of measures 123-141 and the climax of measures 142-148. Additional hints of the impending build-up are provided by the strongly dissonant (though softly presented) minor-ninth chords in measures 115-117, and the crescendo and diminuendo of measures 118-119—both of which suggest a growing excitement that is as yet under control. The build-up and eventual climax, then, form a more gradual and thorough motion in the direction outlined by these earlier gestures —a fulfillment of the commitment they have generated.

The development in the first movement of Mozart's Symphony No. 40 is somewhat more complex than either of those considered to this point—more complex because it contains not just one, but two climaxes, each surrounded by a brief section of reduced intensity. These two climaxes, however, far from seeming independent effects, actually complement each other: the second carries to a conclusion a train of thought left incomplete at the end of the first.

The first climax (measures 134-138) seems too easily—almost mechanically—reached for Mozart's purposes. Were there not something like the second climax (measures 153-160), the subsequent drop in intensity which ushers in the reentry would have seemed only another step in the play of forces rather than an introduction of the major change in dramatic orientation (i.e., restoration of a less restless atmosphere) appropriate for the beginning of a recapitulation. Obviously the first climax sets in far too quickly and does not represent an effect sufficiently striking or powerful in itself to suggest that the play of forces presented during the development has now been consummated and can be called to a halt. Indeed, this first climax ends in much the same way as many of Mozart's bridge passages: with alternating tonic and dominant harmonies over a dominant pedal. And bridge passages, after all, invariably set the stage for respites, rather than for the kind of complete and enduring change in atmosphere required to usher in a recapitulation convincingly.

Thus, the first climax imparts an expectation that there will be another one. The measures that follow function as a delay of that expected outburst and hence lend it additional significance when it finally does come to pass—enough significance to seem to use up the energy generated during the development and make possible a restoration of the more stable atmosphere required for the reentry.

A similar use of a too-quickly reached climax can be found in the opening movement of Beethoven's first string quartet (opus 18, No. 1). The first drive of any consequence (measures 129-150) is already at a strong dynamic level when it gets under way. And, what with the rapid addition of voices, the general upward direction of the lines, and the quickly reached high-tension level of the diminished-seventh chords in measures 133-134, the build-up seems most steep (Example 2a). What follows is not a balancing descent,

Example 2a.

but an abrupt cutback to a single-voice texture. Then the whole passage is simply repeated (transposed and with slight variation), bringing about another sharp rise in intensity. After another cutback to a single-voice texture, still another transposition of this passage—and hence another sharp rise—is presented. This time, however, the diminished-seventh chords are dwelt upon considerably longer than in either of the other passages and are arranged so as to throw into relief a very strong sense of conflict between what seem irreconcilable forces (Example 2b, measures 145-150).

Example 2b.

This driving section comes to an end not with a resolution of this implied conflict, or even a release of the tension generated by these three steep rises, but with a surprise: a sudden change to a calm atmosphere at a low level of intensity (see measure 151 of Example 2b).

The failure to resolve the conflict suggests that the drive is not really over, but that it will resume its motion toward climax after this interruption. And, indeed, something of the same sort is indicated by the steepness of each of the drives and the total lack of balancing descents. For we begin to feel that this expansive force has not been sufficiently challenged to lead appropriately into a strong consummation. To allow a drive to reach a significant climax at this point would seem equivalent to basing a claim to great strength on the ability to lift a two-pound weight.

This, of course, is similar to the procedure used by Haydn to produce a comic effect in the first movement of his Symphony No. 104 discussed earlier. In the Beethoven movement, however, the forceful and almost humorless context virtually rules out this possibility. Thus, as the sharp rises go unrelieved, we begin to suspect that they are setting the stage for a later, more leisurely, and hence more thorough-seeming rise to climax. The surprising quality of the manner in which the third drive is brought to an end (the sudden and unexpected change to a calmer atmosphere) only confirms this interpretation. We are certain now that the calm passage is only a delay; eventually there must be another, better considered move toward climax.

And this is precisely what happens. The calm passage lasts from measure 151 to measure 167; then sforzandi begin to appear, along with an increasing use of sixteenth notes; and finally a crescendo leads directly into the climactic reentry (measure 179).

Like the movement by Mozart, then, this development contains two main climaxes, the second of which completes a train of thought left open by the first. In this case, however, the second seems not so much to use up energy, as to realize the commitment to reach a significant climactic event raised by the first. Since the first climax came as the result of an unrelieved series of very steep rises—too steep to be convincing—and since it failed to release the considerable tension generated to that point, it gave rise to the expectation of a more deliberate build-up and of an eventual significant event which would use up the energy. Both of these conditions are fulfilled by the second climax.

One can almost piece together Beethoven's line of reasoning. The character of this movement in general, and of the first theme in particular, is forceful. It would not do, then, to bring in its reentry in the wake of climax; it should come right *at* the climactic point. Indeed, it could well be the kind of significant event that would signal the climax. The climactic quality could be brought out by a fortissimo dynamic level—a stronger indication than is to be found at any other point in the development—and by presentation of the theme in octaves by the four instruments. To reinforce the sense of significance, however, it might be well to establish the climax itself as a goal—this to be done by introducing a previous build-up which is kept from reaching a satisfactory resolution of its energy. Thus the whole program is accounted for.

A climactic reentry similar to this one is prepared in a somewhat different way in the first movement of the very well-known fifth symphony by Beethoven. The development contains one climax (measures 168-179) in addition to the one that marks the reentry (measures 248-252).

Leading up to the first climax is a series of passages in which a tendency toward rising excitement can be sensed. This tendency is thwarted (by sudden reversions to lower dynamic levels) and suppressed (by maintaining low dynamic levels for almost unreasonably long periods of time), but its presence is undeniable. Thus, the first climax sounds like a realization of a well-defined trend.

This building tendency is carried beyond the first climax, however; the dynamic level is kept very high and the rhythmic patterns continue to drive, indeed pound, forward. An abrupt reduction in the instrumentation, on the other hand, suggests that a new phase of the general build-up is getting under way (from measure 179 on). Presumably, this phase is to lead directly into the second climax.

Beethoven's problem at this point must have been to find means of suggesting that the second climax is of appreciably greater magnitude than the first. To an extent, this is accomplished by dynamic indications: forte and piu forte during the first as against fortissimo during the second. With the orchestral resources available to Beethoven, however, the distinction between levels of volume must not have been too easily perceptible. At any rate, Beethoven took other steps to insure that the second would seem the more climactic culmination. The main step involved presenting a more serious challenge to the building tendency, so that the reaching of the climax this time would seem a more substantial accomplishment.

The challenge to the building tendency takes the form of a prolonged reduction in both rhythmic drive (measure 196 on) and loudness (measures 196-227). In addition to defining the magnitude of the challenge to the building tendency, these specific moves and particularly the lengths to which they are carried give rise to a sense of suspense. Since the energy generated during the drive has never been either used up by a significant event, or balanced by a gradual descent, an explosion is expected. But as measure after measure goes by without it—indeed with an opposing tendency gaining greater and greater control—the conflict between the expected and the presented gives rise to the sense of impatience which is the essence of suspense. We know that an explosion is due, but when will it ever come?

All of these factors, then, plus some others (such as the return to a solidly defined tonality at the start of the recapitulation and the use of fermate at measures 249 and 252) combine to suggest unmistakably that the second is by far the greater of the two climaxes, that everything that has occurred up to that point has had the purpose of defining this as the goal and high point of the entire development.

As was the case for the first string quartet, such a procedure seems well in line with the character of this movement. For this is no longer the underplayed type of emotional representation found in much of Haydn and even to a large extent in Mozart—a type in which highly dramatic qualities are only implied or else used to set up contrasts. The essential qualities of this theme and movement are power, tension, and nervous excitement—a veritable fist-shaking attitude. What better way to bring out these qualities than to place the reentry at, rather than after, the climactic point. Allowing this powerful theme to sneak in *à la* Haydn would have been to destroy its character. Lending it the force of climax, on the other hand, heightens its essential qualities and brings them into bold relief in the movement.

A very different type of organization, and of general character as well, is to be found in the piano sonata opus 53 by Beethoven (the so-called "Waldstein" sonata). The development in the first movement begins with two direct drives (measures 92-101 and 102-105), each cut off abruptly by a sudden reversion to a low dynamic level. What follows (measures 106-114) still has a sense of drive because of the rapid motion, but the sequential descent (by thirds) every two measures makes it seem as though energy is being lost and the motion is settling down. Of course, this is not an appropriate situation for a suggestion of this kind; the movement simply has not reached enough of a high point to make a settling back seem a natural turn of events. It is both expected and welcome, then, when the dynamic level turns upward in measures 112-113, ushering in a new section of considerable force (measure 114 on), as indicated by the forte dynamic marking as well as by the boiling figuration. Thus far, then, every gesture seems to fit into a plan; the transition to a forceful section seems most smoothly and convincingly effected.

The new section begins with three statements (in different keys) of the four-measure phrase shown in Example 3a. This phrase

Example 3a.

can be broken into two parts. During the first two and three-quarter measures, the general rise in pitch and the turn toward triplet eighth-note motion in both voices make it clear that the intensity is building. During the remaining one and one-quarter measures, the falling pitch and the lack of motion in the left hand create just the opposite impression. Thus it seems that an initial rise in intensity is not quite balanced by a terminal descent; or, to put it another way, the lessening of energy at the end is not sufficient to call a halt to the headlong impetus. With the resumption of the upward drive at the start of the second and third statements of the phrase, it becomes clear that the forces of weariness have been overcome.

The situation is changed radically, however, at measure 126. From here on, only the last two measures of this phrase are repeated

Example 3b.

(Example 3b)—in various transpositions, of course. As a result, the balance shifts decidedly toward favoring the descending forces. Now it begins to sound like an impulsive outburst followed by a more reasoned settling down; the driving quality no longer seems a dominating trend, but only a disruptive force—interrupting the tired, settling tendency. This impression is reinforced from measure 138 on by associating the descending portion of the abbreviated phrase with a dynamic indication of piano, while retaining the forte marking for each of the initial outbursts. Finally, the struggle is abandoned as the dynamic level drops gradually to pianissimo (measures 142-144) and the pitch is brought down into a very low register.

The drop in intensity, then, seems most natural, largely because there was a seed of descent in the original phrase (at the end) which eventually took root and flowered. The drive itself, however, has not been consummated, and indeed has not even been carried out at great enough length to make a reaction seem desirable. Thus we have been led through another attempt to reach climax—a more significant and far-reaching attempt, to be sure, than was found in measures 92-114—but one that has not been successful either. As a result, we must feel more acutely than ever a need for an eventual culmination.

And it is just such a culmination that brings this development to a close. It is built up from a static respite obviously designed to suggest a marshaling of forces for the ensuing drive (measures 144-147). The increase itself is brought about by a long crescendo (the only long one in the development) with an abruptly rising pitch in the right hand (measures 148-154), an additional three measures during which the building effect results from increased motion rather than dynamic markings, and finally a fortissimo indication (the only one in the entire development).

In spite of the fortissimo marking, the passage in measure 157 does not at first glance seem to fit into the category of significant events necessary to suggest the release of a great deal of tension. It is not a strong utterance of important thematic material; nor does it involve a powerful cadential resolution. It consists, in fact, of a most commonplace figuration: scales in contrary motion.

Yet steps have been taken—and I think this is sensed intuitively to make this passage seem to release the tension quite fully. In order to understand how this has been accomplished, it is necessary to take into account the fact that the final build-up is almost dominated by static elements. The left hand, for instance, stays in the same register from measure 144 to measure 156. Indeed, it is limited to whole-note G's and repeats of the figure G-C-B-A to measure 154, at which point the high pitch moves first to C♯ and then to D—certainly a very minute change, hardly appreciable in this low register. In measure 156, the only change is in figuration; the compass remains a fifth, G-D.

As for the right hand, although it does move upward, its motion is along the intervals of the G-major triad. So consistently is this carried out, that one is as much aware of the static quality associated with a continuing presentation of the same triad as of the sense of directed motion inherent in the line itself. The chord is changed in measure 154, but, if anything, the static quality is strengthened because the right hand becomes limited to repeats of a three-note figure, D-E-F; there is only a slight addition to this figure in measure 156.

Thus while the steadily increasing rate of rhythmic activity, the dynamic indications, and the rising pitch in the right hand suggest growth of excitement, the specific figurations create an impression of imprisonment within rather confined areas and all of these forces seem bottled up. To go on exploiting these areas much longer would be unthinkable, since the redundance eventually would lead us to abandon our belief that there is some underlying logic to the sequence of events and a point to the narration. Thus, we come to expect some sort of break out of the confining environment. The expectation makes us look actively for some such event, which means that any event that would accomplish this break-out, when it actually came to pass, will take on the function of a goal and hence assume a considerable degree of significance. The scales of measure 157, then, though commonplace in themselves, are invested with significance by the listener's expectations. In this way, they come to seem sufficiently powerful entities to resolve the tension accumulated during the development.

The goallike impression is reinforced harmonically by the presentation of a dominant-seventh chord on G during the last few measures of the build-up, almost to the point of redundancy. The proper resolution to C major at the end of the scale passage then effects a realization of a harmonic commitment that has been long awaited, just as the scale passage itself fulfills what might be termed kinetic expectations of comparable strength. The considerable release of tension brought about by reaching these two major goals at approximately the same time produces the kind of powerful effect suitable for bringing about a basic change in dramatic orientation—a return to the more stable atmosphere needed to set off the recapitulation.

Again the organization is so tight that one can reconstruct a line of reasoning which would account for virtually every action taken merely by considering a single problem: the proper atmosphere for the reentry, and how that atmosphere might be created convincingly. Beethoven may have sized up the situation somewhat along the following lines: because the returning theme is to be softly presented, it would hardly do to bring it back at the peak of a climax. Rather, it should come shortly after the energy generated during the development is used up. Yet the reentry would have to seem a significant enough turn of events to signal a basic change in the dramatic orientation and to bring to a halt the unsettled, restless quality of the development. This was to be accomplished without the kind of exaggerated, almost ludicrous contrast between climax and the following reentry often found in Haydn's music. Since it is not an especially humorous movement, the situation simply would not lend itself to the construction of such a practical joke. The problem was to effect a powerful reentry in spite of these limitations.

Thus Beethoven's first concern may have been to enhance the significance of the reentering theme without turning it into a very forceful utterance. This could be accomplished by making it seem an agreeable reaction to a situation on the verge of becoming intolerable. One of the best expedients for creating a situation bordering on the intolerable, of course, would be a section with a considerable degree of redundancy—perhaps a prolonged passage that was highly repetitive and hence essentially static. The vigorously driving quality of the reentering theme, furthermore, would show to excellent advantage if it took shape very soon after such a redundant passage. The sense of propulsion would gain in attractiveness at this point and would serve to dispel the threat to the entire process of communication posed by the element of redundance.

The next problem, then, was to bring about such a highly redundant section convincingly. If the redundant elements were presented in a very forceful way, Beethoven would have been virtually compelled either to reach a powerful climax, thereby risking a humorously anticlimactic reentry, or else to present the reentry itself very strongly. Neither of these alternatives, of course, would make for the kind of atmosphere envisioned for the beginning of the recapitulation.

If the redundant elements were presented at a low level of intensity, on the other hand, all of the pieces would fit together very well. An extremely forceful event would not be required to suggest the climax that is to follow. And if the build-up to the climax were not too prolonged, some sense of the contrast between the redundant, static section and the vigorous, driving motion of the reentering theme could still be retained.

Now the program begins to take shape: a soft, redundant section near the end of the development, followed by a fairly rapid build-up to an only moderately powerful climax, and then a quick settling into the reentry.

In order to create a climax of rather modest dimensions, furthermore, such powerful effects as a change of key, a strong cadence, or a forceful presentation of important thematic material should be avoided. Rather, the climax should be marked by a milder effect which would still serve to use up the energy unresolved to that point. Such a function could be fulfilled, of course, by any passage which did not seem particularly significant in itself, but which took on added importance because it had come to seem a goal, a fulfillment of a clearly sensed commitment. The element of redundance itself sets up such a goal in mind, namely, any move that would effectively break out of the prison created by the ceaseless round of repetitions. This, of course, is exactly what the scale passage of measure 157 accomplishes.

Beethoven's problem now was to make the softly presented redundant section seem an appropriate turn of events. What better way to accomplish this than to make it appear to be the outcome of an attempt to build up to a climax—a period of exhaustion and recuperation. Of course, this would have to be a major effort to achieve a climactic release, or else it would seem quite inappropriate to spend enough time recuperating to allow the element of redundance to become pronounced. And it would be better if this strong effort actually failed to achieve a release of tension. For this would allow some feeling of unfinished business to carry through the recuperative section, so that the subsequent rise to climax would seem not so much a fresh act of willpower, as a fulfillment of the commitment to culmination left over from the earlier build-up.

A possible expedient for suggesting a strong, but for the time being futile, drive toward climax would involve setting up a section containing a conflict between rising and falling forces. At the end of this section, of course, the falling forces should prevail. This will only come about, however, after a considerable section dominated by the upward thrusts, both to suggest how strong the bid to reach climax has been and to make the eventual victory of the descending forces seem a reasonable outcome of a struggle rather than a motif dominating almost the whole of the section. This, of course, is precisely what happens in measures 114-144.

The advantage of such a conflict of forces for this type of situation is that the struggle can be resolved in favor of the ebbing tide of intensity without implying a real release of tension. No significant event has occurred to use up the energy; the drive has simply ceased—temporarily, we feel—because of exhaustion. We expect, indeed know, however, that it will burst forth again after a period of recuperation—as it does in the final move toward climax.

The only problem remaining, then, is to provide adequate motivation for the section containing this conflict of forces. One way of accomplishing this is to introduce a series of build-ups, each of which would be cut off abruptly, and to follow these with a a section which does not build, at least for a long time. The build-ups would show the basic direction of the forces and lead to the expectation that the following section also would embark upon a course of rising intensity. When it failed to do so, we would begin to feel increasingly eager to hear a fulfillment of our expectations. As more and more time goes by without the anticipated increase in intensity, our eagerness to find it would grow. Some apprehension might be felt as we begin to wonder whether we have misinterpreted the flow of events. Thus we would be in a most receptive mood for the increase in intensity when it eventually does come to pass. And we would be happy and willing to listen to a predominantly forceful presentation for a considerable amount of time. It would seem a result and a gratification; it would take a good deal more time to become sated with the forcefulness than if it had been introduced without such preparation. This, of course, is an ideal situation for introducing the conflict-of-forces section, in which, after all, the forceful element is predominant for a considerable amount of time. Indeed, it permits the forcefully dominated presentation to continue long enough to suggest that, although unsuccessful, this was a major effort to achieve climax.

I do not mean to suggest that this was exactly the line of reasoning followed by Beethoven, or even that rational calculations of this kind entered into his thinking. The stages in his development, and the form they took, may well have resulted as much from intuitive as from rational thought processes. Perhaps, as he shaped his actions and the immediate reactions they called for, he merely kept in the back of his mind an idea of the particular atmosphere required to set the reentry into bold relief. He may have allowed this idea, then, to influence decisions concerning exactly what form reactions should take at given points. Or he simply may have freely invented a series of actions and reactions, looking for an opportune moment for the reentry—possibly making revisions earlier in the score to accommodate the avenues taken once he decided upon the basic contour of the development.

Yet the fact that virtually every move in this complex development can be derived from a series of rational calculations suggests something of the tightness with which the movement is knitted together. From beginning to end, every event seems calculated to set the stage precisely for the events that follow. There are no rambling passages whose relation to past or future events are difficult to comprehend; nor is there any point at which the logical flow of ideas seems to break down. The sections merge into one another so smoothly, so naturally—each a necessary reaction or a plausible outcome to what has preceded—that the progress from point to point becomes not only logical, but virtually inevitable. And yet, each reaction seems to usher in a new stage in the process of setting up an appropriate atmosphere for the reentry. The action-reaction alternations bring a sense not of oscillation between poles, but of genuine progress toward a goal—the reentry.

Such tightness of organization seems all the more remarkable in this case, where there is obviously no intention to create a movement speaking in accents of high drama or of high humor. Such careful structuring of the development would have been a necessity if Beethoven had been out to build an emotional atmosphere to the point where it became overwhelmingly powerful, as in his fifth symphony. That he chose to exert such care in this sonata, where the emotional content is much milder, testifies to the degree to which he was committed to forging a logical flow of ideas. Perhaps it would not be too much to say that logical flow, and the feeling of constantly purposeful motion to which it gives rise, were an integral part of Beethoven's system of values; perhaps he was as much attracted by these qualities as by the sense of emotional intensification that could be wrought from them.

Something similar, though a little closer to Haydn's broad humor, can be seen in the first movement of Beethoven's sixth symphony, the so-called "Pastorale." Here the development consists of three moves toward climax, the first two identical (except for transposition and change of key), and the last quite different.

The build-up in the first two cases is the result largely of the dynamic indication *crescendo poco a poco,* which carries through for a full twenty-four measures each time (measures 151-174 and 197-220). Otherwise very little happens. The same figure

 is repeated over and over, with just a few

transpositions late in the section. Even the accompanying triplet figures do not change much. All of this, of course, merely focuses attention upon the one element that is not static—the dynamics. The crescendo reaches a culmination in a fortissimo passage of four measures (175-180 and 221-225), after which a turn downward is signaled by an abrupt thinning of the texture. The introduction of diminuendi slightly later strengthens the downward trend.

Obviously so little sense of resistance to the build-up of forces is presented in these two curves that the fortissimo measures seem more pretentious than heroic. As a result of this, and because there is no significant event to use up the energy, the turn downward seems not so much a dramatic necessity—a respite after great exertion—as a more or less capricious action: the move is toward lower intensity not to satisfy some longing for rest, but because there is no other place to go. So little of importance has been accomplished that the situation brings to mind the old rhyme: "The king's horses, the king's men/Marched up the street and marched back again."

Obviously there has been a lot of fuss and bustle, but it has amounted to naught—a tempest in a teapot. The fact that this rise and fall is presented twice merely sets the basic pattern of events more firmly in mind and lends emphasis to the obviously comic, or at least nondramatic, atmosphere which these happenings suggest.

What is established by these two unsuccessful attempts to achieve climax is a sensed commitment to try again, with redoubled effort, to bring about some kind of event which would use up the energy generated in the development in a most significant and meaningful gesture. And the rising passages presented in measures 247-271 do seem to constitute a more determined bid to reach climax. The minor cast in measures 257-260 even introduces some darker implications completely compatible with a more heroic effort. Once again the fortissimo level is reached, but this time it is retained for twelve full measures (263-274) while the pitch continues to rise.

Perhaps, then, the promise is to be fulfilled, and a climax capable of releasing the tension will be reached. Instead of a mere, arbitrary turning back, as in the two earlier peaks, this time there will be a sinking back out of dramatic necessity and as a reaction to an accomplishment of some significance.

But Beethoven also builds expectations that he never means to fulfill. Instead of a significant event to cap the climax, he simply allows the bottom to drop out of the whole situation through an abrupt lowering of the dynamic level and a thinning of the texture. Once again we have been led astray—this time more completely and radically than in the other two cases. And thus, the humorous, or at least good-natured, quality has been strengthened. A more serious effort has produced no more significant an outcome: this time the king's horses and men tried harder, but all they could do was march up the street and back again. That this gives rise to an appropriate atmosphere for a reentry of the good-humored first theme seems readily apparent.

One of the few exceptions to the rule concerning placement of the main climax at or near the point of reentry is to be found in the first movement of Beethoven's third symphony, the so-called "Eroica." Here there are two climaxes, the first consisting of a very long, very loud, almost static section of repeated chords (measures 248-279), and the second of a much shorter outburst just before the reentry (measures 396-398).

Qualitatively, there is no comparing the two. The earlier climax carries on for so long at high dynamic levels, and is so often and so strongly dissonant (including the formation of a harmony containing the tones A, C, E, and F, arranged so as to make the minor second between E and F stand out prominently) that it could hardly be topped with the materials at Beethoven's disposal. Certainly there is nothing in the remainder of this movement that even comes close to being so intense a presentation.

This does not mean, however, that the development is devoid of psychological sense, or even that it is padded out beyond its natural dimensions. For there is one thing missing in the first climax that is supplied at the reentry, and that is a sense of finality. Little happens at the big climax to suggest that the energy generated has been used up. There is no significant event to serve as consummation, only a backing down, as shown in Example 4.

Example 4.

The climax at the reentry, on the other hand, comes only after a substantial drive and an enigmatic reversion to a subdued level of excitement (measures 366-395), such as that found near the close of the development in Beethoven's fifth symphony. The drive in particular stands in marked contrast to the build-up to the first climax. For the earlier climax is preceded by a section during which loud passages are juxtaposed against soft ones (measures 178-210), but very little sense of sustained pressure seems to develop. At those points where a drive does get under way, furthermore (measures 166-178, 178-185, and 210-220), it proves short-lived—terminated either by a sudden reversion to a low-level, non-driving atmosphere, or else by an abrupt introduction of a very loud passage. Even the final passage of mounting tension (measures 236-248), which leads directly into the first climax, moves (within just thirteen measures from piano to fortissimo) from two-voice texture to sustained tutti chords. All of this tends to make this climax seem something introduced by a force of will, rather than a natural consummation of prior events. It is a plausible step, to be sure (the music has oscillated so much between loud and soft, and has had so many small build-ups that we might well expect to come across one that went somewhat farther) but it is obviously not the end of the process.

This fortissimo, then, is too suddenly reached to have much of the quality of a goal, and hence it seems lacking in the ability to effect the marked change in dramatic orientation appropriate for a reentry. The second climax, on the other hand, though of much lesser intensity qualitatively speaking, does carry more of the weight of a goal because of a delay of the strongly expected explosion. Thus, the second climax really acts as a complement to the first; it serves to suggest that the energy left unresolved by the earlier climax has finally been used up.

It seems likely that this rather unusual arrangement of climaxes was influenced by an expressive program. Beethoven was trying to produce impressions of forcefulness in an unprecedentedly direct and powerful way. The thematic material, however, seems more easygoing—although in a distinctly masculine sense—than forceful. Thus, there would be no point in bringing the reentry in at the peak of a climax; the theme is not sufficiently charged with drama to lend itself to climactic treatment.

With the orchestral resources at Beethoven's command, it must have seemed advisable to allow the qualities of force to emerge through the implication—of a struggle between titanic elements. The magnitude of the struggle might well be suggested with effects evocative of force (loudness, full orchestra, hammer-like repetition of highly dissonant chords), by prolongation of such a passage beyond all reasonable expectation, and by leaving the impression that there has been no clear-cut victory, merely a cessation of hostilities (an implication of victory might create the impression that the opposition was not really very strong after all).

And, indeed, the first climax of the development is of such quality that one can hardly fail to draw such associations. One can almost visualize two warriors locked in combat, shield against shield, sword blocked by sword. So powerful are these warriors and so evenly matched in strength, that they reduce each other to a state of virtual immobility—one sword keeps the other from moving, one body checks the other. The result is not a yielding by one or the other, but a backing off by both adversaries in order to recuperate. The virtually static quality of this section—the harping on each of the chords presented, leading eventually to four motionless measures of repeated F-E dissonances—suggests the immobility of the extreme strain of force against equal force. The reversion to a minor-ninth chord and then to a dominant seventh, coupled with the decrescendo, thinning of texture, and abandonment of the high register, gives something of the effect of backing off. A suggestion of consummation to this climax, then, would be out of place; it would carry the implication of victory for one of the adversaries. Therefore, the second move toward climax is a virtual necessity. It serves to use up the energy and thus to call a halt to the condition of instability which dominates the development.

This development, then, like the others discussed previously, contains a clear organization of the rise and fall of intensity which is designed to flow logically from point to point and to bring out and strengthen the basic character of the movement. The only novelty is the placement of the dramatic high point within the development rather than at or near its end.

As a final example, let us turn to one of the most fascinating and, judging by the usual standards of performance, least understood of Beethoven's intensity structures, namely, that found in the first movement of his ninth symphony. Here it is no longer possible to consider exposition (recapitulation) and development separately, for the thread of dramatic continuity runs more fluidly through the entire movement than in earlier works. That is to say that the events in the development are not so completely focussed toward creating the proper atmosphere for the reentry, but continue to exercise influence upon the happenings of the recapitulation and coda.

At first glance, there would seem to be nothing out of the ordinary in the organization of this movement. The exposition and recapitulation each contain the usual two climactic passages: at the bridges (measures 63-73 and 327-338) and near the ends of the closing sections (measures 150-158 and 419-427). And, although the development contains several build-ups, it presents only one passage that seems in any sense climactic, and that is at the reentry (measures 301-323). Closer examination, however, discloses something rather unusual about each of these climaxes: the sense of the resolution of tension is never quite appropriate to the circumstances.

The bridge climax in the exposition, for instance, is extremely short, and does not contain that kind of powerful move to a new key which would force a subsequent retreat and respite. Rather, the impression is that the drive has been cut off prematurely merely by slowing the motion, dropping the dynamic level, and allowing the harmony to move in the "soft" pattern of Phrygian cadences (Example 5). In place of the usual respite after a significant

Example 5.

accomplishment (i.e., the definition of the new key), there is a mere reversion to softer sentiments. But this leaves something unfulfilled: a drive toward climax has begun, but no climactic event appears to use up the energy that is generated. Thus, another drive is expected to get under way very soon.

And it does. Even the second theme proper (i.e., after the brief interlude presented in measures 74-79), with its predominantly rising lines and its extra dashes of figuration and off-beat emphasis during the second statement (measures 84-87), suggests a mild increase in intensity. The crescendi of measures 92-93 and 98-101 add to this effect. But it is not until after the opposition between loud and soft passages found in measures 102-110 that the build-up resumes in earnest. This typical classical alternation of loud and soft passages defines a dramatic antithesis which is followed by an attempt to reconcile the forceful and yielding postures, namely, by building gradually from the one quality toward the other.

The build-up is quite deliberate, lasting a full thirty-four measures. It proceeds in distinct stages: a generally rising pitch in measures 116-120; a plateau in measures 120-127 during which there is an alternation between G♭ and G♮ at the topmost point of the main line; a speed-up of this alternation leading into another rise in pitch in measures 128-132; and a faster-moving figure which undergoes a steady sequential ascent in measures 132-138. So deliberate and so prolonged is the build-up that one can hardly help but expect a rather significant climactic event to top it off.

But Beethoven does not provide such an event. Instead, there is only a rather unpretentious cadence formula (measures 146-147 and again in 148-149) which leads into an equally unprepossessing march up and down the B♭-major triad at a fortissimo dynamic level (measures 150-158). To be sure, the significance of this outcome has been heightened by the delay offered by measures 138-145 (Example 6). Nevertheless, one cannot but feel some sense of

Example 6.

disappointment. The march up and down the B♭-major triad simply is not a sufficiently significant event to justify a fortissimo indication, let alone to serve as consummation for so long a build-up of forces. One might ascribe this to miscalculation, possibly the result of deafness or of an untamed imagination—as many of Beethoven's contemporaries probably did. But it is so consistent with the treatment of the other climaxes in this movement that it is difficult to avoid the impression that there was some plan behind these unorthodox proceedings.

The development opens with a slow build-up of intensity, starting from a very low level and eventually reaching a quite powerful utterance (measures 164-192). Just at the point where it gives promise of breaking into the kind of significant pronouncement that would create an impression of adequate consummation, however, it reverts abruptly to the softer sentiments projected by lyrical melodies in a light texture and at a low dynamic level (measure 192; Example 7).

The same process of soft beginning, strong build-up, and

Example 7.

abrupt reversion to lyrical sentiments appears once again in measures 198-215. Indeed, the material is little more than a transposition of that used in the section just described, with minor variants, to be sure.

What follows is one of Beethoven's favorite expedients for building intensity, a fugato. Although the subject (Example 8) is

Example 8.

appropriately forceful in character, the outcome is far from the expected climactic culmination: in the midst of the build-up, there is once again a reversion to a soft dynamic level and to the material used in the two lyrical sections (measure 253 on). By the simple expedient of treating the last note of this figure as an appoggiatura (to the leading-tone), indeed, Beethoven lends almost an elegiac cast to this passage from measure 259 on (Example 9). From this

Example 9.

point forward, at any rate, the music sounds listless, unable to raise much energy. Thus, this build-up has accomplished no more than the preceding two.

In view of the fact that neither of the first two build-ups fulfilled its promise to reach climax, and of the fact that this third build-up began far more energetically, there must be some inclination to interpret this last one as a more determined effort to reach a climactic event of some significance. Its outcome, then, must seem all the more disappointing. At the same time, however, this arrangement gives the strongest kind of evidence of how difficult it was for Beethoven to build from this situation to a satisfactory climax. It implies, most forcefully, that the work is dominated by a kind of lethargy—bordering on depression, it might be said—which is most difficult to shake off. Indeed, just this feeling is reinforced in the following section (measures 275-286), during which the second theme is presented and developed slightly. For this section contains only the mildest hints of any building of intensity—as though there just was not enough vitality left to get much of a drive under way.

Just at the point where this low level of vitality threatens to take over the remainder of the movement, however, a build-up finally takes place (measures 295-300). This build-up, furthermore, even leads to a significant climactic event: the reentry (beginning in measure 301). It would seem, then, that the expectation of a climax finally has been fulfilled; that the long awaited outburst has come to pass; and that the aim all along must have been to bring in a climactic reentry, much as was done in the fifth symphony.

But such an interpretation simply cannot be considered valid. There is one clue in particular that gives the whole thing away: the rapidity of the last build-up. If Beethoven's aim had been to spotlight the reentry, he hardly would have brought it in after the shortest and least significant of the four passages of rising intensity in the development. The suddenly reached climax, of course, cannot well seem a result of processes long in operation; rather, it must have something of the quality of an arbitrary insertion. This is particularly true after so long a period of low intensity during which there is no building of suspense but, instead, a lyrical outpouring of sentiment.

An arbitrarily inserted passage, of course, will function better as a foil, a point of departure for future events of greater significance, than as a consummation. Before it is decided, then, that Beethoven had simply fashioned this reentry clumsily—as many conductors imply when they hold back the tempo and add to Beethoven's instrumentation—it might be well to look for some significant effect for which this climactic reentry could have been intended to set the atmosphere. And one need not look far, only to the bridge passage of the recapitulation (measures 327-339).

Here is one of the most eloquent, the most impressive, most moving passages ever penned. Tschaikowsky, with his complete lack of reserve, his more powerful orchestral and harmonic resources, and his almost total dedication to pathos, can boast few passages of such deep and compelling emotional expression. Only a few moments in Wagner's music can match the evocative force of this section—simple as are its materials. The repeated emphasis on descending figures in this context is certainly one of the most powerfully articulated expressions of an emotional state (perhaps best described as bordering on despair) to be found in the whole body of Western music. There can be no doubt that this is the significant passage which the abrupt rise to climax was designed to throw into relief.

Contributing to this impression is the fact that the high level of intensity is so long maintained, in spite of the short build-up leading into it; it lasts a full twenty-six measures (301-326). Indeed, the tension mounts as this section proceeds, so that a listener virtually must long for any event which will release some of that tension. Even the entrance of the clearly defined portion of the theme (measure 315 on) which is sometimes (erroneously, in my view) considered the beginning of the reentry cannot accomplish this; it is almost drowned in the sheer volume of sound coming from brasses, woodwinds, and timpani. The release of tension, then, becomes a strongly sought after goal. The descents found in the bridge obviously provide something of that sense of release, both because of the implications of lowering intensity associated with consistent pitch descents, and because it is the first time since the reentry began that any clearly defined thematic material, that might seem to use up energy has been allowed to dominate. It is as a strongly desired goal and a strikingly evocative effect, then, that this passage attains such a sense of significance, suggesting not a mere continuation, but an outcome of the struggle now so long in evidence.

Since this outcome is so closely associated with an emotional state which I have described as bordering on despair, it is clear that Beethoven has once again not only brought out the basic mood of the movement, but has intensified it—in this case intensified it greatly. How magnificently structure and individual evocative effects—the narrative and the picturesque—are combined to bring about a strong and ever stronger portrayal of the basic mood.[5]

The remainder of the recapitulation follows the same pattern as the exposition, eventually arriving at the same kind of climactic march up and down a triad (D minor, this time) that is not quite strong enough an effect to suggest an adequate culmination of the preceding build-up.

As we enter the coda (measure 427), then, we have experienced only one climax that in any way seemed significant and appropriate. That single climax, furthermore, was anything but final in character—significant as it was. It brought a release of tension that was absolutely necessary if there was to be any possibility of continuation, but it in no way suggested that the problem had been resolved. It ended, indeed, with a rather sudden reversion to

the lyrical sentiments of the little woodwind and brass passage
(measures 339-344) preceding the second theme proper, leaving
the feeling that there was something more to come in the line of
argument.

Thus, as the coda gets under way, we are still looking for the
main climax, that is, an event of sufficient force and significance
to suggest that the energy generated during the entire movement
and only partially released during the recapitulation bridge, has
been used up to the point where the movement can be convincingly
called to a halt. At first, the coda seems to be continuing the pattern
of the development: allowing build-ups to issue directly into
passages which do not fulfill the reasonable expectations of climax.
In measure 469, a long and quite powerful growth in intensity
gives way abruptly to a soft presentation of the fugato theme from
the development. The presentation of this theme also is built up
to an intense level (fortissimo in measure 489), but, after some
conflict between rising and descending forces, this build-up also
is brought to naught (measure 505). Indeed, in measures 505-512
(Example 10), the whole momentum of the movement seems to be
running down.

Example 10.

What follows is a direct but deliberate build-up over a chromatic ostinato in the bass (Example 11). This one finally issues into
a climactic event of major proportions: a tutti fortissimo statement
in unisons and octaves of the second part of the first theme (meas-

Example 11.

ures 539-547), which brings the movement to a close. For the first time, then, the climactic event seems completely appropriate to the build-up preceding. Indeed, it makes up for all of those points earlier in the movement where no consummating event followed the build-up—so strong an effect is this thundering out of the main theme.

Thus, the movement as a whole can be viewed as an attempt to establish an atmosphere in which this final statement of theme will create a powerful, indeed earth-shaking, effect. The earlier failure to allow growths in intensity to reach adequate climaxes might be interpreted as an expedient to demonstrate the difficulty involved in breaking out of the state of lethargy. The climax at the bridge of the recapitulation, with its emphasis on descending figures, only serves to bring out more strongly the basic mood of depression. All of which makes the final climax all the more remarkable, all the more powerful—an accomplishment against odds, rather than an outcome of a prevailing trend.

As in the case of the reentry and the bridge climax in the recapitulation, performers often seem to have ignored this structural outline, preferring to exploit to the full everything that could possibly be interpreted as a climax. With the romantic orchestra and the commonly made additions to the instrumentation and changes in dynamic indications, of course, it is possible to make a significant climactic event out of a passage from a Czerny exercise. Introduce a crash of cymbals or a few brass at a fortissimo level, and even an obviously insignificant event can assume great importance. And, of course, a sense of consummation also can be brought out of an insignificant event merely by holding back the tempo. By means such as these, many conductors have succeeded in stealing the thunder from the final climax. As a result, the movement often comes to seem little more than a series of almost arbitrary rises and descents in intensity—not much different from the sensation of a ride on a roller coaster, though not nearly so thrilling.

Reasonably interpreted, however, the intensity structure in this movement builds, event by event, to the grand climax at the end. No less than the other works discussed in this essay, it gives evidence of a consummate mastery of dramatic organization and a total dedication to the exploitation of narrative resources.

These examples, of course, hardly begin to scratch the surface of the classic literature. The question is, then, whether the narrative use of intensity is a general characteristic of the sonata-allegro movements of Haydn, Mozart, and Beethoven, or whether it just happens that the pieces studied here were organized in this way.

To this question I can provide only an informal answer. It goes without saying that the examples discussed here were culled from a much larger body of works—just how much larger would be difficult to determine, however. For, in the dozen or so years that this idea has been on my mind, I have not only examined scores formally, but have also evaluated pieces off the cuff, so to speak—that is, the concert hall, in presentations over radio, etc. On the basis of these formal and informal observations, it seems to me that the assertion that the Viennese classic is essentially a narrative art, in which the thread of continuity is provided by the manipulation of intensity, at least represents a reasonable hypothesis. And it is only as such that I offer it. Examples which seem to contradict this assertion are rarely enough found, according to my experience, to qualify as exceptions.

The exceptions, however, are themselves interesting objects for study. I have been able to find three cases which offer evidence of something less than exemplary organization of the flow of time. Some Mozart developments, for instance in several of his piano sonatas, offer so limited a play of intensity and are arranged on so small a scale, that they seem little more than improvisations. Their function seems to be more to allow a breathing space—a period of recuperation—before the reentry and its sense of drive return, than to heighten the sense of drama in any appreciable way. In a work such as the F-major sonata, K 332, the feeling of improvisation is all the more strongly brought out by the presentation at the start of the development of material which seems to be completely unrelated to anything found in the exposition. Here one may well feel that Mozart followed his fingers rather than his head.

An example of a second exception to the classic composers' usual efficiency in the organization of time is provided by some of the emotionally over-charged slow movements by Haydn. In the third movement of his string quartet opus 20 No. 2, for instance, an emotion is depicted in such strongly evocative terms from the start that Haydn must have felt that little more could be done to intensify the effect by a suggested play of forces. At any rate, about halfway through the movement, he introduces seemingly unrelated new material, and the two moods never do come to seem reconciled. The whole movement seems something like a stormy introduction followed by a more reflective aria.

A third exceptional procedure can be found in some works by

Haydn, but in more complex form in some of Beethoven's compositions. In the second movements of the piano sonata opus 53 and the cello sonata opus 69, for instance, the play of implications and commitments is abandoned in midcourse in favor of a fadeaway which prepares for the entrance of the next movement. It is this abruptly introduced fadeaway that does not seem well motivated.

All of these rather isolated instances only serve to point up the importance of the narrative organization of intensity to these three composers. For it seems safe to assert that if Beethoven, Mozart, and Haydn had written only this type of movement, they would not today be recognized as among the most eminent composers in the Western tradition. If they had not been able to forge a vehicle for dramatic intensification (by the arrangement of climaxes and intensity curves) out of what was merely a common practice of their time, there would be little reason for considering their arts in any way superior to those of J. C. Bach, Stamitz, or Filz.[6] When the classic composers failed to calculate carefully in this respect, they had little to fall back upon; there was little left to attract interest.

I would suggest, then, that the classic sonata-allegro movement is anything but the objective exercise in design that it is often said to be. It represents an attempt to intensify a basic mood by a suggested play of forces, much as is the case in the Bach movements described in Chapter 6. Haydn, Mozart, and Beethoven, however, made use of a device not much exploited by baroque composers, namely, indications of gradual changes in dynamic gradation. Where Bach might add to the number of voices, or to their rhythmic activity, or where he might begin to move more rapidly through various keys, or to increase the incidence of dissonance—all to indicate a growth in intensity—the classic composers could merely call for a crescendo and count upon much the same sort of effect. (They never completely neglected these other influences upon the level of intensity, however, as the above descriptions should make clear.)

Perhaps the emotional intent of the classic composers and their commitment to intensification can best be understood by considering an application to a texted composition. In the last act of Mozart's *Marriage of Figaro*, when the barber comes to believe that his bride of a few hours has made arrangements to meet Count Almaviva for an amorous liaison, he gives vent to his feelings in the aria *Aprite un po' quegli occhi.* As the aria begins, Figaro is poised but sarcastic as he sings the text in which he advises men to open their eyes a little and see what fools women make of them. Then, as he begins to enumerate the ways in which women are not the sweet things they seem to be, his blood pressure rises—a rise reflected in the music, of course—so that he ends up with a climax on a repeated high note. After this point of rage, however, he reverts to his earlier cynical attitude to the text: "The rest of it I won't tell." The aria, then, consists of a fluid interplay between the sarcastic but controlled attitude and the almost uncontrolled emotional raging. It ends with Figaro once more in control of himself and sarcastic, but the depth of his feeling has been revealed by the difficulty he has had regaining his composure.

Thus Mozart evidently did not conceive emotion in the stereotyped terms characteristic of much baroque music (although by no means of all baroque music). Gifted as he was with insight into human nature, he must have realized that the ordinary man cannot rage or experience any other strong emotion for very long at a time. In order to portray a particular strongly felt affection, then, he mixed it with appropriate reactions, that is, with material evocative of other emotions. One emotion or the other finally would win out, but, as can be seen in this aria, the winner of the conflict would not necessarily be the emotion most strongly depicted. The conflict of emotions only serves to strengthen the effect of the main one being portrayed, either because the various moods so obviously adhere to an order of mental states appropriate to the situation, or else because some of the attitudes depicted clearly function to challenge the ability to retain a dominant feeling. The implication is that despite all temptations to lapse into other states of mind, the dominant emotion keeps returning with renewed freshness and increased force.

This demonstrates a view of man as a being experiencing a constant stream of emotional changes and modifications, rather than as being in the grip of a single strong feeling for a considerable length of time—a view quite consonant with present-day conceptions. However, the emotional instability, as it might be termed, does not result in a purely arbitrary succession of mood evocations. Quite the contrary, there is a range of appropriateness to the reactions with the various moods centering about a basic attitude—indeed, defining that attitude by their interplay.

Inasmuch as the structure in the instrumental music of the three classic masters is not markedly different from that found in this aria (the climactic passage, for example, resembles the end of a bridge in a typical sonata-allegro movement), it seems reasonable to assume that this conception of the human condition under-lies the more abstract portion of the classic art as well. The play of intensity, no doubt, was intended to evoke a series of moods and modifications of moods which would be appropriately contrasting or complementary, and which in their totality would define and intensify a basic emotional situation.

I would suggest that this is a more reasonable view of the classic art than the one that makes it out to be detached, objective, written for the amusement of a jaded elite. It is an emotional art—an art, in fact, dedicated to the intensification of emotional expres-sion. But it is based upon a fundamental observation concerning human nature: that no pure emotional state can remain dominant in consciousness for very long. The intensification, then, must be achieved by appropriate mixtures of moods which are controlled—indeed, suggested—by the fluid interplay of forces which create different levels of intensity. A mood presented at first in a rather conventional manner, or else only weakly suggested, begins to take on added significance, and hence more personal meaning, as it is subjected to the controlled play of forces, examples of which are described in this essay. Thus, what at first seemed only a tinge of sadness, or a hint of defiance, or even a representation of a neutral state of mind, may have come to be overwhelming in emo-tional impact by the end of a movement.

The classical use of intensity, then, is both a narrative and a characterizational device: it suggests the order to the flow of events as well as contributing to the definition of emotional states. That Haydn, Mozart, and Beethoven could forge convincing, in-deed compelling, works of enduring appeal on these premises virtually goes without saying.

EIGHT

Intensity and the
Romantic Sonata Allegro

ON THE SURFACE, the romantic composers' treatment of intensity seems very similar to the
classic approach. Both make use of dynamic markings as the most
important means for creating fluctuations in the level of excitement;
both lead their ideas into climactic situations quite often; and both
make use of implied reactions to long-presented low levels of intensity as well as to climaxes.

There is one fundamental difference, however: the romantic
composers do not consistently organize the ebb and flow of intensity
into the kinds of large architectural patterns characteristic of the
classic arts. Indeed, they do not seem to have devoted as much
attention to fashioning a convincing sequence of events in this
respect as did the classic composers—presumably because they
could rely more heavily upon the attractive qualities of individual
effects or small groups of effects.

The examples discussed in this essay, which are designed to
illustrate this point, are taken primarily from very familiar works
to avoid the danger of exaggerating the significance of a minor and
thus possibly unrepresentative composition. These have stood the
test of time and hence can be taken to reflect something of the
values of the age of their creation which goes beyond the category
of fads and fashions. The fact that they have achieved fame in
spite of the questionable constructive procedures to be described
makes clear just how little the classic notion of controlled intensity
counted in the romantic aesthetic.

Franz Schubert (1797-1828), a composer very close to Beethoven both temporally and environmentally, already had a different conception than that of the classic masters. The first movement of his eighth symphony (the so-called "Unfinished") offers a convenient starting point for discussion. On the surface, the exposition of this movement seems to bear the classic stamp. It contains the usual two themes plus closing section; the key relations are similar to some used by Beethoven (third relation); and there are even just two climaxes.

There is evidence, however, to indicate something of a lack of the classic composers' concern for creating an obviously logical flow of events. First of all, the change of key takes place after the first climax (measures 35-38) rather than in conjunction with it. This climax, then, seems to close off the first theme, marking it as a complete, self-sufficient unit, and making any continuation really unnecessary.

The second theme (measures 42-61) is much more significant in itself than is usually the case in classical sonata-allegros (Example 1). Indeed, provided with lyrics and inserted into an op-

Example 1.

eretta, this has proven to be one of the most enduringly popular of Schubert's melodies—certainly far more popular than the first theme. And, lovely as it is, it seems something added almost arbitrarily, simply for the purpose of presenting an attractive passage, rather than as a realization of previous commitments (i.e., to serve as a respite) and a step toward future developments. One is led more to forget the original situation than to retain its memory.

An arbitrary quality to the order of the events is brought out once more at the beginning of the closing section (measures 62-71; Example 2), where the intensifying drive toward the close of the exposition seems an interruption of the relaxed quality of the second theme rather than a resumption of activity after a respite.

Thus the first and second themes and the closing passage form three separate and distinct units, each charming in itself, but without much suggestion that they work together to create a logical, unified series of events. To turn to a literary analogy, where the classic exposition could be said to resemble a detective

Example 2.

story or a drama in its commitment to building all details toward a critical point, Schubert's is more like a set of loosely related character sketches.

Indeed, there is something in the quality of the two themes that works against the suggestion of relations between them. Both are so intrinsically attractive and evocative that they tend to absorb all of a listener's attention as they unfold. There is neither need nor stimulus here to question how these melodies fit into a larger plan, what the eventual point may be, or what will be the consequences of any action. One hardly even pauses to wonder about what is coming next. One can only relax and enjoy the sensuous pleasures offered by each passing moment. Lyricism is the watchword—not drama.

Although the scheme in the development is quite readily apparent (two climaxes, the second tapering off into the recapitulation), there are some questionable elements, just as there were in the exposition. The main business of this section gets under way with a gradual building of intensity which requires a full twenty-four measures to reach climax (measures 122-146). The climax is marked by a significant event, an abrupt modulation (via an augmented sixth chord) to a new key. What follows is not the collapse and respite that might have been expected in a classic work, but a more gentle descent in pitch and dynamics (Example 3).

When this descent reaches bottom, there is another, but rather brief, outburst followed by a similar gentle descent (see Example 3), with this entire process being repeated several times more. The outbursts make it clear that the earlier climax did not

Example 3.

entirely succeed in resolving all of the energy generated. The forceful element, however, obviously does not dominate this passage; quite the contrary, it forms a distinct countercurrent to the general atmosphere. Most of the time is spent either descending or at a low level of intensity.

Thus, it seems perfectly natural that the forceful element should regain control as something of a reaction to the low levels of intensity which have dominated for what is by now a rather long time (twenty-four measures). What follows is another twenty-four measure section (from 170 on) devoted entirely to highly agitated, quasicontrapuntal material presented at a fortissimo level. This passage, merely by virtue of the fact that the forceful quality is maintained in it for so long a time, leaves a decidedly more powerful impression than did the first build-up and climax.

The development, then, is very much in the classic tradition: the general trend is toward intensification; the section between the two powerful ones functions as something of an interruption, keeping alive the sense of conflict while allowing space for a recuperation.

There is one bothersome element in the scheme, however, that probably would prove disturbing to anyone attempting to justify this as a classical development. It concerns the ending. For this most powerful passage does not culminate in anything that could be called a climactic event. There is only a seemingly arbitrary introduction of a diminuendo followed by something suggesting a tug-of-war between loud and soft passages, with the latter finally winning out to set the stage for the gentle reentry.

Now if there were a precedent for this (that is, if the earlier build-up had not reached a climax either, but had simply issued into a conflict-of-forces situation), one might well judge that the second forceful section was indeed carrying forward the train of thought started by the first; the ending would seem an amplification of the course of events presented in the earlier build-up, climax, and letdown. But the first build-up does culminate in a powerful climactic event—namely, an abrupt and not quite expected change of key after a period that threatens to become redundant. Compared to that, the outcome of the later section seems tame. This fact leaves us little choice but to conclude that Schubert was counting upon his audience to forget what had happened at the earlier climax; otherwise we would certainly feel some sense of disappointment at the tame outcome. Thus, we cannot help but judge that the two climaxes—if the second can be called a climax at all—are working at cross purposes.

At the end of the second forceful section, furthermore, the conflict seems so easily resolved in favor of the gentler sentiments that one can only feel that it never was much of a conflict in the first place. The forceful element, which, after all, has grown considerably in dimensions up to this point, has not demonstrated its strength by overcoming challenges; indeed, it has been shown to be quite flabby by the ease with which it has been subdued. From the classic point of view, then, the shouting, the heroics, the forcefulness were all bluster rather than expressions of strength and determination.

Indeed, a closer look at the second forceful section (measure 170 on) turns up additional grounds for this feeling. For, in spite of the loudness, the length of time, and the agitation suggested by the quasicontrapuntal texture, this seems anything but a section of mounting intensity. There is little evidence that the level of excitement is any greater near the end of these twenty-four measures than it was at the beginning. Certainly there is not the kind of virtually indisputable evidence to this effect that characterizes classic structures. Schubert has merely indulged in what might be termed musical shouting during these twenty-four measures, without much regard for building up the significance of what he is suggesting or for increasing the sense of tension.

There is even an element of stiffness—almost of caricature— to this section. For the theme (taken from the introduction) which forms its basis does not really seem suited for forceful presentation. Its motion is so circumspect, so much restricted to rather slow conjunct progress along the scale, that little sense of drive can be suggested by it comfortably. The upward move at the beginning is so slow and so shallow, furthermore, that it seems less a bold thrust than a rather halting, mincing step forward. And finally, the rhythm of the theme so squarely outlines the beat-pattern—with but the least suggestion of intensification by increased activity and with none of the sense of strain that might be called up by syncopations—that the whole seems more settled than driving. Therefore the fortissimo dynamic level and the agitated quality of the quasicontrapuntal setting into which this theme is cast do not quite seem to fit comfortably.

It is clear, then, that something is wrong with this development from the classic point of view. The material chosen to suggest the broad line of intensification sounds stiff, static, and almost inappropriate for a forceful evocation. The outcome can only be called a disappointment.

All of which raises the possibility that Schubert did not intend that his audience follow the course of this development in the same way as in a classical sonata-allegro movement. Instead of requiring us to store each detail in memory—gradually replacing the individual impressions with more general ones—Schubert is probably asking us to forget at least some of the previous developments. In fact, it is the most striking event in the development, the one we are least apt to forget (i.e., the climax to the first build-up), that we are asked to put from our minds. In other words, this is not a real use of narration—here all the details gradually begin to drive toward a point—but rather a calculation primarily in terms of reactions. All that we are expected to bear in mind is what has been happening in the immediate past. We should know that the quality has been forceful for some time, and that it is just about the right moment for a reaction to set in. But we do not need to recognize that the later forceful section is stronger than the earlier one, for the more keenly we are aware of this, the sharper will be our eventual disappointment.

It would seem, then, that Schubert was counting primarily upon the element of reaction in fashioning the sequential logic in this work. If forcefulness has dominated for some time, softer material is called into use; when the gentler sentiments have been exploited, more vigorous qualities are brought into play; etc. Schubert's aim in forging this series of actions and reactions might be formulated as the creation of enough contrast in the development to the gentle, lyrical quality which dominates the exposition to make the return to the presentation of the same material in the recapitulation seem all the more pleasant—quite a difference from the intensification which obviously is the *raison d'être* for the classical development.

If evidence of disregard for the classical ideals were present only in this particular movement, one might well suppose that, as its nickname suggests, it really was an unfinished symphony—in the sense that a good deal of polishing and revising yet remained to be done. One could then say that the narrative defects were perhaps errors of judgment.

But evidence of this kind is to be found in a great deal of Schubert's music. Just to take a few examples, the exposition of his sixth symphony could not be said to consist of the kind of drive with interruptions characteristic of the classic sonata-allegro. Roughly two-thirds of its duration is spent at dynamic levels of piano or less, with material that seems more cute than driving. Similarly, the development contains only ten measures which suggest a sense of drive, all at the beginning; the approximately fifty measures remaining (163-211) are all lyrical and soft. While I do not believe in basing aesthetic judgments on numerological calculations, so marked a preponderance of the lyrical element as these figures indicate clearly allows little possibility for any general driving trend (the essential feature of the classic sonata-allegro) to set in. Instead of dominating the movement, the driving sections seem to introduce a needed element of contrast so that the predominant lyrical character can be resumed with refreshed perception.

The exposition in the first movement of Schubert's seventh symphony, to take another example, contains a second theme (Example 4) which is far more attractive and considerably longer

Example 4.

than the first one. As a result, it could hardly be called a respite. On the other hand, it obviously develops very little sense of drive itself.

The bridge leading into this theme, furthermore, is dominated by a dotted-rhythm pattern (♩.♪♩.♪|♩.♪♩.♪) for a full thirty-six measures (94-129). The dotted rhythm, however, does not lend itself easily to the suggestion of a general sense of drive. For the small note (the eighth in this case) drives into the following longer note so powerfully that the latter is thrown quite strongly into relief. This means, of course, that the longer note has little to contribute to any sense of drive toward the notes following, since it is itself something like a goal, and hence seems to ease both tension and attention for the moment. Indeed, it seems an obstacle to be overcome if any sense of momentum is to carry through a passage. Thus, a long series of these dotted rhythms, such as that presented here, actually tends to kill the sense of general drive, focusing attention instead on a series of what can be described as jerky motions from weak to strong notes.

Upon just a few repetitions, furthermore, the next link in the dotted-rhythm pattern becomes so easily predictable that interest tends to diminish. Even the most ardent admirer of this work must wait impatiently for the passage to come to an end instead of looking forward to its reaching a goal. The bridge, then, no less than the lengthy and relaxed second theme, actually helps to dispel any quality of general drive.

Although the development builds to a climax quite clearly, the peak occurs a full thirty-one measures before the reentry. The considerable time remaining is devoted to a diminuendo and some soft passages leading into a gentle return of the first theme. The climax, then, cannot be said to clarify or intensify the quality of the reentry, but rather it seems designed to set up an appropriate atmosphere for a glide down into it. As in the eighth symphony, furthermore, the loud sections seem rather stiff and mechanical—forming an appropriate context for enhancing the attractiveness of the reentering material.

In the first movement of Schubert's fourth symphony, the development is very brief (43 measures to 134 in the exposition), and contains no significant climactic event. After several measures at forte, a diminuendo sets in around measure 160, obviously as something of a reaction rather than as the result of reaching a goal. The development in his fifth symphony has a similar outcome. Like Mozart's fortieth, it contains two loud sections separated by a soft one. Neither forceful passage, however, issues into a significant climactic event. The first (measures 134-146) has no appreciable sense of build-up; it is merely a fairly long section at a high dynamic level. The second (measures 157-160), on the other hand, is so short and begins to taper so soon that it cannot be said to exhaust the energy left over from the previous loud section; it merely

escorts the energy downward without having accomplished anything through shouting and force. Once again there is an extended
fadeaway into a soft reentry (measures 161-171). Obviously, then,
neither of these developments accomplishes the classic ideal of
intensification.

Thus it is clear that Schubert's view of the so-called sonata-
allegro was not that of Haydn, Mozart, and Beethoven. The exposition was not the embodiment of a general drive with just a few
interruptions; it was rather a convenient showcase for presenting
several attractive themes. One changes from the first theme to the
second, not to create a respite, but merely to bring in some fresh
and revitalizing material as a means of avoiding a feeling of satiety.
Similarly, the development is designed not so much to create the
general drive and climax which would magnify the essential qualities of the reentering material, but more to generate a contrasting
atmosphere to that of the exposition, and to extend that atmosphere
to the point where the return would seem fresh and welcome.
Where the aesthetic effect of the classic development might be
likened to the intense play of dramatic forces which leads directly
to the ultimate clarification (of situation, character, or condition),
Schubert's seems more closely related to the fabled experience of
sitting on a tack because it feels so good when one gets off. The
one approach is aiming to build suspense, the other to create an
appropriately contrasting atmosphere.

This is not to say that Schubert's was necessarily an inferior
style to those of the classic masters. His calculations undoubtedly
were correct in many of his works, as is attested to by their enduring popularity. His expositions often are so attractive, for one
reason or another, that for the most part we do not even bother
to reflect on whether the sections fit together nicely or not. His
developments often accomplish their purpose admirably; it does
feel good to get back to the atmosphere of the recapitulation.

But what is responsible for these admirable qualities if the
narrative element contributes so little? Surely there must be other
strong points to his style, or else how can the appeal of his music
and its continued popularity be accounted for?

And indeed there are strong points: a new concern for what
may be termed atmosphere, and a richer, more varied harmonic
palette. In order to discuss the first of these, it is necessary to
attempt to reconstruct something of Schubert's basic attitudes
toward composition.

Schubert, of course, was an expressive composer. To put it

in its simplest terms, his aim was to evoke an emotional response as strongly as possible. Unlike the classical composers, however, he was not willing to defer the strong response to a point well on in the movement. At least this would seem a reasonable inference, judging from the apparent lack of interest in procedures that would produce intensification during the course of a movement. Thus he must have wished to forge a mood as strongly as possible from the outset—without recourse to methods of intensification.

Unlike many baroque composers, furthermore, he evidently was not willing to rely upon semiconventional symbols to create his moods. The thematic material and its context would suggest the basic mood, and suggest it so strongly that one could not mistake it, and, even more important, so that one could hardly resist falling under its spell.

Some idea of the distinction between a semiconventional and an overpowering evocation can be gained by comparing the representations of thunder in Purcell's *Dido and Aeneas* and in Beethoven's sixth symphony. Purcell's "thunder" relies largely upon the imagination of the audience. He provides an effect which might plausibly pass for a symbol of thunder (not too loud or with too many rapidly repeated chords), but which evokes none of the elemental quality of that phenomenon. Beethoven, on the other hand, utilizes a full orchestra at a high dynamic level, with a strongly percussive attack, and the most dissonant minor-ninth chord—all in an attempt to convey powerfully and unmistakably the elemental emotional response aroused by a thunderclap (measure 112 on in the fourth movement). Where Purcell's procedure represents little more than a mild stimulus toward adopting a feeling-tone, Beethoven's is an irresistible summons to experience the emotional impact of an overwhelming natural phenomenon.

Schubert's kinship to Beethoven in this respect can be judged by examining, for instance, the opening few measures of his song *Der Erlkönig*. This is anything but a neutral or mildly suggestive feeling-tone. Right from the start, everything is geared toward suggesting, in the most powerful way imaginable, the sinister, stormy atmosphere of the poem. The same is true of songs expressing such diverse sentiments as *Gretchen am Spinnrad, Die Forelle,* or *Die Post*. In the first of these, we sense Gretchen's confused state of mind; in the second, something of the whimsical element; and in the third, the momentary excitement and high hopes—all without thinking, without reflecting on what we should feel, all automatically and powerfully.

This is equally true of the instrumental music. The "cuteness" at the start of the sixth symphony, or of the second theme in the seventh; the spriteliness in the first movement of the fifth; the dark, passionate quality in the first movement of the fourth; the lyricism of the eighth; the more darkly tinged, almost pessimistic lyricism of the second movement from the string quintet opus 163—all these are moods evoked powerfully, without the need for reflection, or even for much more than a modicum of audience sympathy. The mood is sold to the audience rather than offered to it.

This is what I mean when I assert that one of the strong points of Schubert's style is his ability to suggest an atmosphere. He obviously devoted a great deal more attention than the classical composers usually did to the forging of his harmonic and thematic materials so as to evoke a mood in the strongest possible way. It seems doubtful, for example, that he ever would have chosen material like that in the first movement of Beethoven's third symphony to represent the heroic or the grandeur of a conquering human spirit. Beethoven's themes, after all, are so easygoing and almost neutral in feeling-tone. "How," Schubert might ask, "could these themes be adapted to the depiction of force and greatness?"

Obviously, the forging of a strong atmosphere was not a new conception. One can find a great deal of it in Beethoven (for example, in the first movements of symphonies five, six, and nine, and the third movement from the piano sonata opus 106), and even in Mozart (for example, in the first movements of the twenty-fifth symphony, the twentieth and twenty-fourth piano concerti, and the G-minor string quintet). In these classic works, however, the full emotional impact is realized only late in the movement when the strongly defined mood of the opening becomes even more strongly and compellingly delineated. In many of Schubert's works, on the other hand, the depth of emotional expression is as great at the beginning as it ever becomes in the course of the movement.

This is not to suggest that Schubert was not as well schooled or as perceptive a musician as the classic masters. One need only examine certain of his compositions—particularly some of his songs —to see how skillfully he could arrange materials to heighten emotional impact. Just to take an example at random, in *Gretchen am Spinnrad,* the confused, restless, and unhappy state of mind is not only suggested by the whirring accompaniment, but is intensified by pitting sections of relative composure against more agitated outbursts, and allowing the dimensions of each outburst to grow larger, so that it seems that the restoration of composure becomes

more and more difficult. This is not the work of a person unaware
of the possibilities of intensification; on the contrary, it is a most
skilled and convincing use of a narrative technique. The fact, however, that Schubert saw fit not to build such structures into some
of what are undoubtedly his finest works only demonstrates how
different the bases of his aesthetic calculations were from those
governing classic creativity and how much he relied upon atmosphere rather than narration. A narrative technique was no longer so
important a thing to Schubert that he would incorporate it into
all of his significant movements; it was merely one among many
compositional tools to be used only in works where it would seem
particularly appropriate.

The second point of strength in Schubert's style is his treatment of the harmonic element. This is a far richer-sounding harmony than is to be found in the works of the classic masters. It has
more frequent and more striking moves to unexpected keys, for one
thing. Where, for instance, the move to the Neapolitan area in the
third movement of Beethoven's piano sonata opus 106 (for example
in measure 14), although most striking in effect, represents an
isolated instance of harmonic surprise, comparable procedures seem
almost the rule in Schubert—where interest seems about to lag,
there will be an unusual modulation.

For another thing, Schubert is far freer than the classical
composers in his use of what is perhaps the most seductive pair
of sonorities in the entire Western palette, the major- and minor-
ninth chords. In the first movement from his eighth symphony, for
instance, a minor ninth is introduced and dwelt upon after the
very first phrase of the first theme. How effectively it is used also
in bringing the development to a close (measures 214–218)! In the
sixth symphony, just to take another example, the charm of the
development—a charm sufficient to draw attention from the fact
that it is not really going anywhere—can be attributed largely to
the major-ninth chords which are presented every few measures.

With a colorful harmony and a new ability to forge an atmosphere, Schubert probably was simply not concerned with
problems of structure—a readily understandable attitude, given his
gifts. He did not need intensification to make his points. His was
a reactive art, then, which drew heavily upon particular picturesque
effects and used the principle of reaction as a means for refreshing
the taste for these effects. It probably would not be too much to
say that it would have been a waste of effort for him to go to the
trouble of forging a classical type of sonata-allegro movement when

he could evoke such arresting qualities at a stroke.

Another composer often considered very close to the classic ideal is Felix Mendelssohn (1809-1847). Again, however, the structural organization in some of his most significant works seems to indicate a very different basis for calculation.[1] The first movement from his fourth symphony ("Italian") can serve as an illustration.

To a classic composer, the organization of the first theme itself might seem faulty. The opening set of "gestures," after all, projects a distinct contrast between the vigorous, boiling, assertive quality presented in the first five measures and the more hoppy, dancelike and certainly less assertive atmosphere of the next four (Example 5a). But Mendelssohn does little to capitalize upon this

Example 5a.

contrast. He does not repeat the statement of contrasting segments so as to strengthen and clarify the sense of conflict between states of mind, nor does he do anything to suggest that the dimensions of this conflict are growing broader. Instead, he goes over to the kind of questioning, tearing apart of the first element that, in the classic view of things, would be properly used only after a situation had been most carefully established, usually by means of a repeat (Example 5b). Thus, this type of passage would be in place after the

Example 5b.

double bar (i.e., after the repeat of the first part) in a minuet. Its function in such a position would be to reopen a question previously considered closed: where the first section is equivalent to an assertion that this is the way things are, with the repeat merely adding emphasis to that assertion, the passage immediately following the double bar seems to question whether it really is the way things are. In this movement by Mendelssohn, however, it is clear that no situation has been established well enough in mind to call for this kind of questioning posture. Indeed, what promised to develop into a dramatic situation (i.e., an opposition between contrasting states of mind) has been completely ignored. What is there to be questioned, then? There is no escaping the impression, according to classic tenets, that the passage is completely inappropriate for the situation—something in the nature of the kind of utterance for which Mrs. Malaprop was noted.

Thus, within less than twenty measures, Mendelssohn has done things that would both disappoint and surprise a classically oriented audience—the former by failing to develop what had promised to become a central dramatic situation, and the latter by introducing a passage inappropriate to the context. As a result, there is a sense of looseness to the connection between events. The listener cannot stop to worry about these things, of course, but neither can he turn all of the details into a sense of emerging drama. His only recourse is to forget many of the previous events and the puzzled attitude they may have raised in his mind, and become more absorbed in what is happening at the moment.

Finally, this first statement of a theme that started so full of vigor and dash comes to an end with the weakest kind of material (Example 5c). This posture that seemed so brave and full of prom-

Example 5c.

ise ends in a series of mincing, rather effeminate convolutions. The first assertion of strength comes to seem hollow; the great hero has turned out to have the spirit of a mouse, as the exuberance gives way to a sense of over-refined delicacy.

To a romatically oriented musician, however, these criticisms probably would have seemed irrelevant. The important element in this theme, such a person might argue, is not the contrast between the first two sections, but the quality or the atmosphere so strongly evoked by the material of the first five measures. The aim here was to bring this most significant material back a little later (measure 51 on) in a setting which would make it appear even more powerful; that is, in something akin to a climactic situation. Of course, it would have to sound fresh when it returned in this powerful setting. How better could it be made to sound fresh than by allowing it to emerge as a reaction to a passage of strongly contrasting character in which the dynamic level is held low for a considerable period of time and the forward motion is brought almost to a standstill. If this is to be effected, however, the first statement of the theme has to end weakly to make a reasonably smooth transition to the low levels of action and volume that are needed to set the stage for the reaction. The weak ending to this statement is not an admission of a lack of determination; it is a ploy, a prudent retreat so that a more overwhelming build-up of forces may take place a little later.

As for the failure to exploit the contrast, the romantic might continue, it is not really important. A listener will tend to forget about these loose ends because he will become absorbed in the strong reentry and the sense of suspense that builds up just before it. He will know that a thunderclap is coming, and will become more and more impatient to hear it.

Here, then, are entirely different bases for calculation, the one from a primarily narrative point of view, the other from a more picturesque orientation. Where the classic masters would think primarily in terms of actions and reactions that should gradually build up a dramatic situation, Mendelssohn seems more interested in building a story line which would show particularly intriguing effects to their best advantage. Where it would have been a cardinal sin to the classic composers to evoke an impression which did not contribute directly to the logical line of development, to Mendelssohn it must have seemed perfectly legitimate to present effects whose main contributions to the story line were to kill time and to facilitate a reasonably smooth transition, so long as it all contributed to the emergence of a truly stunning effect.

In this particular case, concerning the structure of this first theme, the romantics would seem to have the better of the argument. For recasting this theme according to classic tenets certainly seems anything but an improvement. In Example 5d, I have reorganized this theme so that it contains an immediate repeat of the contrasting segments; and I have altered the cadences (exchanged tonic for dominant at the end of the first segment, and dominant for tonic at the end of the second) in order to avoid a harmonic dead

Example 5d.

spot between the two statements of this material and to avoid a sense of redundance between the cadences of the two contrasting segments. Clearly, the greater clarity of dramatic definition has been achieved at the expense of all that makes this theme attractive. It seems doubtful that this symphony would have found so enduring a place in the standard repertory if it had been recast along Haydnesque lines. All of which merely demonstrates once again that romantic music is not to be considered a degeneration of a classical tradition, but rather is the result of a supplanting of basic assumptions; the primarily narrative orientation of classical composers gives way to a more picturesque view of things.

Much the same kind of thinking seems to underlie the construction in the development section of this movement. As was the case in Beethoven's fifth symphony, it contains only two climaxes, the second at the reentry. These two climaxes, however, do not give anything like the impression of coordination (one serves as a stage in the journey toward the other) so readily apparent in Beethoven's scheme.

The first climax comes at the end of a long build-up (almost 100 measures) which moves in an almost unbroken line from a soft and thin to a very loud and full presentation. It is capped by a long section during which the high dynamic level is maintained without relief. The rise into the reentry, on the other hand, is far more abrupt (about fifteen measures). Separating the two is a fairly long, soft, almost static passage—a pause to catch one's breath—obviously thrown in to prepare the way for the resumption of the vigorous motion at the recapitulation.

The point of interest here is the nature of the first climax. It is not marked by any significant event which would give the impression of using up the energy generated to that point. On the other hand, neither is it an abrupt reversion to a low level of intensity which would leave a strong expectation of a rise to a genuinely climactic event; indeed, even if the break were more abrupt, the amount of time devoted to the soft, static presentation would do much to wipe this expectation from memory. All Mendelssohn does to bring the long section of high intensity to a close is to turn the line downward, thin the texture, and decrease the volume—all to a rather unprepossessing arpeggiated line (Example 6). This

Example 6.

manner of leaving the climax—by a descent too gradual to plant a commitment to return to the high level of excitement and too innocuous to suggest using up the energy generated—can contribute but little to the effectiveness of the subsequent climax (at the reentry).

The arpeggiated descent, as a matter of fact, seems so out of keeping with the atmosphere already established in the development, as well as with the events that follow, that one cannot help but be brought up short by it. For a moment, the so-called seams of construction show through; the sense of connection between moments breaks down. If we are to enjoy the piece as a whole, it is clear that we must overlook this passage, and if we cannot, we must at least forget it as quickly as possible. Such a requirement, of course, bespeaks a style in which the narrative element is not of overriding significance.

This is not to suggest that Mendelssohn did no planning at all in this respect. Obviously he recognized that the vigorous, boiling motion at the reentry would be most effective if it seemed to grow out of a prolonged section of low intensity and almost static quality—these being almost diametric opposites to the essential characteristics of his theme. This low-intensity passage, in turn, would seem a reasonable continuation if it were preceded by a climax of considerable significance.

A program of this kind, however, represents a calculation not in terms of narrative principles (i.e., of cumulation), but rather in terms of actions and reactions or of establishing a climate appropriate for the next major move which would then be in the nature of a reaction to that climate. The lack of coordination between climaxes, the incongruity of the descending passage after the first climax, the extent of the amorphous section between the two climaxes—all become perfectly understandable if Mendelssohn is viewed as a composer interested primarily in the play of gross actions and reactions, rather than in the piling of detail upon detail to forge a continuous line of development. Mendelssohn's style, then, can be said to be balanced toward the picturesque. It is obvious, after all, that he took considerable care to design material that would prove intrinsically evocative and appealing; the boiling, vigorous motion of the first theme in this movement hardly can be resisted. But this is a picturesque style which nevertheless makes use of a strong element of reactive structure. The action-reaction schemes, of course, are constructed to show the inherently attractive qualities in the best possible light, from the best possible angle.

Just how unimportant the classic ideal of cumulation had come to be for romantic composers can be judged even more clearly from the works of Robert Schumann. Even the questionable practices of Schubert and Mendelssohn seem highly polished compared to the way Schumann sometimes treats the flow of time. The development from the first movement of his B♭-major symphony ("Spring") can serve as illustration.

This development opens with a pair of oppositions between loud and soft sections (measures 134–149), followed by a series of passages embodying a build-up from a soft presentation to a climax (measures 150–178). The climax itself is marked by a strong statement of significant thematic material (the opening four measures of the first theme: measures 178–181). Except for the fact that this is not the right key—something that probably would go unnoticed by most of Schumann's audience—this climax might well be taken for the beginning of the recapitulation. For the first theme continues to be presented, in an almost exact transposition of the way it appeared in the exposition, for some twenty-four measures.

Now this first theme also contains a set of oppositions between loud and soft passages. Thus, no sooner does the sense of climactic culmination begin to be felt than there is an abrupt reversion to a quieter atmosphere, followed by another loud-soft alternation. After just a few more measures, furthermore, Schumann goes about repeating the sequence of events with which the development opened (though in different keys, of course). As a result, another set of loud-soft oppositions comes to be heard in very short order. This time, however, there is a subsequent attempt to build the intensity, just as was done in the beginning of the development.

Instead of issuing into a climactic reentry of the first theme, as the previous build-up did, this one is cut off abruptly by a sudden reversion to a low dynamic level and a thin texture while a new variant of the theme is introduced and tossed about by various instruments. Perhaps Schumann felt that by now the almost continual alternation between loud and soft passages was in danger of becoming a little tiresome. To go into a reentry at this point, of course, would mean presenting another pair. In addition, it might be difficult to suggest that the coming climax offered anything sufficiently new to prove rewarding for an audience since the earlier build-up and climax had gone over essentially the same ground. The solution, he may have reasoned, would be to insert a passage that would delay the explosion, thereby lending it added significance.

If this was indeed Schumann's intention, the passage in question (measures 246–298) must be counted one of his more notable failures. For it lasts much too long, introduces too great an element of novelty, and contains far too many repetitions of a well-defined thematic contour to permit it to act as a delay. The excesses are so pronounced, indeed, that I don't think one could well claim that these are subjective judgments or reflections of a personal standard of taste. By the end of fifty measures, after all, all memory of the culmination which this passage was supposed to delay certainly would be dissipated. The climax that follows clearly has its roots not in the commitment left over from the unrealized reentry designed to take place at measure 246, but in the processes developed in the delaying passage itself.

The introduction of a considerable element of novelty further undermines the sense of delay. The novelty is introduced by the particular variant of the main theme whose repetitions and transpositions form the substance for this section. For this variant, although retaining the rhythmic pattern of the main theme, describes an entirely different trajectory: a rising scale (Example 7). The mood it evokes is so unlike that of the theme from which it is de-

Example 7.

rived that one cannot but interpret this as a novel and not quite expected turn of events. The element of novelty, of course, tends to make one look for a return to the original situation fairly soon.

By the end of fifty measures, however, this expectation has gone so long unfulfilled that it must be pushed from memory by the flood of subsequent impressions. Anything that hinders the action of memory in this way must create a certain amount of confusion, and any source of confusion, needless to say, undermines that feeling of clarity of interpretation required to effect a sense of delay. One's attention is distracted; one's ability to concentrate on seeking out the delayed effect is diminished.

Added to these factors is an almost mechanical quality resulting from excessive repetition of the novel thematic variant. This figure is presented in full and without significant change in contour or rhythm some thirteen times within a space of thirty-four measures. By any reasonable standards, this must be considered so redundant a situation as to kill all sense of logical progress. One cannot help but feel that the composition is floundering at this point, flailing about aimlessly, wasting time until it should seem appropriate to bring in a more interesting effect. So prolonged a breakdown in the sense of logical progress, of course, must distract attention from any temporal calculation, including that of delay. The only expectation induced is more in the nature of a hope, that this section will soon be over.

It may well be, of course, that the clumsiness merely reflects a lack of intention to fashion a delay. My imputation that this was his purpose may have been incorrect. In that case, one can only wonder why the commitment to a climactic reentry of the first theme at measure 246 was not honored. Why should a long build-up be cut off just at the point where culmination was expected if delay was not the purpose? This would mean that a very strongly sensed commitment remains unfulfilled. The implication is that it is to be forgotten in the subsequent stream of events; it is a loose end contributing little or nothing to the fashioning of a sense of logical flow.

No matter how one looks at it, then, this simply could not be taken for a classical development organized along narrative lines. There is too much alternation between loud and soft passages to allow for any suggestion of overall direction, and the one passage that could be interpreted as an attempt to break away from the tyranny of these alternations is so clumsily executed that it could not possibly have been successful.

In this case, perhaps, can be seen the result of attempts to imitate a classic procedure from the viewpoint of a changed set of values. For Beethoven, Mozart, and Haydn often initiate a process of growth with the kind of loud-soft-loud-soft pattern found in the development. Almost invariably, furthermore, this pair of theses and antitheses will be followed by a crescendo, which might well be termed an attempt at synthesis, much as is the case in Schumann's movement. The sense of conflict between the two levels of intensity seems to set the stage for the following crescendo, which may be interpreted as an attempt to bridge the gulf between the two states of mind. In classic works, however, this build-up is channeled into a climax, ordinarily marked by a strong cadence, suggesting that the conflict has been resolved, at least temporarily. Thus what follows the whole process is a respite—a far cry from the restatement of the conflict introduced again and again by Schumann. If Schumann was indeed following classic models in the shaping of this development, it is clear that he only imitated external features without understanding the purposes they served in the style as a whole.

This is obviously far less sensitive and effective planning than was found in the Mendelssohn movement discussed earlier, or in those by Schubert, for that matter. Although it, too, is based on the principle of reaction—the loud setting the stage for the soft, the sharp contrasts between loud and soft establishing an appropriate atmosphere for the crescendo—the principle is applied on a much smaller scale. Instead of calculating reactions, as Mendelssohn and Schubert must have done, in terms of the development as a whole (for instance, a whole section building, and another stagnant to balance the one preceding as well as to set the stage for what follows), Schumann obviously limited his calculations to the areas contained in the subsections of the development. His planning, no doubt, was in terms of immediate contrast, with little concern for, or concepion of, the effect of the development as a whole. As a result, the point of strength in Mendelssohn's and Schubert's movements, the reentry, is exactly the point of weakness in Schumann. Schumann apparently has not attempted to plan toward a forceful reentry by means of the reactive type of organization—something which Mendelssohn and Schubert had conceived superbly. The reaction is something more like an end in itself, a source of refreshment for a palate that might otherwise become jaded.

That there is an awkwardness to the reentry in the first symphony seems readily apparent. For Schumann is no closer to bringing the continual alternation to a head—to deciding the suggested opposition of forces in favor of the one or the other—by the end

271

of the development than he was at its beginning. The expedient adopted to achieve some sense of conclusion—the fortissimo statement of the opening of the first theme in augmentation (measures 294-300), followed shortly by an even louder ritardando section (measures 311-316)—seems arbitrarily introduced, and rather lame; it is not really able to top preceding events appreciably. This impression is reinforced by the fact that there is an immediate return to the loud-soft opposition.

Since the applications of reactive organization are so limited in scope, it seems reasonable to suppose that Schumann relied primarily upon picturesque resources for appeal. He must have counted upon a listener becoming so engrossed in the moods called up by the individual sections that he would be quite willing to pay little attention to any line of development which would link those sections together. Apparently he was not even too concerned about using the line of development to set an atmosphere against which the evocative material would show to best advantage—certainly he was far less concerned with this than Schubert or Mendelssohn.

Many of the songs, among them the most significant ones, show somewhat the same indifference to the large line of development. In some cases (for example *Der Nussbaum* or *Mondnacht*), small phrases are repeated so often with little or no change that no sense of progress can develop. Even when the pattern of repetition is broken in these pieces, the change is so mild in degree as to seem almost inappropriate; what Meyer [2] called the element of saturation virtually demands a more radical step at this time. As a result, a quality of sameness attaches to these pieces—a feeling that the basic mood has been presented, extended, but not intensified or even subjected to stress. Indeed, there is little to suggest the emergence of any trend larger than the phrase.

In a composition like *Widmung,* on the other hand, two contrasting moods are presented, the first and last exuberant, and the middle far more restful—a contrast-full situation which seems to promise, indeed require, working out by means of trends. The execution, however, makes it clear that this was far from Schumann's intention. For, once again, a commitment to climax is left unfulfilled. The drive that should culminate in a climax gets under way with what is obviously a determined rise in intensity at the third and fourth lines of text (*Du meine Welt, in der ich lebe, Mein Himmel du, darein ich schwebe*). The music set to the next line of text, however, breaks off this build-up abruptly (*O du mein*

Grab . . .) in favor of a descent. If ever any move was designed to
be interpreted as a delay, this must be it: the promise of climactic
culmination is so clear, the breaking off so abrupt. What is expected, then, is a return to the upward motion followed eventually
by a significant outcome—a climactic event powerful enough to
suggest that the drive has reached its goal. What follows, however,
is just the opposite: a section of extreme calm (*Du bist die
Ruh'* . . .).

How is one to interpret this in the scheme of development?
Undoubtedly what was expected—and strongly expected—has not
occurred. The first thought might be that this is yet another delay.
But the commitment to return to the sense of exuberance just at
this point of change is so strong, the new mood endures so long
(sixteen measures), and the change in atmosphere introduced at
this point is so striking that an interpretation of this kind seems
out of the question. There is a decided quality of the arbitrary
to this turn of events—although the poetry does indeed call for
such a change in mood here—a quality which tends to dispel any
sense of logical development, focusing attention instead upon the
three major sections as separate entities related but tenuously to
each other. From the narrative standpoint, so radical and long-
enduring a change in mood so early in the piece and so completely counter to expectations can only be interpreted as a *faux
pas*. Far from contributing to a line of logical development, it
raises problems in interpreting just what the line of development
is to be. The fact that these problems are never really resolved
only serves to indicate how little Schumann's calculations had to
do with the narrative element.

Sometimes there is even a clumsiness to the introduction of
what was undoubtedly intended to be the climactic event—a
clumsiness which unmistakably carries an impression that the
climax did not really grow organically out of the musical situation,
but rather was inserted arbitrarily, perhaps because the text seemed
to call for it. In the same *Widmung*, for instance, the music to the
final line of text (*Mein guter Geist, mein bess'res ich*) does not
seem the outcome of the readily apparent sense of drive so much as
an interruption of it. It is only because the closing formula and
the postlude contain material intrinsically suggestive of termination that the piece seems to end at all convincingly; by narrative
calculations, it might be expected that the drive continue until
some more significant and appropriate outcome has been suggested. In a similar way, the climactic line of *Der Nussbaum*

(*Flüstern von Bräut'gam und nächstem Jahr*) hardly seems to flow naturally from the preceding context, in this case because very little sense of drive, or even of direction, has developed within the piece, what with the inordinate number of repetitions and the fact that almost every move toward increased tension has been resolved almost immediately.

Much of the piano music offers additional evidence of indifference to narrative possibilities, both in the small and large forms. The obvious predilection for short pieces strung together to form a larger one itself bespeaks a mind preoccupied with the immediate mood. The treatment of these brief pieces, moreover, suggests this even more clearly. For Schumann does not take the view that brevity requires a great concentration of events, or so much happening so quickly that an ending can sound convincing before too much time has gone by. Rather, the rhetoric in these pieces gives every indication of a prolixity which is simply cut off in midcourse. The themes are often not particularly short; they are repeated, sequenced, and transposed in full, sometimes almost to the point of saturation, and then often just dropped without much of a sense of termination.

In many of the larger piano pieces, Schumann simply seems to have been out of his element. The occasional long passages of dotted rhythms introduce so mechanical a quality that the sense of progress seems lame and halting. The frequency of the moves toward climax, furthermore, the extended duration of the intervening soft sections, and the general lack of ability to suggest greater or lesser degrees of intensity at the various climaxes all combine to assure that no general line of development will be impressed upon the listener—only a succession of individual sections.

Sometimes even the way in which moods are juxtaposed seems rather puzzling. The earthy, forceful opening of *Aufschwung*, for instance, gives way, after a very short time, to a theme so much more delicate in quality that one can only wonder what relation can possibly exist between the two moods. This is simply too much of a contrast to permit any moves toward a resolution of the tension created by the opposition. It seems more an either/or proposition than a first/and then situation.

Once again, it may be well to stress that I am not attempting to assert that Schumann was an unskilled composer. Despite their puzzling elements, the pieces I have discussed remain among the most frequently played and probably best enjoyed in the modern repertory—and quite rightly, in my opinion. The point I am trying to bring out is that these pieces owe their value to something other than narrative organization. Schumann simply does not seem to have been interested in intensification, or in working out a conflict-full situation dramatically. Indeed, he does not even seem to have cared much about setting up an atmosphere against which a basic mood would show to best advantage, as Mendelssohn and Schubert apparently did. For all of the considerations raised in connection with his works suggest that his aim was to evoke a mood, extend it to an appropriate length, and then drop it in order to avoid satiety and go on to another.

This means, of course, that Schumann's main problem with respect to time was the question of how to extend a mood to the proportions required to register it properly in mind, rather than how to work out an opposition of forces, how to intensify a dominant mood, or how to set the stage for a reentry. It is proper timing that counts and that becomes the subject for direct calculation. One could imagine him thinking—perhaps as a modern cinematic composer might—that thirty seconds of a particular mood would be needed, and then considering what actions would purchase those thirty seconds. And he would have judged the need for this amount of time not on the basis of preparing the atmosphere adequately for a subsequent event, but rather of extending the mood long enough for it to take hold well.

There is the implication here that Schumann had considerable confidence in the musical value of mood evocations. He must have felt that he could organize his materials to evoke mood associations powerful and intriguing enough to attract and hold the interest of a listener; and he must have felt that he could do this merely through the application of thematic, harmonic, and other materials —that is, without recourse to processes of intensification.

It is not at all difficult, furthermore, to find solid grounds for such confidence. Schumann, after all, was attempting to depict a new range of emotions in music—a range which might be termed "poetic," with all the implications of delicacy, sensitivity, nuance, and of the out-of-the-ordinary that the word must have carried during his time. Compared to him, Beethoven, Haydn, and even Mozart must seem plain-speaking men whose interests were far more earthbound. It is understandable, then, that enthusiasm for new expressive possibilities would come to govern his thinking, and would thus divert his attention from other constructive aspects.

Schumann's position becomes even more understandable when one realizes that he forged a musical idiom almost ideally suited for evoking these novel sentiments. By a combination of textural and harmonic practices, along with a tendency toward complexity in the organization of small details, he was able to project a varied range of sentiments eloquently, as well as to produce fine shadings of meaning.

The treatment of texture is marked by a new degree of imaginativeness applied to accompanimental figures. In his piano music, for instance, such stereotyped figurations as the Alberti bass, repeated arpeggiations within the range of an octave, and scale passages are avoided in favor of freshly invented figures appropriate to a specific mood evocation. Upward arpeggiations often go well beyond the octave, reach a peak, and then subside, making possible a sense of surge and retreat within a small time span—a figuration that would lend itself well to many of the new moods being depicted. The addition of nonharmonic tones, further-more, and a general blurring of the distinction between the impor-tance of the harmonic and nonharmonic tones, made it possible to suggest various degrees of smoothness and vagueness to this arpeggiated figure, as well as to create various degrees of cantabile quality. And by allowing the high points of the arpeggios to enter into an obviously purposeful motion (for example, down the scale) at some points, it became possible to suggest an emergence of clarity and direction from a vague context.

These, of course, are only a few of the new possibilities, but it is easy to see how even these few devices would have served to widen expressive horizons. It is as though Schumann realized that by paying attention to this aspect of construction—an aspect largely neglected by the classic masters—he could achieve a variety of expression and a precision in depicting nuances that were both entirely novel and appropriate to his poetic aims.

The essentially novel features of Schumann's harmonic prac-tice are the free and frequent use of second and third inversions of dominant-seventh chords, and the ease with which keys are changed. In the opening section of *Widmung*, for instance, much of the tone is set by a descending bass line over which the pro-gression IV-V$_2$-I$_6$-V$_4^3$-I unfolds. The second and third inversions of the dominant-seventh chord and their subsequent resolutions which dominate this passage, lend it a quality of smooth, gentle, yet almost irresistible drive. It is like coasting down a hill compared to the obvious up-hill struggles characteristic of classic harmonic practice. The advantages of this type of progression for evoking the mild restlessness and vagueness so intimately associated with the concept of the poetic are readily apparent.

As for the change of key, the notable thing is that it takes place so smoothly, almost unobtrusively, and that it is nevertheless so relatively significant in effect. To turn again to the opening portion of *Widmung*, once the harmony departs from tonic (measure 8), there is no return to it until just two measures before the end of the first section. This is no mere excursion away from an established tonic; it is a pilgrimage which carries its own sense of significance. As a result, the return to the tonic sounds less like a return than simply another change. In other words, the harmony is not used to create the kind of tectonic quality so evident in much of Bach's music, nor even to reinforce such a tectonic quality, but rather to create atmosphere; the moves to the various keys are so strong that the location of the tonic becomes only a dim memory. Nor can the contrast be drawn between tonal stability and instability, because the opening move away from tonic (to the subdominant) sounds most stable, while the return to tonic, with its strong element of surprise (a rather unexpected I_6-V-I cadence),

does not. [4]

Almost any excerpt from Schumann's works will demonstrate how he loved to slip in and out of keys almost unobtrusively. The basic pattern repeated so often in *Der Nussbaum*, for instance, goes through the relative minor, back to the tonic, on to the dominant and the subdominant before settling into tonic again—all within a space of some twelve measures, just nineteen different chords. To put it another way, the key changes with every fourth chord, on the average. To turn to purely instrumental music, the first statement of the theme in the first movement of the piano concerto (a point at which little modulation is expected) contains moves through the dominant and subdominant keys before ending with a move to the dominant—all within just eight measures. The passage following the bare presentations of the theme (measures 20-32) moves through the following set of keys: A minor, D minor, A minor, D minor, C major, E minor, C major, and G major—better than one key change every two measures. Later on (measures 67-95), in a section of relatively settled character (i.e., not bridgelike), the sequence runs: C major, D minor, E minor, C major, G major, E minor, D minor, G major, C minor, G minor, B minor, and C major—once again close to one key change every two measures.

While such rates of key change are to be found in some baroque music where the harmonic rhythm is much faster, there is nothing comparable in the classic literature. Even in the classic development sections, so quick a series of changes stretching over so long a time is seldom to be found. The result is a far richer-sounding harmonic idiom than that of the classics, with a consequent increase in the range of evocations and the capabilities for nuance.

A most significant source of Schumann's poetic evocations is the complex organization of small sections and details, particularly the presentation of complex entities right from the start of a composition. Sometimes it is the harmony that introduces the element of complexity. In *Der Nussbaum,* for instance, the opening chord turns out to be not the expected tonic or the second choice dominant, but the subdominant. Schumann, then, requires that our mood picture be formed out of a reevaluation of our first interpretation, and out of the whole progression IV-V_7-I. The picture is further complicated by a long-held appoggiatura over the dominant. All of this must register before we begin to be certain of the basic mood—quite a difference from the almost outspoken quality at the beginning of classic pieces.

In other cases, the complexity is introduced by the rhythmic configuration. Perhaps the best example of this kind can be found in the opening theme of his third symphony (Example 8) in which

Example 8.

a good deal of the character results from the play between figures which define $\frac{4}{4}$ and $\frac{3}{4}$ meters.

Still another source of complexity is the structure of the theme or small thematic section. Where classic composers' themes tend to have a simple outline—often developed from a repeat of a small motive or of a contrast—many of Schumann's show the breadth of conception and the refinement of calculation so conspicuously absent on the larger scale. The first theme from the third symphony (see Example 8), for instance, seems a veritable structural micro-cosmos, with its rapid rise to climax (measure 3) and its following gradual descent; and which, by the principle of reaction, sets the stage nicely for the climactic ending. In *Der Nussbaum,* to take just one more example, the line of development can be sensed through each of the ten-measure segments that undergoes repetition: the second phrase within each of these segments seems a retreat from the first, but only to set the stage for the move toward climax which brings the section to a close. The following interlude then helps dispel the energy left over from the climax.

Thus, there would seem considerable justification for Schumann's reliance upon the value of mood expression *per se.* The new array of musical materials and processes adaptable to his program, no less than the new range of evocations it made possible virtually invites concentration on the charm of the moment. Schumann could well afford to say to his audience: "Never mind how they are joined together; are not the individual sections—the tableau—attractive?" Whatever his justification, however, it certainly is clear that the narrative organization characteristic of classical composers was quite far removed from his way of thinking.

Even the works of that most classically minded of all the romantic composers, Johannes Brahms (1833-1897), show evidences of the temper of the times, both in loose organization of the narrative element and in greater concern for quality of mood. In the first movement of his third symphony, for instance, the first climax comes within the first theme proper rather than near the end of the bridge—just as was the case in Schubert's eighth symphony. The considerable energy generated during the presentation of that theme comes to seem completely used up by the climactic approach to the cadence and the subsequent tapering of intensity. In spite of this, almost the entire bridge (measures 15-35) is devoted to suggesting settling down into the second theme; there is only a very slight build-up at the beginning of the bridge, with the rest of this rather long passage clearly settling down. As a result, there seems little reason for sustaining a quality of ebbing intensity for so long. It could not well be interpreted as a natural consequence of an exhaustion of energy because the build-up was much too minor to suggest the kind of effort that might go into creating a sense of exhaustion. The tapering undoubtedly is an effect put in at this point not because it was called for by the context that had developed, but rather for its own sake, or possibly to set the stage for the events to come. This lack of motivation, I would suggest, is easily perceptible; the seams of construction show through.

As a result of this questionable calculation, the build-up in the closing section seems less a resumption of a previous tendency than a new idea—an appropriate reaction to a section that has remained serene for a long time. It has been so long, after all, since the previous climax was consummated (more than forty measures).

The impression that the closing drive is not really a continuation of the opening one is further enhanced by the inherently attractive quality of the second theme itself, as well as by its considerable length. For it is so lyrical, its basic idea so fully developed (its form can be diagramed as *a a b a'*, with a small climax in the *b* section), and the whole rounded off with such polish (a return of the original theme in a kind of inversion), that it virtually begs to be enjoyed and evaluated not as a cog in a mechanism, but as a significant entity in its own right.

Apparently Brahms sensed the difficulty that would be involved in getting up momentum again for the closing drive. For he prepared for this new undertaking in a most sensitive and effective way. Into this soft atmosphere extending well beyond the close of the second theme proper, he inserted a gradual surge of energy (measures 56-58)—a surge which is cut off abruptly, to be sure (measures 59-60), but which nevertheless predicts the more general and enduring move toward intensification taken slightly later (measure 64 on). Effective as this device is, it only serves to emphasize how little Brahms must have counted upon the memory of the earlier drive to climax (within the first theme; measure 11) to remain in mind and to contribute to the shaping of further expectations. For there would have been no need for so careful a preparation if this memory was still active; the resumption of drive would have been a thing expected.

Similar instances are to be found in other of Brahms's expositions. In the first movement of the first symphony, the climax in the bridge (measure 97) is followed by a very long tapering of intensity (measures 99-130) and an almost equally long second theme (measures 130-156), most of which is presented at a very soft level. In the first movement of the second symphony, the second theme (measures 82-109) is preceded by a fairly extended passage (measures 66-81) whose essential purpose clearly is to taper off from the climax. The final stage of this tapering process, furthermore, consists of an almost awkward broadening of a figure

formed by the punctuating chords of the accompaniment in measures 71-78. All of which seems to indicate that Brahms was less
interested in following out previous commitments and building an
impression of a cause-effect relationship, than in finding a way to
bring in his new theme effectively. And this second theme is one
of those extended lyrical out-pourings that cannot but draw attention to itself and wipe any vestige of an underlying drive from
memory. In these cases too, then, the closing drive seems less a
resumption of an underlying current than a reaction.

In the first movement of the fourth symphony, on the other
hand, Brahms escapes this problem by moving directly from the
climax in the bridge (measures 53-57) into the second theme
(measures 57-73), and by limiting himself to two statements of
the theme before the closing drive sets in. Even this exposition,
however, is not entirely free of lesions in the sense of narration.
For with what should be the closing drive well under way, a
gradual tapering of intensity is introduced (measures 80-86), followed shortly by an extended passage of markedly lyrical quality
(measures 91-106). The lyrical passage even tapers again as it
draws to its close (measures 103-106). These twenty-seven measures
of an essentially relaxing character (one-fourth of the composition
to this point) could not well be said to constitute merely a challenge to the dominant trend toward intensification; rather, they
seem to represent a complete conquest of it. To revert to the driving quality, then, requires considerable care, which, as previously
noted, would not really have been the case if the underlying current
were still felt. The care in this case takes the form of going to
great lengths to set up an especially soft climate against which the
drive toward intensification would seem an appropriate reaction,
and of planting some seeds of the rise before it actually takes
control (measures 110-113).

The developments, too, show signs of the romantic temper.
In the third symphony, for instance, the planning seems very similar
to that discussed in connection with Mendelssohn: a driving opening that reaches a climax of minor proportions (measure 90) and
then gives way to a gradual tapering of intensity. The tapering
leads into a soft and almost static passage (measures 101-119)
which sets an appropriate atmosphere for the emergence of the
powerful quality of the reentry. The amount of time and the
obvious effort involved in getting up momentum for the reentry
again indicates that Brahms had little confidence that the memory
of a preceding drive would engender an expectation of its resump-

tion. Thus, his calculation was primarily in terms of reaction rather than of resuming a clearly sensed trend.

In the first movement of the fourth symphony, the opening build-up in the development is cut off by a rather unexpected event—conventionally unexpected, to be sure—namely, a deceptive cadence (measure 184). The expectation is that the drive will resume—and it is a strong expectation. Brahms seems to be following out this commitment when he introduces the little fanfare figure very shortly after this deceptive cadence (measure 188); in spite of the fact that it is presented *sotto voce*, its own driving character gives the impression that a return to the building of intensity is imminent. What follows, however, seems to ignore this commitment completely; the music lapses into a prolonged passage of lyrical quality and of a very low and even gradually decreasing dynamic level. It is from this low ebb of intensity that the drive gets under way again (measure 206). The length of the soft section separating the two driving ones (twenty-two measures), the very slow motion which dominates most of it, and the tapering of intensity toward the end all seem to indicate that Brahms was not as interested in fashioning the impression of a resumption of activity, as he was in establishing a favorable climate to which the section of forcefulness and drive would seem a most welcome reaction.

It might be argued that this is a scheme much like that discussed in connection with Mozart's fortieth symphony in Chapter 7,[3] in which, it may be recalled, the second of the climaxes performed the function of using up energy left over from the first one. Quantitative considerations, however, make such a comparison extremely dubious. In the Mozart movement, the fact that the soft section lasts only slightly more than half as long as the preceding forceful one (twenty-four measures of drive to fourteen less intense ones) creates the effect of a respite. These proportions are almost exactly reversed in this movement by Brahms (fifteen forceful measures to twenty-two soft ones). As a result, the less intense element seems the more significant one and in effect nullifies any tendency to interpret the drive as a dominant current. That the return of the forceful quality seems well motivated is due not so much to any remembrance that the earlier drive had failed to reach an adequate culmination, but more to the new expectation of a reaction engendered by the prolonged presentation of a particular quality.

Even where a narrative program is easily recognizable,

Brahms' obvious predilection for lyrical qualities and for the states of mind associated with long gradual declines in intensity sometimes jeopardizes the perception of the basic plan. The sections devoted to these qualities are so long and are fashioned of such compellingly evocative materials that we tend to become absorbed in them and to drop from memory the commitments and implications of earlier trends and events. Such is the case, for instance, in the first movement of the first symphony. Here the development contains three forceful sections separated by passages of soft and even ebbing intensity. The first of the forceful sections is a bold utterance to open the development (measures 189-197); the other two involve preceding build-ups. Since the second one involves a short build-up (measures 225-232) and a long sojourn at the high level of intensity (measures 232-268), while the third has a long, gradual build-up (measures 300-320) and an only slightly shorter stay at the top (measures 321-343), the impression is created that the last section is a more deliberate and serious attempt to achieve climactic release than was the second section. In the second one, after all, the high level of intensity may seem to have been too easily achieved to suggest adequately the forcefulness of the characterization Brahms desired. It would be the business of the third passage, then, to deepen the dimensions of force by seeming to overcome a more determined opposition to the rise.

This impression is reinforced by the fact that the third passage seems much stronger qualitatively, largely because of the orchestration: full orchestra virtually all of the time in the last forceful section as opposed to an antiphonal play between strings and woodwinds in the second one. And the third passage is the only one that achieves any considerable sense of resolution of tensions: where the first merely drops back abruptly from a very high to a very low dynamic level (measure 197), and the second simply introduces gradually lower dynamic markings into the antiphonal play (measure 268 on), the third is channeled directly into a strong, well-prepared cadence (measures 321-343)—an effect which seems to use up a great deal of energy.

Thus, there is no mistaking a trend toward more and more significant climactic passages as the development runs its course—at least there is no mistaking this trend on paper. In performance, this is another question. For the intervening soft sections are so long and so filled with heavily charged effects—such as a long diminuendo over an organ point (measures 274-290), chromatic key changes through the (again conventionally) unexpected augmented-sixth chord (measures 210-211, 214-215), and a surfeit of diminished-seventh chords (measures 197-210)—that there is an almost unavoidable tendency to devote one's attention to the atmosphere created by these effects, to luxuriate in the emotional overtones. The result is that the memory of the preceding events tends to fade away so that there is no longer any basis for comparing the magnitudes of the various climaxes. It is questionable, then, whether the constructive program so clearly present in the score actually plays any significant role in the aesthetic experience offered by this development. This point may be argued, of course, and, indeed, various listeners with different memory capacities might come to diametrically opposed conclusions. It seems clear, however, that the evidence of primary reliance upon the narrative element is not nearly as clearcut as is usually the case in classic compositions.

The development in the first movement of the second symphony, on the other hand, offers a program that seems to work quite well in narrative terms, largely because Brahms avoids the prolonged descents and soft sections which dominate his other symphonic developments. The program is somewhat different from those usually used by the classic masters, however. The conflicting elements, the forceful and the more lyrical qualities, are arranged not so as to allow one to dominate, with the other serving as contrast and relief, but rather to effect a gradual change in dominance: the forceful, driving element governs the early part of the development, but gradually gives way to the softer one. Although the opening drive actually lasts from measure 195 to measure 249, there are two spots within it where an abrupt reduction in texture plants the seed of an eventual turnabout: measures 225-226 and 231-232. The quality of reduced intensity is given greater play slightly later when the dynamic level is reduced considerably, and the resulting soft section is allotted roughly seven measures (249-256). Still later, the dimensions allotted to the soft presentation are expanded to include approximately nineteen measures (261-279). Separating these two sections, furthermore, is a forceful one that lasts only about four measures. The tide obviously is turning in favor of the soft element. There is another flareup (measures 281-288), but by now the downward trend is so firmly established that this merely acts as a countercurrent, lending more authority to the close of the development which follows the return to the descending quality.

This is the way analysis goes in Brahms. In some cases the flow of time is beautifully organized; in others there is at least some question; in still others, there are obvious signs of breakdown in the logical chain of expectations and fulfillments. The significant thing is that it would be most difficult to assert that movements which made exemplary use of narrative organization were superior in quality or emotional impact to movements in which this element is more loosely organized. To Brahms, a finely conceived narrative structure obviously offered little advantage; often, indeed, as in the second movement of the third symphony, it simply indicated a more modest expressive intent. For Brahms clearly shared the romantic composers' confidence in the evocative powers of their materials and in the intrinsic value of these evocations. Since such powerful moods could be evoked merely with a harmonic turn, a fortissimo stroke of the orchestra, or a descending intensity line, and since intensification of these moods could be suggested most forcefully by qualitative means (such as a more dissonant harmony, a more rapid harmonic rhythm, a fuller orchestration), there would be little gained by engaging in a complex process of calculation designed to produce powerful effects by means of a smooth play of currents and counter-currents.

It must be admitted, furthermore, that there seems ample justification for such confidence. For one thing, Brahms's harmonic palette was far broader than even Schumann's. The freedom in using third relations, in the borrowings of chords from the relative minor, in the use of augmented sixths, and in the forging of often prolonged chromatic movement in the basses, all provided a new store of associations and nuances. Coupled with this was a new concern for execution; in particular, a tendency to play a percussive type of attack against a legato. The application of various dynamic shadings to these modes of execution also could produce a wide variety of mood evocations, from a heavy, earthbound quality sometimes termed bearlike, to a light, jocular effect, to a passionate lyricism, to a more serene, contemplative quality—all done at a stroke, so to speak; the mood is powerfully suggested before three seconds have elapsed.

Then, too, Brahms was most sensitive to rhythmic nuances. The disruptive power of a cross-rhythm and its usefulness in indicating an imminent drive while yet holding it in check, the tension associated with weak-beat accents (for example, temporarily putting the main accent on the third beat of a triple measure), the sense of controlled power inherent in a dotted rhythm, particularly when presented staccato, the quality of consummation that could be suggested by holding a significant melodic note considerably longer than expected—all of these possibilities were appreciated and exploited by Brahms to an unprecedented degree. And, of course, these procedures could be combined with those previously enumerated to achieve evocations and shadings of various kinds and strengths.

The climax itself became a major weapon in Brahms's arsenal. With the stylistic elements described above, as well as the expanded orchestra and the more sonorous piano, it became possible both to control the rate of growth of the drive to climax and to consummate the various drives with a variety of truly stunning effects. The climax and even the drive toward it became soul-stirring effects. In some cases, a climax much stronger qualitatively than any preceding is placed near the end of a movement, as in the first movements of the third symphony (measures 183-201) and the clarinet quintet (measures 195-200). When this happens, the effect sometimes seems so charged with drama and significance as to approach catharsis. There can be no doubt that the generation of tension and its release were among the most treasured of Brahms's evocations.

Although additional examples, drawn from the works of these and other composers, can be adduced without difficulty, these few seem adequate to suggest that romantic composers did indeed take a quite different view of the need for organizing the flux of intensity into rational patterns than did their predecessors. They simply did not find it necessary, for one reason or another, to organize the ebb and flow of intensity in such a way as to suggest the kind of logical motion from event to event that would lead to a gradually heightening quality of suspense.

The question naturally arises, then, whether any other steps were taken to create the quality of suspense; whether, for example, the harmonic organization fulfills this purpose almost by itself as was shown to be the case in some works by Bach. This question is by no means easy to answer inasmuch as a work of art is susceptible to so many types of organization that one may well overlook a feature of considerable significance. It may be surmised, however, that such is not the case here. For the rise and fall of intensity is one of the most powerful and easily perceived of musical effects and, as such, claims the foreground of attention no matter what else is going on. An apparently aimless series of rises and falls would divert attention from virtually any other conceivable method of organization, such as the harmony, no matter how ingeniously this other factor is patterned. As soon as composers begin to toy with the intensity—to raise it out of a neutral state or rigid organization—they are almost obliged to organize it or give up any idea of heightening suspense as the movement unfolds.

It would seem, then, that romantic composers simply were not interested in the cumulative properties of music, at least on the large scale. A large composition, to them, must have seemed little more than a series of sections, each of which was to be made as appealing as possible in and for itself. The care with which these sections were connected varied with the composer, from the meticulous craftsmanship of a Brahms or Mendelssohn to the awkwardness of Berlioz, Schumann, Wagner, or Mahler. Even the conception of how logical connection can be effected seems to have changed. For this is no longer, as it was to the classics, a matter of organizing music into predominant trends to which all events can be related, but rather a matter of calculating toward the establishment of an atmosphere against which a particularly significant event will show to best advantage as a reaction. This, of course, is a much looser kind of organization. No matter how careful the composer, it is evident that he counted upon the listener's patience at various points. "Just hear me through this spot," he seems to say, "and I'll present something beautiful and significant that will make it seem worth your while to have endured this roughness." It is the quality of the individual sections that forms the primary point of appeal in this music rather than the cumulative effect of the piece as a whole —the picturesque rather than the narrative.

I think it can be easily recognized that the procedural differences formulated in connection with what I have termed the conservative romantics (Schubert, Mendelssohn, Schumann, and Brahms) are equally applicable to the music of the more radical composers of the nineteenth century. Indeed, evidence of this kind is even more apparent in the works of the more consciously rebellious composers. In the music of Liszt, Wagner, Mahler, Bruckner, Franck and Schoenberg, climaxes are so easily embarked upon, so often reached, and so little differentiated from each other as to give an impression akin to that experienced on a roller coaster. Even more than for the conservatives, the climax for these composers must have been little more than an effect, a color, a way of producing forceful or nervously irritable evocations rather than a means for creating suspense and a sense of continuity.

It is perhaps ironic that the climax itself should have become one of the major means for achieving that kind of powerful evocation which no doubt contributed to the decline of interest in narrative organization. Yet this seems perfectly understandable. The new resources of instrumental color and power made it possible to build climaxes more often and to make them extremely significant as ends in themselves. Where Beethoven probably could not have been sure that the difference between forte and fortissimo would have been appreciated, Mahler could be certain enough of the volume-resources of his orchestra to use a whole range of dynamic indications from pppp to ffff. With these new resources, the climax could be a rewarding experience without relation to previous or future events, simply for its overpowering ability to evoke strong, primitive responses.

The technical changes described in this essay, important as they are for reaching an understanding of the composers' intentions, hardly seem to offer sufficient justification for marking off an era, let alone for giving it a name so charged with emotional connotations as romantic. Some inferences can be drawn from these new technical practices, however, which seem to indicate a quite different approach from that underlying the classic arts to fundamental human problems. The new outlook has to do with the question of emotional representation.

Although, on the surface, the romantic view of emotion in music looks very similar to the classic (both schools, after all, are interested in evoking moods and in playing appropriately contrasting feelings against each other rather fluidly) the conceptions actually are quite different. Where the classic composer builds upon these conflicting moods, heightening the suspense and the sense of conflict between them by the technical means described in Chapter 7, until one or the other wins out, the romantic composer tends to present an emotion, wring it dry, and then go on to another one, giving more thought to delineating the individual emotion than to creating a sense of logically progressing conflict. This is the crux of the difference between the two points of view: the classic composer views emotion as transitory, an individual affection capable of being experienced only for a short time, and therefore hopes to obtain strong response only as the piece develops; while the romantic composer becomes enveloped in the emotion presented at the moment and aims at obtaining a more immediate and direct response to his material. For the classic composer, the strong response results from the arrangement of the play of emotions in such a way as to suggest that the conflict between a set of them comes to seem much magnified during the course of a movement. To the romantic composer, on the other hand, the response is not dependent to so great an extent upon the context.

In a way, the romantic view of emotion seems reminiscent of late-baroque values in that it involves concentration on a single affection at a time [4] as though the classic conception of an interplay between similar and contrasting evocations had never existed. There are some significant differences, however, having to do with the number of emotions presented in a movement, the manner of projecting emotional representations, and the means for achieving intensification of these representations.

In the late baroque, of course, only one emotion generally was depicted in a movement. Composers such as Corelli, Vivaldi, J. S. Bach, and Handel used motives consistently within a movement—spinning them out into variants, repeating at certain points, but seldom introducing anything that can be construed as a contrasting figure. Some of the *da-capo* arias, to be sure, have rather radical changes of mood in their middle sections, but in many the contrast seems rather mild in degree; the middle section represents a continuation of the basic thought rather than an opposition to it. Romantic composers, on the other hand, obviously had no eye for such consistency. Within a single movement there are often motivic and thematic materials so different in configuration, rhythm, and implied intensity that they can only be construed as materials intended to evoke different emotions. These very different kinds of evocations, furthermore, are freely intermingled: departure from a specific mood does not at all imply that there will be no return to it later in the movement; indeed, there may be many returns. This is a much more flexible treatment of emotions than is to be found in late-baroque music.

The projection of an emotion in the late baroque apparently involved something like a symbolic process. By its rhythm, speed, and general contour, a theme probably was intended to represent a particular affection much as a symbol represents a specific entity. Presumably, the composer counted upon his audience's recognition that a specific theme was, for instance, a ragelike configuration, but that another was more apt for the expression of sorrow, and still another resembled an expression of joy or humor. He probably felt little need to convince his audience that a particular emotion was being projected, but rather felt confident that this would be recognized from the nature of his theme. Recognition of the nature of a theme, furthermore, would be as much the result of the rational as of intuitive processes.

The romantic, on the other hand, seems to have adopted something of the attitude of a salesman—a high-pressure salesman, at that. His material must not just symbolize, but must evoke the mood being projected in a most powerful and unmistakable way. He was out to convince his audience, to persuade it to adopt his state of mind, right from the outset. Accomplishing this, of course, required additional resources for producing evocations. Thus, whereas the late-baroque composer relied primarily upon his theme to set the mood, the romantic worked hard not only on the fashioning of an appropriate theme, but also on the figures designed to accompany that theme, the harmonies underlying it, and the pattern of intensity growth and decay that it would follow, forging what I have termed an atmosphere right from the beginning and in the most compelling of terms. Thus the romantics took elements that often came to assume importance only later on in a late-baroque composition (harmony, texture, intensity pattern), and applied them at the beginning of a piece for the purpose of influencing and strengthening emotional representation.

The intensification of an emotional representation was a complex affair in the late baroque—the result of a manipulation of many factors. The conflict between the memory of a tonal center and the challenges to that memory produced by modulations, by the use of various degrees of dissonance, by the various rates of rhythmic activity and of harmonic rhythm, and even by the changing numbers of voices were organized to suggest a general sense of motion toward a climactic point which would then create the sense of intensification of the basic emotion. It is noteworthy, furthermore, that this is an art of pressure and expansion that is almost always moving in the direction of increased intensity. Even in the most lyrical of movements, one would be hard put to find anything like a long, gliding descent in which the intensity tapers off to a whisper.

The romantic, on the other hand, simply could instruct performers to play more loudly in order to achieve intensification, or else could increase their number at climactic points—obviously a classic influence Although this may seem less sophisticated than late-baroque practice, it made possible new dimensions in sheer, direct power. And, of course, the romantic direction sometimes seems just the opposite of that of the late baroque: many nineteenth-century composers obviously luxuriated in the long descent and tapering off, using outbursts and build-ups to climaxes largely to set the stage for the projection of their favored softer sentiments.

In general, then, the romantic practice seems less a reversion to baroque values than an infusion of them with a new and more powerful source of vitality. This new type of treatment involved evoking moods strongly rather than symbolizing them, and presenting not necessarily one, but possibly a series of such mood evocations, any or all of which could be heightened to an overpowering point.

It is this new ability to evoke and to overwhelm, along with the power, directness, and immediacy of the response sought, that distinguishes the romantic from the baroque musical art. The romantic composer seems to demand that his compositions be able to persuade even uncooperative, unthinking audiences. Whereas the late-baroque and classic arts almost require a certain distance and a critical attitude for full emotional involvement to take place, (one must at least keep track of what has happened and reflect continually on what is yet to come to experience the depths of feeling), romantic compositions actually seem to suffer if the listener attempts to reach too far beyond the impression of the moment. Romantic music is an art of ecstasy, not of reflection.

In a sense, the romantic musician's handling of emotion is deeper than the classic: the power of some feelings to seize, grip, and control, even to destroy, an individual seems much better recognized. On the other hand, it represents a far less practical view of the human being: it is only an extraordinary personality experiencing extraordinary emotions who can maintain a mood for any considerable length of time. As soon as this element of the extraordinary ceases to be sensed or valued, the romantic is indeed on shaky ground.

The evidence, then, seems to indicate that there was indeed a major change in musical viewpoint during the early decades of the nineteenth century—a change of such scope and dimension as to justify a comparison with similar developments in other arts implied by the use of the term romanticism. Assuming music to be a flow of meaningful sound-effects in time, this change can be understood as a shifting of emphasis to the term sound-effects in this formulation as opposed to the classic predilection for the flow of time. It seems to reflect a change in the conception of the human condition: from the dominance of man, who is assailed by many transitory emotions, to the dominance of the emotion, which is capable of overwhelming man.

Perhaps the substance of this change in viewpoint is best summed up in the bargain struck between Faust and Mephistopheles in Goethe's great dramatic poem. For instead of the pacts found in the various versions of the legend and in the earlier dramatic settings, Goethe employed a wager, a wager which was made contingent upon a view of time, and reflecting satisfaction as opposed to the eternal human striving. One of a series of clauses in the verbal contract runs:

> Werd' ich zum Augenblicke sagen:
> "Verweile doch, du bist so schön!"
> Dann magst du mich in Fesseln schlagen,
> Dann will ich gern zugrunde gehn!
>
> Should I ever say to the moment:
> "Stay, thou art so beautiful!"
> Then you may throw me in chains,
> Then will I gladly go to ruin!

The romantic composers, I would suggest, succumbed to this allure of the moment, creating thereby a priceless artistic treasure, but leaving behind, when their time had passed, a rather tangled intellectual legacy: a conception of music in which the role of temporal relationships was neither appreciated nor understood.

NINE

Schoenberg the Prophet

W ITH ALL THAT HAS been written about the innovations of Arnold Schoenberg, the critical
significance of one fact seems to have been largely overlooked. That
is, that Schoenberg was not advancing a system designed to stand
or fall on its own merits, but rather was basing his claim to justification on certain predictions concerning the future development
of the human ear, the human mentality—and their aesthetic
ramifications. He seems to have formulated his practices because
he felt that they fulfilled aesthetic conditions whose emergence in
the future was inevitable. His was a voice, not of expedience, but
of prophecy.

As a prophet, however, Schoenberg was truly a product of
his time. For his claim to understanding the future was not based
upon absolute principles, or upon some kind of revelation; it was
based upon history. Schoenberg was attempting to read the future
from a knowledge of past developments. Since historical calculations played so significant a role in his thought, it would seem only
reasonable that any attempt to evaluate Schoenberg as an historical
figure should begin with a study of his grasp of past developments,
and of his grounds for believing that the future could be read from
them. This would mean examining the body of data at his command, his interpretation of these data, and the historical philosophy
which made him feel so confident about predicting the future.

Fortunately, Schoenberg left a small body of writings which
outlines his views and aims with some degree of clarity. From

these writings (notably his book of essays *Style and Idea*,[1] his text *Harmonielehre*,[2] a set of interviews included in the volume *Schoenberg* compiled by Merle Armitage,[3] and his fairly recently issued *Briefe* [4]), it is possible to reconstruct his line of thinking at least approximately.

It is regrettable that Schoenberg's style of writing was more aphoristic than expository, and heavily charged with emotion. As a result, there often appear to be gaps in the structure of his thought: seemingly unrelated ideas are juxtaposed in surprising ways while causal connections are implied between remotely related entities. The whole begins to make sense, however, if one considers certain theoretical notions and intellectual beliefs current duing Schoenberg's formative years which he may have felt constituted a body of common knowledge. At several points, then, I have introduced common conceptions of this kind in order to make Schoenberg's position clear and understandable. I can only hope that this has not led to any distortion of his thought.

Schoenberg himself has traced his doctrine to a theory which he has called the "emancipation of the dissonance." His argument runs to the effect that consonance and dissonance are not really matters of agreeableness and disagreeableness, but rather of different degrees of comprehensibility.[5] A chord which does not seem to require any resolution, a chord which is understood without reference to anything else, is easily comprehensible and therefore consonant. One which somehow seems incomplete or unstable by itself and requires some resolution is incomprehensible by itself and therefore dissonant.

Schoenberg maintains that in the course of history, a line of development can be observed in which more and more combinations of sounds gradually lose their connotations of dissonance and come to be considered consonances.[6] He cites as evidence the early predilection for the "empty" intervals of octave, fourth, and fifth, the later admission of the third, and the increasing acceptance of more and more complicated chord structures through the late nineteenth century. To a seventeenth-century audience, the famous chords at the beginning of *Tristan und Isolde* would have been incomprehensible as they stand; each of them would have had to be resolved before they made any sense. With the growing sophistication of the human aural consciousness, however, a nineteenth-century audience could accept and understand at least the last of these chords without resolution.

Schoenberg goes so far as to postulate a directing force

behind the gradually widening range of consonances. That directing force, he asserts, is the overtone series.[7]

The overtone series, of course, is the result of a physical phenomenon: the tendency of a string or air column to vibrate in equal parts (halves, thirds, quarters, etc.) at the same time that it is vibrating as a whole. Each vibrating segment produces a pitch distinctly different from that of the original string as a whole or of any other division into segments. Thus, the plucking of a string will produce a whole series of pitches: the division into halves producing the upper octave, the division into thirds sounding a fifth above that, the division into quarters adding the double octave, etc.

Schoenberg's assertion, then, is that, with the passage of time and the growth of sophistication, man has been able to progressively increase his capacity to understand and assimilate the sonorities formed by the division of a string into smaller and smaller parts. In early civilizations, he certainly would maintain, nothing beyond the interval formed by the string as a whole and its division into halves could be understood. In these times, men sang and played in unisons and octaves. Later, the sophistication of the human mind increased to the point where the interval formed by the division of a string into three equal parts became acceptable as a consonance. Then music ran in fifths or fourths as well as octaves. The intervals formed by the divisions into five and six parts (the thirds) were accepted only around the thirteenth century, leading to the tertian harmony with which we are all familiar. So Schoenberg reasons that the judgment that an interval is dissonant at any given time in history merely indicates that the interval lies in an as yet unfamiliar portion of the overtone series. To the average man of the ninth century, for example, the interval formed by the fundamental pitch and the division into five parts (major third) would have seemed totally unfamiliar, therefore incomprehensible and dissonant. By the fifteenth century, on the other hand, this was a perfectly familiar combination of pitches (one could feel so much at home with it that no resolution was required) but the division into seven parts formed an interval which was still incomprehensible.

This gradual exploration of, and familiarization with, the intervals found only in the more remote reaches of the overtone series, Schoenberg maintains, is not just something to be observed in the past, but something which will continue on indefinitely into the future. If human consciousness really is expanding, after all, there seems little reason to believe that it will stop self-contentedly at any particular point in its development. As a result, eventually there will be no such thing as a dissonance. Every possible combination of partials will be familiar, understandable, and therefore consonant.

Schoenberg's own formulation is as follows:

> In my *Harmonielehre* I presented the theory that dissonant tones appear later among the overtones, for which reason the ear is less intimately acquainted with them . . . Closer acquaintance with the more remote consonances—the dissonances, that is—gradually eliminated the difficulty of comprehension and finally admitted not only the emancipation [i.e., disappearance of the need to resolve] of dominant and other seventh chords, diminished sevenths and augmented triads, but also the emancipation of Wagner's, Strauss', Moussorgsky's, Debussy's, Mahler's, Puccini's, and Reger's more remote dissonances.
>
> The term *emancipation of the dissonance* refers to its comprehensibility, which is considered equivalent to the consonance's comprehensibility. A style based on this premise [i.e., of increasing comprehensibility of remore overtones] treats dissonances like consonances and renounces a tonal center.[8]

All of these ideas seem quite clearly and logically organized and easily understandable, with the notable exception of the very last phrase: ". . . and renounces a tonal center." What does the question of consonance and dissonance have to do with the matter of a tonal center? Why would the obliteration of the consonance-dissonance distinction necessarily lead to renunciation of a tonal center?

Perhaps the first impulse is to wonder whether Schoenberg believed that the only function served by the definition of a tonal center was to provide a means of suggesting resolution of dissonance—certainly a far-fetched idea. Something more substantial and logical seems to be involved here, however. In order to reach an understanding of it, it is necessary to examine another of Schoenberg's basic tenets, the doctrine of musical space. His own formulation of this doctrine runs as follows:

> *The two-or-more dimensional space in which musical ideas are presented is a unit.* Though the elements of these ideas appear separate and independent to the eye and the ear, they reveal their true meaning only through their cooperation . . .
>
> The elements of a musical idea are partly incorporated in the hori-

zontal plane as succesive sounds, and partly in the vertical plane as simultaneous sounds. The mutual relation of tones regulates the succession of intervals as well as their association into harmonies . . .[9]

The key sentence in this passage is the last one, which deals with the mutual relations of tones governing harmonic and melodic phenomena. It becomes clear from the entire tenor of Schoenberg's writing that his conception of relations between tones, at least in the music of the so-called period of common practice, is very closely tied in with the notion of the scale. Indeed, the primacy of the scale is a fundamental tenet of theoretical thought from around the turn of this century, and even down to the present day. According to this view, it is the scale that gives logic to the arrangements of musical tones. There are certain laws inherent in the scale, and these are manifested in both harmonic and melodic construction. Because the scale is evident in a melody (that is, because a listener recognizes where the tonic is and where the melody is in relation to it at any time, the listener feels comfortable, he feels oriented, and he knows what is going on. Similarly, it is because the harmony is arranged to point up the inherent properties of the scale that one feels at home and oriented in the harmonic dimension. Thus it is the scale which is the source of logic, or better orientation, for both the melodic and the harmonic aspects of music.

The scale, however, in Schoenberg's view (again, the view behind much speculation of his time [10]) must have seemed a natural derivative of the overtone series. As the more remote reaches of the overtone series became more familiar, then not only would there be less and less of the need to resolve dissonances, but also less and less need to rely upon the recognition of location within a scale to make melodic or harmonic progression intelligible. A particular note or harmony would yield its message directly (i.e., in relation to the other notes or harmonies presented) without any need to be related to its location in the scale. When all members of the overtone series come to be equally well considered and comfortable to us, we can savor and understand any conceivable individual harmony, or any conceivable melodic configuration, just by evaluating its place in and effect upon its immediate context. We would not require the mediation of a suggested relationship to a tonal center to make sense out of it. Thus, any definition of tonal center will become superfluous.

This, then, is how Schoenberg must have arrived at his fundamental position concerning the eventual abolition of the distinction between consonance and dissonance, and hence the eventual renunciation of a tonal center. Here, in the premise regarding the evolution of what might be termed aural consciousness along the lines of the overtone series, and the premise regarding the unity of musical space through the subservience of harmony and melody to the scale, must have been the link between the two seemingly unrelated questions of dissonance treatment and the abolition of tonal center.

Now a man like Arnold Schoenberg would never be satisfied merely to cater to a contemporary audience's taste, or even to follow his own inclinations if they conflicted with his beliefs; he speaks often, after all, of how reluctantly he turned prophet, and how destiny forced him to this position. His appeal would be to the ages. Thus, around 1908, he began to adopt his own program and to write the music of the future, music which played with many kinds of dissonance freely while it refrained from giving much sense of orientation by means of a tonal center.

But Schoenberg does not really seem to have been satisfied with his works of this period. He would present what he considered to be highly evocative musical effects, abruptly juxtaposed in many instances, since he believed that future man would be able to understand the meaning of these effects instantaneously. But he had difficulty weaving these effects into a sustained composition of any duration. He tried using text to suggest continuity over a longer span,[11] but making his chosen art subservient to nonmusical considerations must have been repugnant to a man as innately musical as Schoenberg. Shortly after the close of World War I, his thoughts turned again to theorizing, this time a theorizing that dealt with the logic of progression in a positive way, rather than in the negative manner of his early formulations.

If the scale were to be deemphasized as an agent for orientation, he reasoned, then some other factor would have to be strengthened to compensate. In this way, there would again be a possibility of suggesting relations between moments, a possibility that would be a virtual necessity for a work of any considerable duration. Looking at the established literature, he found one other factor making for intelligibility: thematic relationship. Every masterpiece, Schoenberg seemed to think, is based upon some kind of variation of a single theme. And, indeed, he presents a plausible example of this kind from Beethoven's opus 135 before going into a discussion of his own works.[12]

Now the important thing is not that he made this observation, but that he seems to have assumed that some value attached to this procedure. For he speaks of his own compositional problems in terms suggesting just such an assumption. In discussing his work on the Chamber Symphony opus 9, he mentions having had doubts about the validity of the second theme because it did not seem related to the first. Many years later, he goes on to say, he realized that his instinct in not discarding that theme actually had been correct. With the aid of a few manipulations (inversion, rhythmic changes, omission of notes), he was able to see that he had unconsciously derived that theme from the first one, and therefore, he implies, it was good and suitable.[13]

Thus, Schoenberg reduced musical logic to two factors: scale and thematic relationship. If the influence of scale was undermined, then that of thematic relationship had to be strengthened to provide some sense of logical progression. His solution was to derive all materials from what might be called a basic shape: an ordered series of the twelve different pitches available in the tempered octave. Since any sense of center would tend to make the music sound old-fashioned, it is hardly surprising that a rule was built into this system with the express purpose of preventing any one note from seeming more significant than the other eleven so that it might come to seem a tonic. The rule was to allow no note to appear twice within the basic shape. The basic shape, by the way, is not to be confused with the motivic organization. Rather, it should be considered purely an organization of pitches or, better, of intervals in which rhythmic arrangement was left out of consideration. The rhythm was to be decided upon by superimposing upon this shape a motivic organization not unlike Beethoven's. The motivic organization also might call for the immediate repetition of any note in the basic shape.

In order to insure the relationship between moments, Schoenberg adopted the practice of deriving virtually all of his materials from this basic shape or a permissible variant thereof. The variants permitted are the inversion, the retrograde and the retrograde inversion, as well as any transposition of the whole shape, and octave-multiple transpositions of individual notes within the basic shape. In other words, the order of pitches could be read forward, backward, upside down, or backward and upside down, with any single pitch at any octave, and with the whole starting on any of the twelve tones of the chromatic gamut.

Schoenberg's justification for permitting just these transformations gives something of the idealistic quality of much of his thought, and is thus worth quoting at some length:

> . . . the validity of this form of thinking is also demonstrated by the previously stated law of the unity of musical space, best formulated as follows: *the unity of musical space demands an absolute and unitary perception*. In this space, as in Swedenborg's heaven . . . there is no absolute down, no right or left, forward or backward. Every musical configuration, every movement of tones has to be comprehended primarily as a mutual relation of sounds, of oscillatory vibrations, appearing at different places and times. To the imaginative and creative faculty, relations in the material sphere are as independent from directions or planes as material objects are, in their sphere, to our perceptive faculties. Just as our mind always recognizes, for instance, a knife, a bottle or a watch, regardless of its position, and can reproduce it in the imagination in every possible position, even so a musical creator's mind can operate subconsciously with a row of tones, regardless of their direction, regardless of the way in which a mirror might show the mutual relations, which remain a given quantity.[14]

Thus, the justification seems to be partly a matter of analogy with optical phenomena, and partly a matter of confidence in the ability of the fully evolved aural consciousness to perceive the identity of relations no matter what the order of their presentation.

In line with his theory of the unity of musical space, furthermore, Schoenberg also derived his harmonies from this basic shape. The first chord in a passage, for instance, might contain the first four notes of the basic shape, the next chord the following three notes of the basic shape, and so forth. Or an inversion or retrograde inversion might be used for the derivation of the harmonies.

It is not the mechanics of Schoenberg's system, however, which are so interesting aesthetically, but rather, on the one hand, his belief in the necessity or value of thematic relationship, and, on the other hand, his injection of still another consideration: the basic shape as substitute for the scale. For his feeling seems to have been that once a sequence of pitches was chosen for a composition, it would do more than provide thematic relationship between individual moments; it would also function as a scale, infusing the lines and harmonies—the dimensions of his musical space—with the same properties of logic, coherence—in a word, unity—which the diatonic scale imparts to compositions by Bach, Mozart, Brahms, etc.:

The main advantage of this method of composing with twelve tones is its unifying effect . . .

. . . In music there is no form without logic, there is no logic without unity . . .

I believe that when Richard Wagner introduced his *Leitmotiv*—for the same purpose as that for which I introduced my Basic Set—he may have said: "Let there be unity." [15]

This view also probably was based on an evolutionary conception. Presumably, when aural consciousness had progressed sufficiently, a listener would be able to grasp even an arbitrary arrangement of pitches and recognize where he was within the arrangement—that is, orient himself—much as an eighteenth-century listener would find his bearings by relating melody and harmony to the scale and its center. Just as an eighteenth-century connoisseur might have said (if he verbalized what was essentially a fleeting and intuitive perception) that the melody is now at the supertonic degree of a major scale and the harmony is at the dominant, so a listener of the future might judge that the melody is at the seventh note of the retrograde inversion of the basic shape, while the harmony consists of notes three to ten of the inversion.

Curiously enough, however, Schoenberg apparently believed that this recognition would take place automatically; he did not seem to place any value on recognizing the basic shape and its mutations. When Kolisch wrote to him saying that he had discovered the basic shape in this third string quartet, Schoenberg replied (in a letter dated July 27, 1932) that this was not particularly important; he wished to be remembered as a twelve-tone *composer* rather than as a *twelve-tone* composer.[16] Unless we can assume that Schoenberg was beginning to feel confined by his theory—which seems doubtful—I think we must conclude that he expected the basic shape to accomplish its purpose automatically, that is, to infuse the music with a unity that the fully developed aural consciousness would appreciate without even thinking about it.

At any rate, Schoenberg and his disciples (such as Krenek and Leibowitz) developed an interesting interpretation of an historical process of scalar evolution: the major-minor system ousted the earlier church modes, and, in turn, is now in the process of being displaced by the twelve-tone "scale." [17] It should be noted that this is not advanced as a possibility, or even as a likelihood; rather it is considered an evolutionary certainty.

In condensed form, then, Schoenberg's arguments could be phrased as follows: There are in music certain effects which are comprehensible in themselves, and others which are compehensible only in the light of other effects (resolutions). The range of effects comprehensible in themselves is expanding along lines derived from the overtone series, and will continue to expand indefinitely. Eventually, therefore, all the effects contained within the overtone series will be self-understandable and will require no relational processes to convey their messages.

Two types of effects are influenced by the increasing familiarity with all reaches of the overtone series: the consonance-dissonance distinction, and scalar organization. With increased familiarity of the overtone series, then, the need for relational practices in both these respects must diminish to the point where such practices would become entirely superfluous. Eventually, therefore, no purpose will be served either by resolving dissonances (since all possible combinations of pitches would be self-understandable), or by suggesting relations of pitches to a tonal center (since the pitches would be understood directly in relation to one another without any need for the mediation of a tonal center).

In addition to the scale, unity is effected by another factor: thematic relationship. Since the influence of the relation to a center (a property of the scale) is to vanish in the future, this factor of thematic relationship should be strengthened to retain the qualities of order and coherence. This is to be accomplished by deriving not just the themes, but all pitch relationships (harmonic and melodic), from a predetermined ordering of notes. To facilitate the avoidance of a tonal center such as might make the music sound old-fashioned, the predetermined set of pitches should include all twelve notes available in tempered tuning, and should avoid repetitions of any of these notes. An arrangement of this kind also would develop something of the orientational advantages of a scale.

Schoenberg's prophecies, then, can be said to be based essentially upon three assumptions: that the aural consciousness of the human being is evolving, that the overtone series provides the direction for this evolution, and that the factors making for musical comprehensibility (a term Schoenberg uses interchangeably with unity) can be reduced to scalar and thematic relationships. It is clear, furthermore, that his positive formulations—his ideas concerning the basic shape and the twelve-tone system—can be valid only if all three of these assumptions are demonstrably correct. If any one of these should prove of questionable validity, his predictions and program would come to seem more arbitrary than necessary.

The problem, then, is to determine whether evidence currently available will support these assertions. The additional knowledge gained since the time Schoenberg formulated his theories may well provide some indication of just how justified his position was.

Perhaps the easiest of the assumptions to deal with is the one concerning the reduction of the sources of comprehensibility (unity) to scalar and thematic relationships. With respect to the latter, it should be noted that Schoenberg has in effect made two assertions: that thematic relationship *can* be used to effect a sense of unity, and that it *has been* so used in those compositions that are commonly known as masterworks.

Both of these questions have been treated most perceptively by Jan Nordmark,[18] in relation to very similar assertions advanced by Reti. One of Professor Nordmark's main points is that the criteria by means of which themes are judged to be related or not related are very loose. Indeed, there are few themes that could not be considered related by standards such as these.

It must be admitted, furthermore, that Schoenberg's judgments in this respect are as much open to question as Reti's. Some idea of how much license he was willing to permit can be gained from his own description of the previously mentioned relation between first and second themes in his chamber symphony opus 9.[19] To condense the argument, the first theme of this work is shown in Example 1, with what Schoenberg considered to be the important

Example 1.

notes marked. Example 2 shows how this was (subconsciously)

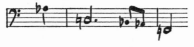

Example 2.

converted to the shape of the second theme by inversion of these important notes.

The question is how Schoenberg came to choose these five notes from among the many notes contained in his first theme as more significant than the others. The first of these, the G♯ (equivalent to the A♭ with which the second theme begins), undoubtedly is important in that it occupies the first strong beat in the theme. The E (which inverts to C) at the beginning of the next measure also can be taken to be important because of its stressed position. But what about all of the notes in between these two? Does it not seem arbitrary, if not capricious, to eliminate all of these from consideration at one stroke? In the second full measure, to continue, the half note G♯ (inverts to A♭) could well be considered significant because of its duration, but the F♯ (inverts to B♭) preceding it is but a fleeting, insignificant passing tone. If Schoenberg could claim that this is an important note, it becomes all the more difficult to see how he could justify omitting all but one of the notes in the first full measure. Similarly, the B (inverts to F) in the third full measure seems anything but significant, particularly because it is touched so fleetingly. There would seem little reason to consider it more significant than, for instance, the A♯ which precedes it.

Thus, there is no apparent rationale to Schoenberg's choice of notes. Neither duration, nor rhythmic stress, nor importance in the contour seems to have entered into his calculations in this respect. One can hardly escape the conclusion that Schoenberg found the relationship between these two themes not because it was there, but because he was looking for it. With this degree of license, of course, the idea of relationship becomes so broad as to be virtually meaningless. Certainly, then, the assertion that thematic relationships have been used in that body of music known as masterworks cannot be taken seriously.

As for the question of whether thematic relationships *can* be used to effect a sense of unity, I would suggest that Schoenberg's formulations in this respect are based upon a semantic confusion. Dr. Nordmark has put his finger upon the source of this confusion admirably:

> . . . Reti and the Schoenberg school use the word unity in two different senses, one very general and one highly specific. In the first, the term indicates that an art work is an organic whole, that "the sum is more than the parts." Second, unity means that one basic thought provides material for an entire work.[20]

It is the unity described in the first of these definitions, of course, that makes for the sense of comprehensibility envisioned by Schoenberg. According to this definition, the various details in a work are less important for their own sake than for their contribution to the effect of the whole. Each event is designed, first and foremost, to fit in with the context as it has already developed to that point, and to contribute to its further unfoldment in a logical and efficient way so that one is left without a question about the purpose served by any particular action. It is in this sense, I would suggest (the sense of being left with no question about purposes served or the line of development being followed) that unity can be considered to increase comprehensibility.

The method adopted by Schoenberg, however, clearly has nothing to do with this conception. It is obviously designed to fulfill the conditions imposed by the second of these definitions, namely, to provide a common source for all the material in a work. How this common derivation might effect a sense of subordination of details to the whole seems something of a mystery. For the sense of aesthetic unity (i.e., of the subordination of details) is a matter of the sequence into which events are arranged rather than of derivations. It results from the efficient functioning of what I have termed the procees of reduction,[21] a process in which more general impressions constantly are being substituted for larger numbers of smaller, more specific ones—essentially a matter of logical sequence, of course. Indeed, it is easily conceivable that a reference to prior material might actually disturb the sense of comprehensibility, or unity, if it seemed inappropriate to the situation as it had developed or if its introduction seemed badly motivated. The key question in determining whether a particular event contributes to aesthetic unity obviously has to do with pertinence rather than with ancestry.

Thus, Schoenberg's linking of aesthetic unity (the kind that makes for comprehensibility) and thematic relationship simply cannot be taken seriously. It is perhaps the result of semantic confusion, as Dr. Nordmark suggests, or possibly a remnant of the interest and belief in the unifying powers of cyclic construction shown by many romantic composers—those, as I have suggested, whose grasp of the problems and possibilities of creating logical sequences of events is by no means beyond question.

Schoenberg's second source of comprehensibility, the scale, also seems rather puzzling. This is not to deny that the scale is a help in determining one's orientation in relation to the cadence in a great deal of music. Everyone knows how much of a help it is in the typical Verdi cadence shown in Example 3. But it is difficult to see just why so much significance should be attached to the kind

Example 3.

of mutual relations between tones implicit in Schoenberg's conception of the scale, when the function of a given pitch in a melodic line, or of a given harmony in a progression, may be changed merely by the repetition of certain notes, or by altering duration, rhythmic emphasis, or position. Repetition of a given note, for instance, may cause it to be recognized as something in the nature of a tonic (a point of reference against which other moves are measured) despite the fact that that pitch obviously does not represent the starting point for those arrangements of tones and semitones known as the major and minor scales. In certain circumstances, furthermore, pausing upon a note will make it sound like a supertonic which is about to resolve to tonic—a device frequently employed by Ockeghem in shaping his basses.[22] To cite just one more instance of this kind, the passage shown in Example 4 would

Example 4.

seem to define C as tonic. If, however, the positions of the last two notes were exchanged, the D probably would come to seem the tonic, the point of repose. On the other hand, if the last three notes were exchanged as shown in Example 5, F obviously would be the tonic.

Example 5.

Similar considerations apply to harmonic orientation. A triad that has been heard very often—perhaps as a base against which several excursions unfold—may come to carry the sense of a tonic even if it is never approached by way of a dominant and obviously is not the first chord in either a major or a minor scale. Similarly, dwelling upon a chord or consistently introducing a caesura after it may well tend to define it as tonic, no matter where it lies in the scale. As simple a thing as introducing an up-beat to down-beat rhythm may help lend a sense of tonic to the second chord.

The point is that all of these definitions of function can be achieved without introducing a new pitch; the relationship between pitches has not changed, yet it has been possible to produce quite different interpretations of where the tonic lay. If durational and positional factors can exert so profound an influence upon the assignment of tonic function—the function that is the very essence of the scalar relationships—it is difficult to see how orientation can be considered purely a matter of relations between tones.

Of course, a follower of Schoenberg could object that the variants I have introduced actually constitute violations of the laws of the scale—an entirely inadmissible reversion to a modal practice long since discarded in the evolutionary process. These might be considered clumsy applications of a valid law rather than legitimate usages which call the law into question. The fact remains, however, that the psychological impression of a frame of reference or point of repose—the essential characteristics of the conception of a tonic—can be created and modified by means of procedures having nothing at all to do with scalar relations. And there seems little ground for asserting that practices such as these are outmoded or in any way inferior in effect to those produced by dominant-tonic relationships. Indeed, such a view seems little more than a reflection of the smugness often considered characteristic of the late nineteenth-century mentality.

Perhaps the artificiality of Schoenberg's reduction of the sources of comprehensibility to scalar and thematic relationships can best be brought home by some simple experiments. Imagine a performance of a work by Beethoven in which all dynamic gradations were suppressed—the whole being presented at an even mezzoforte. Or imagine a work by J. S. Bach in which no rests were permitted and in which all rhythmic gradations were eliminated, every voice moving evenly in quarter notes. The result in either case would be far removed from the eloquence and coherence suggested by the original composition. Certainly other influences for order must be at work in these compositions if the elimination of such entities as rhythmic gradation, rests, and changes in volume can damage the sense of logical flow so badly. In fact, as was brought out in earlier chapters, if one were to try to find one principle governing the construction and the interest in all of this music, it would have to be the play of intensity rather than thematic or scalar relationships. Tonality and thematic identification probably should be considered only expedients designed to set in motion and effect a process of intensification.

Thus, the reduction of the sources of comprehensibility to scalar and thematic relationships seems completely unjustified. If its implications were to be followed out strictly in performance (i.e., by suppressing other constructive factors), the effect would be to make highly eloquent masterworks into almost unintelligible sequences of sound. In addition, it is clear that the factors of scalar and thematic relationships, which Schoenberg supposed would account for the comprehensibility, actually seem to be far from preponderantly significant in this respect. This one of Schoenberg's fundamental assumptions, then, must be considered totally invalid.

The second of the fundamental assumptions, the one concerning the overtone series, is presented in a formulation that seems almost bizarre in the context of modern, more or less scientific modes of thought. Indeed, his conception seems a direct outgrowth of eighteenth-century speculations.

Schoenberg apparently believed that the overtone series was the progenitor of the scale, but not in any direct way. In an interview with Merle Armitage,[23] he asserted that the major scale resulted from the addition of the tones of the three main triads (tonic, subdominant, and dominant). Thus, the C-major scale would draw C from tonic, D from dominant, E from tonic, F from subdominant, G either from tonic or dominant, A from subdominant, and B from dominant. These tones, he goes on to say, represent the fourth, fifth, and sixth partials of the three fundamental degrees (tonic, subdominant, and dominant). These three fundamental degrees, in turn, are related by the fact that each one occurs as the third overtone of the one lying a fifth below it, so that c' is the third overtone of F, just as g'' is the third overtone of c'.

Interestingly enough, Schoenberg believed that these relationships could be sensed:

> The natural origin of these fundamentals of the main degrees, of the three main triads constructed on them, and of the resultant major scale from these components, as well as the circumstance that we actually to some extent hear and to some extent feel this relationship in every sounding tone . . .[24]

In physical terms, this would seem to imply something like the following line of argument. A sounding fundamental produces six audible pitches: let us say *C, c, g, c', e'*, and *g'*. The third of these, however, would itself act as a fundamental and generate another series of six pitches: *g, g', d'', g'', b''*, and *d'''*. Finally, the third of these pitches also would act as a fundamental and generate six pitches of its own: *d'', d''', a''', d'''', f♯'''''*, and *a''''*. The G-major scale, then, would be obtained by combining all these notes, with octave transpositions, of course. The ear, furthermore, perceives each of these relationships to some extent.

Clearly there is an element of the arbitrary to this kind of formulation. Why, after all, should only the third partial act as a fundamental and generate another series? Why not the fifth partial as well? Even more to the point, why should each of these series be cut off after the sixth partial? For a string sounding the pitch C generates not only the tones *c, g, c', e'*, and *g'* mentioned by Schoenberg, but also a *b♭'* that is considerably flatter than the one incorporated in the tempered scale, another *c''*, a *d''*, etc. Why not include these also? Their omission certainly cannot be due to inaudibility, since Schoenberg asserts, in effect, that the forty-fifth partial is recognized by the ear (an *f♯''''* which is the fifth partial of the third partial of the third partial of the fundamental C in the above discussion). If this were granted, how could inaudibility of merely the seventh partial be justified?

I think we must conclude, then, that the cut-off after the sixth partial was arbitrary. Inasmuch as the next partial provides a note which doesn't fit into anyone's system of tuning or consonance, it seems safe to say that at this point the physical reality and the aesthetic experience have parted ways. This, in turn, suggests that the correspondence between aesthetic preference and the physical law underlying the overtone series was a coincidence all along; that we have only projected a hierarchy of aesthetic values onto the physical fact of the overtone series; that this series never was of any real significance in the processes of scale-building or consonance-dissonance distinctions.[25]

If the overtone series has so little to do with matters aesthetic, and cannot even be shown to govern the formation of the major scale in any convincing manner, it seems most unlikely that it would act as the directing force behind an ongoing process of evolution. If it does not even give evidence of having entered into the formation of presently used scales and practices, how can one reasonably assert that its influence is to prevail in the future? Thus, the second of Schoenberg's fundamental assumptions seems at least highly questionable. Indeed, his reasoning is so shot through with inconsistencies and irrelevancies that it is difficult to find any reason at all for taking his formulations in this respect very seriously.

Schoenberg's remaining assumption (that human aural consciousness is evolving) seems to be based upon historical observation. At least it is difficult to imagine why anyone would formulate an evolutionary doctrine about music unless there was some historical data that would seem to require "explanation" in this way. He and his followers, at any rate, consistently refer to three historical developments as offering evidence in support of an evolutionary interpretation: the late admission of the thirds to the ranks of consonances, the displacement of the ecclesiastical modes by the major and minor scales, and the general growth in the use of dissonance and chromaticism through the late nineteenth century.

Now if a theory of this kind is to be invested with any more significance than that attached to idle speculation, it must be shown to be one of the most plausible of possible views. It should account for the phenomena observed in a more satisfactory way than other conceivable theories.

With respect to these three developments in particular, I would suggest that this simply is not the case. Knowledge acquired since the time Schoenberg formulated his theories indicates that each of these developments represents a rather complex question, a question probably influenced by sociological factors and by changes in conceptions of value, as well as by the necessarily inadequate store of information available to the historian. The conditions are so involved and so much hidden by insufficiency of data, indeed, that a self-respecting historian probably would hesitate to attempt any conclusive formulation of the mechanics of these changes.

A number of interpretive possibilities have been raised, however, which seem more closely related to the facts now at hand than would any sweeping attribution to so amorphous a conception as evolution. The theory has been advanced, for example, that a tuning problem may have been responsible for the late admission of the third. Professor Hans-Heinz Draeger suggests that the major third consigned to the ranks of the dissonances by medieval theorists was the interval obtained by Pythagorean tuning (ratio 81:64) —a sound which is considerably less gratifying than the just third (ratio 5:4), even to present-day audiences, when the two notes forming the interval are presented simultaneously.[26] On the other hand, Professor Draeger reports that this size of major third is invariably the one preferred when the two notes forming it are presented successively. He claims, further, that the Pythagorean third is so much better suited than the just to melodic construction that it virtually always has been used in monophonic music; conversely, the just third has always been the one used in harmonically oriented music: "historically monophony has generally called for the cyclic [i.e., Pythagorean] third, whereas part-music has generally called for the divisive [i.e., just] third." [27]

Thus, it may well have been a problem, or possibly some confusion, engendered by the gradual transition from monophonic to harmonic ways of thinking that brought about the late acceptance of the thirds. Or, as Dr. Draeger has put it: "The medieval theorists and composers were correct in calling the simultaneous cyclic (Pythagorean) third a dissonance. . . . It is not the human ear that has changed down the years; it is the thirds." [28]

Another argument that might bear upon this question is more sociological in nature. It may well have been that people of the middle ages associated the same qualities with the thirds (at least the just thirds) that we do today—let us call them "sweet" for convenience—but that this type of evocation may not have been socially acceptable for some time. Perhaps the evocations of these intervals were considered too lascivious, or too seductive in drawing the contemplating mind away from heavenly delights, or too much in conflict with the church's authority. Church authority, after all, supported a view of consonance formulated at a time when polyphony did not exist, and in which value was derived as much from numerological speculations concerning the inherent order behind the universe as from aesthetic qualities of sensuous pleasure.[29] It may well have been, then, that the theorists who first admitted the third into the ranks of the consonances were simply recognizing the fact that a new standard of value was assuming influence: sensuous gratification. Interestingly enough, similar developments seem to have taken place in the practice of the graphic arts at approximately this same time.

The displacement of the ecclesiastical modes by the major and minor scales also can be explained plausibly without reference to any hypothetical evolution of aural consciousness. For one of the distinctive features of the major and minor scales is the possibility of using the sonority of the tritone to create a sense of driving toward the final, where this is not possible if the intervallic structure of the ecclesiastical modes is adhered to strictly. As I pointed out in Chapter 3, no one really knows why, but the tritone seems to carry a connotation, for Western listeners, of a tension that can be resolved satisfactorily in only one way: by motion to a triad one-half step above one of its notes. Thus, the combination B-F virtually requires resolution to a triad whose root is C.[30]

As long as attention was focused on the designs of individual lines within a texture, this tritone drive offered no particular advantages. But once composers began to place more emphasis on the design of the texture as a whole—the harmonic logic, we would call it—the tritone drive became most useful since it could suggest that the texture as a whole was moving purposefully (i.e., toward a cadential release of tension). It is thus perhaps more than coincidental that composers came to modify modal arrangements to produce major and minor scales just at the time when the new conception of texture began to make itself felt.

It may well have been a sense of advantage, then, an advantage traceable to the new harmonic conception of texture, that led to the general adoption of the major and minor scales, and not a matter of inevitability. Thus there seems little reason for preferring an evolutionary interpretation here either.

As for the third evolutionary argument, the growing use of dissonance and chromaticism through the late nineteenth century, all that can be said is that there is only one way that Schoenberg could have arrived at such a belief: by examining the music of two or three selected composers (Bach and Wagner, perhaps), and shutting his eyes to the practices of the rest. For it is difficult to see how one could very well consider Beethoven either a more chromatic or a more dissonant composer than Bach. Certainly Bach used dissonance far more frequently than Beethoven, and, if anything, was far less fussy about resolutions. Occasionally bold chromatic strokes in Beethoven, furthermore, can be more than matched by equally arresting moves in Bach. This applies equally well, if not better, to Haydn, Mozart, and the other composers of the latter part of the eighteenth century. It is difficult to see how any conception of a general pattern of increasing use of dissonance or chromaticism can be justified. Schoenberg appears to have projected the romantic taste for more and more interesting harmonic colors into past eras.

All of these considerations must raise some doubts about the wisdom of viewing history in evolutionary terms. And, if one examines other historical deveolpments, these doubts are more than confirmed. Even the limited knowledge available today makes it clear that stylistic changes have occurred frequently in the history of Western music, and that these changes are not usually in the nature of increasing refinement of a basic approach, but rather involve changes in emphasis. Sometime between the seventh and eleventh centuries—possibly earlier—a melodic art of considerable refinement flourished. At least some of the people responsible for the creation of what are now known as the Gregorian melodies appear to have known exactly how to balance melodic curves in a very subtle, sophisticated, and yet clearly perceptible way. If one examines the Introit Antiphon for the first Sunday in Advent, *Ad te levavi,* for instance, one can hardly avoid the impression that this single line embodies a superbly conceived and executed drama in miniature. Each of the archlike curves into which this line can be divided seems to contribute almost perfectly to the sense of unfolding dramatic action, carrying further the move toward increased tension, easing the level of tension, subjecting the resolving tendency to greater strain, etc.—all in a most convincing way. The calculations of this composer—and this is by no means an exceptional composition in this repertory—were sure and skilled. The result is that one can feel a sense of logical progress from curve to curve as the dramatic situation is built up.

In the twelfth and thirteenth centuries, all of this highly sophisticated melodic art was abandoned. The melodies of this time become thin, stilted, and repetitive, as composers apparently shifted their attention to something else, something which had not been much exploited before these centuries: polyphonic rhythmic organization. In the fourteenth century, after a considerable development of rhythmic skills and capabilities, a new art based on a fusion of rhythmic differentiation and concern for melodic design came into being—the secular polyphonic art of Machaut discussed in Chapter 2. Toward the end of the fourteenth century, composers appear to become carried away with their new rhythmic possibilities as they were developing an art of extreme rhythmic complexity and subtlety. And then at the start of the fifteenth century this approach was abandoned—a dead end again—apparently because the composers became interested in another new possibility, one involving the blending of voices in a texture to form a kind of harmonic effect. Indeed, a harmonic logic of great refinement emerged toward the end of the fifteenth century, as was suggested in Chapter 3, to be lost again in the sixteenth, when composers turned their attention to textual expression and, as a tool for accomplishing this, chromaticism.

So history is full of dead ends. Particular lines of thought or practice undergo refinement only to a point and then are discarded as composers seem to tire of them, or else to seek territory less worked over. That an evolutionary doctrine could be reconciled with these data seems highly unlikely.

Indeed, there is something in the nature of the conception of evolution that would make its application to anything like what I have termed the development of aural consciousness rather dubious. For the conception of evolution must necessarily be tied in with some kind of plausible explanation of how the whole system works. Darwin's theory, for instance, is based upon the idea of natural selection, according to which only the species that can adapt to their environments and conditions for subsistence would survive. Even after he had formulated his theories, Darwin still was not satisfied with his work because he could advance no satisfactory explanation for the way the characteristics of a species might undergo change—a problem resolved, to some degree, by Mendel.

What kind of mechanism of natural selection can be offered in connection with the idea of musical evolution? Little survival value, after all, can be attached to the development of a keen aural consciousness or of the ability to understand directly the relationships presented by the more remote reaches of the overtone series. The idea of a competition for limited food supplies, or of a continual conflict between predators, or even of a difference in ability to adapt to environment between the aurally developed on the one hand, and the aurally underdeveloped on the other, seems ludicrous. That the former should be consistently victorious in this struggle seems an unrealistic assertion. It is clear, then, that Schoenberg was generalizing the practical biological conception of evolution to a metaphysical principle which was supposed to permeate all of nature. Such a generalization would have been easy enough to justify during the late nineteenth century, when Schoenberg's ideas were being formed, but is difficult to accept in the context of present-day thought.

Each of Schoenberg's assumptions, then, seems at least arbitrary. There is little reason to believe that human aural consciousness is evolving in any particular direction, let alone in the direction outlined by the overtone series, and there can be no question but that the reduction of the sources of comprehensibility to scalar and thematic relationships was not justified. What grounds remain, then, for any confidence in the prophecies of Arnold Schoenberg?

Perhaps the element of his thought most directly jeopardized by the weaknesses of his assumptions is that concerning the use of a basic shape—the row, as it is usually termed. For this conception is so intimately bound up with Schoenberg's historical thought (it is so obviously designed to satisfy the conditions he projected into the future) that any flaws in his interpretation immediately would call its validity into question.

Certainly it must be admitted that the basic shape could not accomplish what Schoenberg assumed it would. It is hardly conceivable that it could have served as a means for effecting comprehensibility, since the notion of comprehensibility envisioned by Schoenberg is largely a matter of the sequence into which events are arranged rather than a matter of common origins. Indeed, the influence of a row is so subtle, that it goes virtually unperceived by most present-day musicians. How, then, could it possibly be considered a source of comprehensibility? I think that one would have to be either so idealistically inclined as to discount the role of perception in musical value—a position that I suspect few would care to defend today—or else willing to credit the idea that aural consciousness eventually will reach a state of perfection, in order to maintain belief in the efficacy of the basic shape in this respect.

There is also another sense in which the device of the basic shape does not seem to fulfill Schoenberg's expectations. For it really does not guarantee that any sense of tonic will be avoided. By choice of the order of the twelve tones and of the transpositions used, as well as by the emphasis that may be imparted by rhythmic organization and by the immediate repetition permitted in the system, it is quite possible to suggest that a particular note dominates a passage, a section, or an entire composition.

This is not to suggest that the use of the row may not have served such a function to a generation of composers so indoctrinated with nineteenth-century conceptions of harmony as to require some such crutch to avoid falling into familiar patterns based upon the idea of tonic definition. But that it should continue to serve this purpose when nineteenth-century modes of thought have been discarded seems open to question. It is perfectly feasible to write music in which the definition of a tonic is unimportant or avoided altogether without recourse to the row, just as it is possible to write tonic-defining music by means of this device. It is difficult, then, to see what value can be attached to it in this respect either.

In another respect, however, Schoenberg does seem to have

spoken in truly prophetic accents. He recognized that the musical thought current during his early years had reached a *cul-de-sac,* and that one would have to strike out boldly in new directions to avoid the automatic and unthinking application of established procedures that would bring about a sense of posturing in music. He realized that music need not be limited largely to triadic conceptions of harmony (as it had been for some five centuries), and that every chord did not have to be interpreted as tonic, dominant, or subdominant. Along with other musical thinkers of this time, Schoenberg opened new vistas in the more expressive use of harmony: the quartal harmonies, the chords built on seconds, those various combinations which cannot really be reduced to simpler models or even catalogued, but which seem appropriate for specific situations. All of these likely would not have come into general use without the activity of Arnold Schoenberg. In a very real sense, he worked to free the harmonic element from the romantic clichés of chromatic alteration and continual modulation on the one hand, and from the restriction to tonic-dominant relationships on the other. If not for Schoenberg, Karl Goldmark and Richard Strauss might still today be considered among the foremost of the modern composers.

It must be admitted, furthermore, that his initial conclusions seem to have been borne out strikingly thus far in the twentieth century. For a great many composers—even those who are not direct followers of Schoenberg—clearly treat all dissonances as consonances (that is, they do not take pains to resolve them), and either pay little attention to definition of a tonic, or else avoid it completely.

In a sense, then, Schoenberg seems a genuine prophet, much in the spirit of the Old Testament: he recognized a situation that required remedial action and he advocated such action most forcefully. That he ran into difficulty trying to formulate a positive program that would effect the needed reforms can be traced to his inability to rise above the nineteenth-century modes of thought which dominated most of Europe during his formative years. His concept of musical evolution, after all, bears a decided resemblance to the kind of social Darwinism so widely accepted during the latter part of the nineteenth century and the early part of the twentieth. Both are characterized by an uncritical acceptance of an idea formulated to account for discoveries in another and quite alien field, without pause to consider whether there was an appropriate equivalence of rationale—a reasoning by analogies rather than by a combination of inductive and deductive processes.

Similarly, Schoenberg's exaggeration of the importance of the scale seems little more than an echo of the kind of overly abstract theorizing characteristic of a good deal of the writing of the late nineteenth century. To reduce so many complex phenomena and relationships as are to be found, for example, in a composition by Beethoven or Wagner to a set of "laws" inherent in the major-minor scalar system—the natural approach of nineteenth-century writers —seems virtually inconceivable today. The undue stress upon the factor of thematic relationship, finally, probably was a reflection of the romantic preoccupation with cyclic techniques.

There is one more respect in which Schoenberg remained bound to the thought of the nineteenth century: that is, in relation to the conception of continuity. Schoenberg seems to have trusted to his device of the basic shape to carry the element of continuity (the narrative element, in his music); that is, to suggest that individual events are strung together in so logical and compelling a way that suspense as to the outcome might grow as the composition unfolds. If, as I think I have shown, this expectation seems unfounded, it might just be that the element of continuity did not play a significant role in his thinking.

This, I would venture to suggest, is precisely the impression left by much of Schoenberg's music. Even in his very early works, different materials are juxtaposed abruptly, often in bizarre ways, suggesting sudden and strange shifts in mood. There is little evidence of an attempt to generate trends or to set up and intensify any basic mood, or to create a play between just a few basic moods. Every moment seems to bring its own message, which does not add to previous messages to produce a sense of narration, but which rather introduces a quality of shock. So frequent are the shocks, indeed, that there can be little chance for any sense of cumulation to develop; for each shock tends to focus attention on itself—on its own unexpected qualities—and thereby draw attention away from any role it might play in a larger design.

This apparently was what Schoenberg expected. He must have believed that listeners would understand the implications of individual effects and the associations they would call forth. Each interval, each chord, each melodic leap, each dynamic gradation, and each combination of any or all of these factors (or more) would call up a certain state of mind. All the composer need do is juxtapose states of mind, ordinarily in a rather bizarre way. Value was a matter of recognizing the various states of mind and coming to appreciate the condition in the soul of another human being. In a way, this seems an approach to the human condition similar to that formulated by another compatriot and contemporary, Sigmund Freud.

It is the deemphasis of the narrative element, I would suggest, that ties Schoenberg to the intellectual legacy of the romantic century: the absorption in the individual evocative effect, the seeking satisfaction in the moment. Indeed, he seems not only to have adopted this romantic approach, but to have pushed it to its limits. For he did not base his art, as the romantics did, on effects that were sure to elicit strong and agreeable associations. He simply seems to have assumed that any and every effect would evoke some sort of response; whether it would prove attractive or not was unimportant. It was his business as a composer merely to choose from among all possible effects those which he felt best corresponded to his own state of mind. The value presumably lay in the confession of a soul and the listener's sympathetic understanding of it, rather than in any great human issues.

As a prophet, then, Schoenberg falls somewhat short of biblical standards. He was able to recognize that the situation of his time required reform, and could even sketch out some of the remedial actions needed. He was too closely bound to the thought patterns of his own day, however—the thought patterns against which he was attempting to revolt—to be able to formulate a workable program which would truly accomplish the refreshment of the sources of musical creativity that he so earnestly desired.

APPENDICES

APPENDIX A: *Phrases in the chorale harmonizations by Bach in which the bass can be reduced to the shapes of scale, arch, or inverted arch.*

In this appendix and those following, each chorale harmonization is designated by the number assigned to it in the Breitkopf and Kalmus editions. The figures to the right of a decimal point refer to the number of the phrase. With the exception of the cases noted in footnote 15 of Chapter 5, a phrase is considered to be defined by each fermata. Thus, for instance, the second phrase in a particular chorale is the one lying between the first and second fermate.

1.2, 1.3, 1.6, 2.2, 2.5, 3.1, 3.2, 3.5, 4.3, 5.1, 5.3, 5.4, 6.4, 7.2, 7.3, 7.5, 7.6, 8.1, 8.2, 8.3, 8.6, 8.7, 8.8, 9.3, 9.4, 9.6, 10.4, 11.2, 11.4, 11.12, 13.1, 13.4, 13.6, 14.4, 14.7, 15.4, 15.5, 16.1, 16.4, 17.2, 18.2, 20.1, 20.2, 20.5, 20.6, 21.2, 21.3, 21.5, 21.6, 22.1, 22.3, 22.4, 22.5, 23.2, 23.3, 23.4, 23.5, 24.4, 24.6, 25.1, 25.2, 25.3, 26.4, 26.5, 27.5, 28.2, 28.4, 29.1, 29.3, 29.4, 30.3, 31.1, 31.2, 31.4, 32.5, 35.2, 36.4, 37.1, 37.5, 39.1, 39.3, 39.5, 40.3, 40.6, 44.1, 44.2, 45.1, 47.1, 47.3, 48.3, 49.2, 49.5, 49.6, 50.3, 50.4, 50.6, 51.3, 52.3, 52.7, 53.4, 55.4, 57.3, 57.5, 58.2, 58.3, 59.2, 60.1, 60.2, 60.3, 60.5, 60.6, 61.1, 61.2, 61.6, 61.8, 62.3, 63.3, 63.4, 63.6, 64.1, 64.2, 64.5, 65.2, 66.5, 67.3, 67.6, 69.7, 69.11, 70.3, 70.9, 71.1, 71.3, 71.4, 71.7, 72.4, 73.1, 73.2, 73.3, 74.1, 74.2, 74.5, 74.6, 76.1, 76.2, 76.3, 76.6, 78.4, 79.1, 79.6, 80.2, 80.4, 80.5, 80.6, 81.1, 81.5, 81.6, 81.8, 82.2, 82.5, 82.7, 83.2, 83.6, 83.8, 84.3, 85.4, 85.8, 86.2, 86.3, 86.7, 87.2, 89.1, 89.4, 90.3, 90.4, 91.1, 91.7, 91.9, 92.1, 92.2, 92.3, 94.3, 94.5, 95.4, 97.4, 98.2, 98.4, 98.6, 99.5, 99.6, 100.2, 100.4, 100.5, 101.3, 101.4, 103.3, 103.4, 103.6, 104.3, 105.1, 105.4, 106.3, 106.7, 106.8, 107.6, 108.3, 108.4, 108.6, 109.7, 110.3, 110.6, 112.3, 113.1, 113.8, 114.5, 115.2, 115.6, 116.4, 116.6, 116.8, 117.3, 117.4, 117.5, 117.6, 118.2, 119.4, 119.7, 120.5,

120.6, 121.1, 122.4, 122.5, 122.6, 122.7, 123.3, 125.2, 125.4, 127.1, 127.5, 128.6, 130.2, 131.1, 131.4, 132.2, 132.16, 132.18, 134.1, 134.3, 134.4, 135.2, 135.6, 135.8, 137.1, 137.2, 137.5, 139.1, 139.4, 140.2, 140.3, 141.1, 142.2, 142.6, 142.8, 144.1, 145.1, 145.2, 145.3, 146.1, 146.2, 146.3, 146.4, 147.3, 148.2, 149.3, 149.4, 150.4, 152.6, 153.4, 155.2, 155.3, 155.4, 155.6, 156.1, 158.1, 158.2, 158.5, 158.6, 158.7, 159.3, 160.3, 161.3, 162.3, 162.5, 162.6, 165.1, 165.2, 165.3, 166.1, 166.7, 167.6, 167.7, 168.2, 169.2, 169.4, 169.5, 169.7, 170.1, 171.2, 171.4, 171.7, 171.8, 172.1, 172.2, 172.4, 172.6, 173.4, 173.6, 174.1, 174.5, 175.1, 175.4, 176.4, 177.2, 179.4, 180.1, 180.2, 181.1, 182.1, 182.3, 182.5, 183.1, 184.1, 184.2, 184.4, 185.1, 185.4, 186.2, 187.2, 189.2, 189.3, 193.5, 194.5, 196.6, 197.4, 197.7, 197.16, 198.5, 200.1, 200.2, 200.4, 200.6, 200.7, 200.8, 201.4, 201.7, 201.8, 201.9, 202.2, 202.4, 202.7, 203.2, 203.4, 203.6, 205.4, 205.11, 205.16, 206.4, 206.7, 208.3, 210.5, 210.6, 211.3, 212.3, 212.4, 212.5, 212.7, 213.3, 214.8, 214.10, 215.1, 215.4, 215.8, 216.5, 216.6, 216.9, 218.1, 218.6, 220.1, 221.1, 221.3, 221.4, 221.5, 222.1, 223.8, 224.4, 225.1, 225.3, 227.6, 227.7, 228.1, 229.6, 230.1, 231.4, 233.2, 233.3, 233.4, 233.6, 235.1, 235.5, 235.8, 236.4, 237.4, 237.8, 238.3, 238.4, 239.1, 240.2, 242.6, 244.1, 244.2, 244.3, 246.3, 246.4, 247.2, 248.2, 248.4, 248.5, 249.2, 250.1, 250.2, 250.3, 250.5, 250.6, 251.2, 252.4, 252.6, 252.8, 253.1, 253.2, 253.5, 254.1, 254.2, 254.6, 255.8, 258.3, 258.4, 260.2, 260.4, 260.5, 261.1, 262.1, 262.2, 262.3, 263.1, 263.6, 264.2, 264.6, 266.1, 266.2, 266.3, 267.2, 267.3, 269.1, 269.5, 270.6, 271.4, 272.2, 272.5, 272.6, 273.2, 273.3, 273.5, 275.3, 275.4, 278.2, 278.3, 279.3, 280.3, 280.4, 281.2, 284.3, 285.1, 285.2, 286.2, 287.1, 288.2, 289.3, 289.6, 290.5, 291.2, 291.6, 291.8, 292.3, 292.4, 292.5, 292.6, 293.2, 293.5, 294.1, 294.2, 294.5, 296.3, 296.6, 296.10, 297.7, 298.1, 298.2, 299.5, 301.1, 301.2, 303.3, 303.4, 304.1, 304.2, 304.4, 304.6, 310.2, 310.4, 311.2, 311.4, 311.6, 312.8, 314.3, 314.4, 314.6, 315.2, 315.6, 316.3, 316.5, 317.2, 321.7, 322.3, 322.4, 322.6, 323.2, 323.3, 323.7, 324.1, 324.4, 325.1, 325.3, 325.5, 325.6, 326.2, 329.1, 331.2, 331.3, 332.2, 332.5, 333.7, 335.2, 335.3, 335.4, 336.1, 336.2, 336.4, 337.3, 337.6, 337.8, 338.2, 339.3, 339.4, 340.6, 341.2, 341.3, 341.6, 341.8, 343.3, 343.5, 343.6, 345.2, 345.4, 345.5, 347.1, 347.2, 348.1, 350.3, 350.4, 351.1, 351.6, 352.4, 352.5, 355.3, 355.6, 360.3, 362.4, 362.5, 363.3, 363.4, 363.6, 365.2, 365.3, 365.4, 366.1, 366.6, 367.1, 367.2, 367.5, 367.6, 370.4.

APPENDIX B: *Phrases in the chorale harmonizations by Bach in which the bass represents a moderately embellished scale, arch, or inverted arch.*

1.1, 1.5, 2.4, 2.6, 4.2, 6.1, 9.5, 10.3, 11.9, 11.10, 12.2, 13.7, 14.6, 15.1, 16.5, 19.1, 19.2, 19.3, 19.5, 22.6, 24.1, 24.5, 25.5, 26.1, 26.2, 27.3, 27.4, 28.1, 28.3, 30.2, 31.5, 33.1, 33.3. 33.4, 34.3, 34.6, 35.1, 35.3, 35.4, 36.1, 36.3, 36.6, 37.4, 39.4, 39.6, 41.5, 46.1, 46.3, 47.5, 48.4, 48.5, 49.1, 51.1, 58.4, 58.5, 59.1, 61.4, 61.5, 62.1, 62.2, 64.4, 66.6, 66.7, 67.4, 68.4, 69.1, 69.4,

69.9, 70.2, 70.5, 71.6, 72.2, 73.5, 75.2, 76.5, 77.2, 77.6, 79.2, 81.7, 83.3,
85.5, 89.6, 90.1, 91.2, 91.3, 92.5, 95.2, 95.3, 95.5, 95.6, 96.3, 96.4, 96.5,
97.6, 99.3, 101.2, 103.2, 104.1, 104.4, 105.2, 106.6, 109.2, 110.5, 112.2,
114.3, 115.3, 115.5, 116.2, 116.7, 116.10, 119.8, 119.9, 120.2, 121.6,
123.4, 123.5, 125.5, 127.4, 129.2, 129.4, 129.5, 131.2, 132.9, 132.12,
133.3, 133.7, 133.10, 133.13, 134.6, 135.3, 137.6, 138.2, 138.5, 138.6,
139.8, 140.6, 142.4, 142.5, 143.1, 143.8, 144.2, 144.3, 145.5, 148.1,
148.4, 149.1, 151.1, 151.3, 153.2, 153.6, 156.2, 156.3, 157.3, 158.8,
161.1, 163.1, 163.2, 164.1, 164.4, 166.4, 166.6, 167.4, 169.3, 169.8,
170.4, 172.3, 173.7, 176.2, 177.4, 179.2, 179.5, 183.4, 183.5, 188.2,
188.4, 189.4, 190.1, 190.2, 190.3, 192.2, 194.1, 196.4, 197.2, 198.7,
202.9, 205.8, 205.18, 205.22, 205.23, 206.9, 208.6, 209.4, 210.4, 211.5,
213.1 213.2, 213.4, 214.1, 215.2, 215.3, 215.5, 215.9, 215.10, 218.3,
218.4, 220.3, 220.4, 221.2, 222.6, 225.5, 227.2, 227.5, 227.8, 230.2,
232.8, 239.2, 239.4, 240.3, 241.2, 241.3, 241.4, 242.5, 243.5, 244.7,
246.1, 246.2, 247.3, 249.3, 249.5, 251.1, 251.4, 251.5, 252.1, 252.2,
252.7, 252.10, 254.4, 255.2, 255.3, 255.4, 255.5, 255.6, 258.6, 258.8,
260.1, 261.4, 263.2, 264.1, 265.4, 265.5, 267.1, 267.4, 267.5, 267.6,
268.2, 268.3, 268.4, 269.3, 269.6, 270.5, 271.1, 271.2, 274.2, 275.2,
276.1, 276.3, 277.5, 277.6, 277.9, 279.6, 281.1, 281.4, 285.3, 287.2,
287.3, 287.4, 288.1, 288.4, 289.2, 289.5, 291.1, 297.5, 298.5, 299.1,
299.2, 301.3, 301.5, 303.2, 303.5, 312.2, 312.3, 312.4, 312.5, 312.6,
316.1, 316.4, 317.3, 321.4, 322.2, 323.6, 324.5, 329.2, 329.3, 329.5,
330.5, 331.1, 331.4, 332.6, 333.5, 335.5, 337.1, 337.2, 337.5, 340.1,
342.3, 343.2, 343.4, 350.2, 350.6, 351.3, 352.1, 352.2, 352.3, 352.7,
355.1, 355.5, 356.2, 357.1, 359.5, 359.7, 360.6, 362.1, 364.1, 364.6,
366.3, 368.4, 369.4, 369.6, 370.3, 370.5, 370.6, 371.1, 371.2.

APPENDIX C: *Phrases in the chorale harmonizations by Bach in which
the bass consists of a series of scales suggesting amplification or condensation.*

3.3, 16.2, 30.1, 30.4, 34.4, 37.3, 41.1, 45.5, 52.4, 52.6, 55.3, 56.3, 77.3,
83.5, 86.1, 122.3, 124.3, 132.11, 132.14, 133.2, 181.3, 181.4, 192.3,
199.4, 201.3, 207.2, 226.4, 235.10, 264.7, 273.6, 275.6, 278.7, 279.5,
281.6, 286.4, 315.4, 317.5, 332.3, 360.4, 369.3.

APPENDIX D: *Phrases in the chorale harmonizations by Bach in which
sequential motion is a prominent feature of the bass.*

8.4, 8.5, 8.9, 11.11, 13.5, 14.5, 16.3, 25.4, 25.6, 31.3, 38.1, 38.2, 38.6,
39.2, 41.3, 41.6, 44.4, 52.5, 55.6, 58.6, 58.9, 65.5, 66.4, 68.2, 70.6,
83.7, 89.5, 91.5, 91.12, 93.4, 94.2, 94.4, 99.4, 107.7, 112.1, 114.2, 114.4,
114.6, 116.1, 118.6, 119.6, 121.5, 124.5, 128.4, 128.5, 132.10, 134.2,
136.4, 137.4, 137.7, 137.11, 138.1, 138.4, 140.4, 140.5, 145.4, 151.4,
152.2, 155.5, 166.5, 168.5, 176.3, 179.3, 180.3, 198.1, 201.2, 211.2,
220.2, 222.4, 231.6, 235.6, 238.2, 239.7, 243.1, 247.4, 249.1, 250.7,

253.4, 254.3, 258.5, 264.3, 268.10, 269.4, 277.6, 280.7, 281.5, 283.6, 285.5, 286.5, 291.4, 297.8, 300.5, 324.6, 327.3, 333.2, 334.4, 348.2, 348.4, 356.6, 357.8, 362.2, 362.3, 365.6, 370.1.

APPENDIX E: *Phrases in the chorale harmonizations by Bach in which the bass does not suggest any sense of drive.*

5.7, 5.8, 11.8, 14.2, 14.3, 16.7, 17.4, 18.1, 19.4, 20.7, 21.4, 34.2, 37.2, 40.1, 42.3, 45.2, 45.4, 47.2, 48.1, 48.2, 49.3, 50.2, 53.1, 54.3, 55.1, 55.2, 56.4, 57.1, 58.1, 66.1, 68.1, 69.3, 69.6, 69.8, 70.7, 71.5, 72.1, 75.1, 78.2, 78.3, 79.4, 86.4, 86.5, 87.4, 89.2, 89.3, 94.1, 97.1, 97.2, 97.5, 98.5, 101.1, 102.2, 102.3, 102.5, 107.2, 107.3, 107.8, 109.1, 109.3, 109.5, 118.1, 119.3, 121.2, 122.1, 122.2, 123.1, 124.1, 124.6, 128.1, 128.3, 129.3, 132.7, 132.13, 133.1, 133.4, 133.6, 135.4, 135.7, 137.9, 139.6, 140.1, 141.3, 141.4, 141.5, 147.5, 147.6, 150.1, 150.2, 150.5, 150.6, 154.3, 157.1, 157.2, 159.1, 159.2, 161.2, 161.4, 162.2, 163.4, 166.2, 167.5, 167.8, 168.3, 171.1, 171.3, 173.1, 173.2, 174.3, 175.2, 176.1, 177.1, 181.2, 181.5, 182.4, 183.3, 184.3, 184.5, 185.3, 186.1, 186.3, 186.4, 187.1, 188.1, 188.3, 190.6, 192.1, 192.4, 193.1, 193.2, 194.2, 197.5, 197.14, 200.3, 205.3, 205.6, 205.7, 205.10, 205.12, 205.14, 205.15, 205.20, 206.1, 206.3, 206.5, 207.4, 208.1, 208.4, 209.1, 210.1, 211.7, 212.6, 215.12, 216.7, 216.10, 217.2, 217.3, 219.2, 222.5, 223.2, 223.7, 223.10, 224.3, 226.3, 227.4, 229.1, 229.2, 229.3, 229.5, 230.3, 231.2, 231.3, 232.1, 232.4, 232.5, 234.1, 235.2, 235.7, 236.1, 237.1, 237.3, 237.7, 238.1, 241.1, 241.9, 242.1, 245.1, 245.4, 247.1, 248.1, 252.3, 252.5, 255.7, 261.6, 263.4, 263.5, 268.6, 268.8, 270.1, 271.5, 272.3, 274.3, 276.4, 277.1, 278.4, 278.5, 279.1, 280.6, 286.3, 286.6, 288.3, 288.5, 293.4, 294.4, 296.9, 298.6, 299.6, 311.3, 311.5, 316.2, 320.2, 321.3, 321.5, 321.6, 323.4, 323.5, 327.4, 327.7, 332.7, 333.3, 341.1, 342.1, 344.1, 344.2, 345.1, 346.6, 346.7, 350.1, 351.5, 357.6, 358.2, 358.4, 366.4, 368.1, 369.2.

NOTES

Chapter One

1. This is not to imply that specific associations are necessarily inherent in particular sounds. I only wish to assert that meaning depends upon an ability to draw some analogies from acoustical phenomena. Specific meanings may vary with cultural influences—indeed, the range of effects considered meaningful would be different in different cultures.
2. See Leonard B. Meyer, *Emotion and Meaning in Music* (Chicago, 1956), pp. 37, 45-46, and 54-59 for a formulation of this view.
3. A similar formulation can be found in Meyer's *Emotion and Meaning*, p. 28.

Chapter Two

1. An ingenious discussion of some of the ways of achieving a sense of function (i.e., of generating and fulfilling expectations) at this time may be found in Richard L. Crocker, "Discant, Counterpoint, Harmony," *Journal of the American Musicological Society*, XV (Spring 1962), 1-21.
2. Heinrich Besseler, *Bourdon und Fauxbourdon* (Leipzig, 1950), pp. 29-31.
3. Guillaume de Machaut, *Musikalische Werke*, ed. Friedrich Ludwig (Leipzig, 1926-1943).
4. Machaut, *Musikalische Werke*, I, 1.
5. *Ibid.*, p. 2.
6. *Ibid.*, III, 58-61.
7. *Ibid.*, pp. 68-70.
8. George Perle, "Integrative Devices in the Music of Machaut," *The Musical Quarterly*, XXXIV (April 1948), 176.
9. See Sarah Jane Williams, "The Music of Guillaume de Machaut" (Ph.D. dissertation, Yale University, 1952), pp. 108 and 113.
10. Armand Machabey, *Guillaume de Machault, La vie et l'oeuvre musical* (Paris, 1955).

11. Machaut, *Musikalische Werke,* I, 88.
12. *Ibid.,* p. 47.
13. See Gilbert Reaney, "Voices and Instruments in the Music of Guillaume de Machaut," *Revue Belge de Musicologie,* X (1956), 6.
14. The canonic ballade *Dame, par vous-Amis, dolens-Sanz cuer m'en vois* (Machaut, *Musikalische Werke,* I, 16-17) represents an exception to this assertion, of course.
15. This, indeed, is one of the basic principles upon which Meyer erects his whole structure of thought. See Leonard B. Meyer, *Emotion and Meaning in Music* (Chicago, 1956).
16. Schemes differing from this one only in details can be found in *Dame, par vous* (No. 17) and *Se quanque amours* (No. 21). In both of these, an opening curve containing a considerable measure of descent is followed by another one in which a descent seems cut off prematurely—by a cadential return to the starting note in No. 17 (measures 5-6), and by an abrupt leap downward in No. 21 (measures 6-10). The climax that follows immediately, then, represents a similar kind of affective reaction and sets the stage nicely for the subsequent resolving descent.
17. Since this is a vocal art, rather minute differences in the high range almost certainly would register quite strongly in this respect. The greater amount of strain required to proceed even a half-step higher at this portion of a vocal range is readily apparent. Thus I have taken even the reaching of a pitch only a second higher as a reflection of climactic intent. Practically, however, this is a negligible problem, inasmuch as, with but one exception (No. 17), the stay at the highest note or register is appreciably longer or else the previous climax is bettered by a third.
18. In two of the ballades (No. 17 and No. 21), it is perhaps taking some liberty to speak of a climax immediately following the second ending; the climactic level is approached by means of a fairly short buildup instead of being reached at once. In view of the relative brevity of these rises, however, the idea of offering a stronger challenge to the will toward resolution still seems in effect. Hence I have included these ballades in this category.
19. Very similar arrangements can be found in *On ne porroit penser* (No. 3), *Nes que on porroit* (No. 33), and *Gais et jolis* (No. 35).
20. A similar high ending can be found in *Doulz amis* (No. 6). In this case the approach is more direct: a series of curves put progressively more emphasis on the rising element. Still another scheme of this kind can be found in *Se quanque amours* (No. 21) where an especially long descent at the end of an arch (measures 28-34) engenders a reaction in the form of a fairly direct rise from the low to the high register. There is a slight difference to the quality of the ending: the high point reached by this rocketlike rise becomes a foil, setting the stage for a leap down to the middle register and an understated ending—a familiar enough dramatic device.
21. An even simpler type of organization can be seen in *De petit po* (No. 18) where the entire second part consists of two descents interrupted by a brief passage dominated by the rising element.

The second of these descents is so much more leisurely (it is outlined by the successively lower high points reached) that it carries an unmistakable suggestion of resolution. Equally simple is the scheme in *Dame, par vous* (No. 17), which consists essentially of two arches, the second lying lower than the first and so much shorter that it seems little more than a countercurrent or a final flare-up designed to enhance the finality of the subsequent cadence. In *Ne penses pas* (No. 10), finally, the sense of climax is created, not just by a single high pitch or by a series of them in adjacent measures, but rather by a long inverted arch (measures 24-33) which begins and ends on a pitch (A) higher than any found elsewhere in the piece. What follows, then, is a succession of curves in which the descending element gradually gains the upper hand.

22. This is the figure arrived at by including the ballade and baladelle from the *Remède de Fortune*, but leaving out of consideration the works listed as No. 37 and No. 41 by Ludwig, the former because it is not set to music, and the latter because it is not Machaut's composition.

23. This is what is sometimes called a double ballade, that is, one in which two of the voices are provided with different texts. In this case, only the one labelled "B" by Ludwig was by Machaut. Since the melody to which this text is set seems somewhat more clearly shaped than the one bearing the text that begins *Quant Theseus,* I have chosen to treat it as the main melodic line, a fact I have designated by using the number 34B. For an account of the "contest" which led to this double text, see Williams, "The Music of Guillaume de Machaut," p. 250.

24. This is what might be called a triple ballade. I have used the symbol 29A to indicate the melodic line set to the text labelled "A" by Ludwig.

25. Something similar was noticed by Gilbert Reaney, whose formulation is as follows: "It is significant that the main part of the melody tends downward, while the middle section strives upward. This, however, is a feature of almost all Machaut's ballades and virelais." See "The Ballades, Rondeaux and Virelais of Guillaume de Machaut: Melody, Rhythm and Form," *Acta Musicologica,* XXVII (1955), 44. As is clear from this study, however, this assertion applies only to a few of the ballades; Reaney's generalization is completely without foundation.

26. The plans of *Donnez, signeurs* (No. 26), *Une vipere* (No. 27), *J'aim mieus languir* (No. 7), *Ne Quier veoir* (No. 34B) and *Il m'est avis* (No. 22) differ from this only in details. In the first, the main rise is found at the beginning of the second part (measures 17-25), and is followed by a period of rather circumscribed motion during which little sense of direction either way is developed (measures 26-30). Once again the issue is resolved by the return of the motto which formed the second ending. In *Une vipere,* the rise is found farther along in the second part (measures 46-51) after a play of forces seems about to be resolved (too easily) by a long descent. The return of the descending passage which ended

the first part once again effects the resolution. In *J'aim mieus languir,* the rise (measures 22-27) attains such significance that it assumes the function, at least temporarily, of a main current, with the brief descent of measures 28-30 unable to suggest anything more than a delay of its progress. Appropriately enough, the resolution is effected only after a considerable conflict between the rising and falling elements. The proportions of the rising and descending elements are almost reversed in the two parts of *Ne quier veoir,* as the second part is dominated by a series of rises (measures 23-33) with the resolution supplied by the long descending passage which brought the first part to an end. Finally, the only significant rise in *Il m'est avis* is to be found in measures 38-44. In this case, it is more than counterbalanced by the protracted descent that follows— the whole serving to set the stage nicely for the return, as a welcome reaction, to the high-lying motto which brought the first part to a close.

27. Similar considerations apply to the ballade *Dame, de qui toute ma joie vient* from the *Remède de Fortune.*
28. This figure includes the rondelet from the *Remède de Fortune,* but not rondeau No. 16 in Ludwig's edition since it is not set to music.
29. Reaney, "The Ballades, Rondeaux and Virelais of Guillaume de Machaut: Melody, Rhythm and Form," *Acta Musicologica,* XXVII (1955), 52.
30. See, for instance, Heinrich Besseler, *Die Musik des Mittelalters und der Renaissance* (Potsdam, 1931), pp. 138-139; or the same author's *Bourdon und Fauxbourdon* (Leipzig, 1950), p. 29; or Jacques Handschin, "Les Etudes sur le XVe siècle musical de Ch. Van Den Borren," *Revue Belge de Musicologie,* I (1947), 95.
31. Besseler, *Bourdon und Fauxbourdon,* p. 29. Translated from the German for this volume by John W. Grubbs, The University of Texas at Austin.
32. George Perle, "Integrative Devices in the Music of Machaut," *The Musical Quarterly,* XXXIV (April 1948), 169-176. Gilbert Reaney, "The Ballades, Rondeaux and Virelais of Guillaume de Machaut: Melody, Rhythm and Form," *Acta Musicologica,* XXVII (1955), 40-58. Sarah Jane Williams, "The Music of Guillaume de Machaut."
33. Reaney, "The Ballades, Rondeaux and Virelais," p. 56.
34. Perle, p. 169.
35. Reaney, "The Ballades, Rondeaux and Virelais," pp. 53-54.

Chapter Three

1. Leipzig, 1950.
2. Paris, 1955.
3. Sylvia Kenney has suggested that this represented not so much a change in conception as a new interest on the part of continental composers in the cultivation of discant—a well-known category of composition in which the choice of vertical combinations was largely restricted to consonances. According to Miss Kenney, this type of composition was neglected by continental composers during

the fourteenth century but flourished in England, from where it spread back into France near the turn of the fifteenth century. See "English Discant and Discant in England," *The Musical Quarterly,* XLV (1959), 26-48. See also Miss Kenney's book: *Walter Frye and the "Contenance Angloise"* (New Haven, 1965).

4. The performance practices of the time seem to point toward the same conclusion. Were a blending of the individual lines a part of the musical conception of the time, it is doubtful that *ad libitum* mixtures of voices and instruments would have been practiced. Free mixtures of timbres, however, is readily understandable if aesthetic values are considered as vested in individual lines rather than in the texture as a whole.

5. The Masses *Caput, Se la face ay pale, L'homme armé, Ecce ancilla Domini,* and *Ave regina coelorum.* In a recently published study, *A Chronology of the Works of Guillaume Dufay, Based on a Study of Mensural Practice* (Princeton, 1964), Charles E. Hamm places the first two of these within the years 1435-1450, and the others between 1454 and the year of Dufay's death. On the other hand, he places most of the chansons before 1433. Inasmuch as the texture and bass in the later chansons are treated much as they were in the earlier secular pieces, it might well be that the stylistic differences were more a matter of genre than of chronological development.

6. The Masses *Caput, Ecce ancilla Domini,* and *Ave regina coelorum.*

7. It is interesting to note that Hamm also found some instances of notational archaisms in this Mass (Hamm, *A Chronology,* pp. 143-145).

8. Hamm, *A Chronology,* pp. 143-145.

9. "The Approach to the Cadence in High Renaissance Music" (M.A. thesis, University of California, 1943).

10. Since it stands between two G's (with but a slight decoration), and since it forms a sixth expanding to an octave with the bass at an obvious cadence point.

11. For the reasons cited in footnote 10.

12. Movements such as the *Kyrie* from *Missa Prolationum* and the *Sanctus* from *Missa Caput,* and entire works such as *Missa Au travail suis* and the two three-voice Masses.

13. "Tonality," in *Harvard Dictionary of Music* (Cambridge, 1951), p. 752.

14. Uncertainties concerning *musica ficta* make it virtually impossible to speak for the entire body of Obrecht's works.

15. See Jacob Obrecht, *Opera omnia,* ed. A. Smijers (Amsterdam, 1953-1957), I, 121-126. In view of the length of this excerpt and the availability of this new edition, I have taken the liberty of not presenting it in a musical example.

16. There does not seem to be much reason for flatting any of them.

17. Both described, along with the patterns found in several others of Obrecht's movements, in this writer's dissertation: *The Masses of Jacob Obrecht: Structure and Style* (Ann Arbor: University Microfilms, 1959), Chapter XI.

18. Concerning the number of Masses actually contained in the com-

plete edition, see Gustave Reese, *Music in the Renaissance* (New York, 1954), p. 195, footnote 59.

19. Jacob Obrecht, *Werken,* ed. J. Wolf (Amsterdam, 1912-1921), fasc. 5.
20. See Manfred F. Bukofzer, *Music in the Baroque Era* (New York, 1947), pp. 220-221.
21. See pp. 94-96, above.

Chapter Four

1. August W. Ambros, *Geschichte der Musik,* 3rd rev. ed. (Leipzig, 1893), III, pp. 203-237.
2. Notably Hugo Leichtentritt, *Geschichte der Motette* (Leipzig, 1908); Gustave Reese, *Music in the Renaissance* (New York, 1954); Myroslaw Antonowytch, "The Present State of Josquin Research," *International Musicological Society, Report of the Eighth Congress* (Kassel: Bärenreiter, 1961), I, 53-65; and Helmuth Osthoff, *Josquin Desprez* (Tutzing, 1962-1964).
3. Ambros, *Geschichte der Musik,* p. 229. Translated from the German for this volume by John W. Grubbs.
4. Antonowytch, "Present State of Josquin Research."
5. Osthoff, *Josquin Desprez.*
6. Heinrich Besseler, "Von Dufay bis Josquin," *Zeitschrift für Musikwissenschaft,* XI (1928-1929), 1-22.
7. Reese, *Music in the Renaissance.*
8. *Josquin des Prez, Werken,* ed. A. Smijers (Leipzig, 1921-).
9. Ambros, *Geschichte der Musik,* p. 229. Translated from the German for this volume by John W. Grubbs.
10. Leichtentritt, p. 64. Translated by John W. Grubbs.
11. Osthoff, II, 26-27. Translated by John W. Grubbs.
12. Ambros, p. 231. Translated by John W. Grubbs.
13. Osthoff, II, 47. Translated by John W. Grubbs.
14. E. E. Lowinsky, *Secret Chromatic Art in the Netherlands Motet* (New York, 1946).
15. The E in the altus probably would have been flatted to avoid a noncadential tritone, as well as in accordance with the old rule concerning an E between two D's.
16. The E almost certainly would have been flatted.
17. Osthoff, II, 26-27.
18. This is a view that I have advanced in my dissertation: *The Masses of Jacob Obrecht: Structure and Style* (Ann Arbor: University Microfilms, 1959).
19. Leichtentritt, *Geschichte der Motette.*

Chapter Five

1. See Allen I. McHose, *The Contrapuntal Harmonic Technique of the Eighteenth Century* (New York, 1947), pp. 3-18, or the same author's *Basic Principles of the Technique of Eighteenth and Nineteenth Century Composition* (New York, 1951), Chap. 22.

2. The essentially harmonic arts described in Chapter 3, of course, are clearly exceptions to this rule.
3. Whether similar considerations should be applied to the diminished triad with a minor seventh (the so-called half-diminished) seems open to question. For this chord carries so distinctive a quality that it seems to draw attention to itself more than it produces a commitment to resolution. In the interest of obtaining conservative results, at any rate, this chord has not been considered a dominant substitute in the calculations contained in this essay.
4. See Chapter 3, above.
5. I have considered a change of chord to take place only upon the introduction of what today would be called a new root, or upon the conversion of a major triad to a minor, or vice versa.
6. This figure is arrived at by omitting the twenty-three duplications contained in the standard collections of 371 chorale harmonizations. According to the numbering of the Breitkopf edition (or the Kalmus), these duplicates can be designated as Numbers 88, 126, 178, 195, 204, 256, 257, 259, 282, 295, 302, 305, 306, 307, 308, 309, 318, 319, 328, 349, 353, 354, and 361.
7. Again following the numbering in the Breitkopf and Kalmus editions, these would be Numbers 1, 3, 9, 21, 27, 33, 37, 40, 45, 57, 58, 59, 68, 71, 76, 81, 89, 90, 92, 94, 103, 105, 131, 135, 136, 137, 141, 144, 145, 146, 149, 156, 158, 159, 161, 171, 172, 174, 180, 184, 190, 192, 193, 194, 198, 202, 207, 208, 212, 216, 218, 225, 228, 236, 238, 240, 242, 251, 253, 254, 265, 275, 279, 287, 303, 311, 315, 317, 321, 322, 325, 327, 331, 336, 339, 340, 356, 363, 364, 371.
8. Numbers 59, 94, 141, 161, 180, 192, 198, 242, 279, and 340.
9. Numbers 12, 15, 16, 24, 42, 47, 51, 55, 62, 63, 67, 72, 75, 78, 83, 99, 100, 101, 102, 106, 108, 110, 122, 127, 140, 155, 169, 173, 175, 182, 183, 196, 200, 203, 206, 211, 213, 214, 217, 222, 224, 226, 229, 230, 237, 252, 255, 266, 276, 281, 283, 284, 289, 290, 294, 297, 299, 300, 304, 314, 320, 330, 332, 333, 337, 351, 358, 365, 369.
10. Numbers 2, 4, 5, 6, 7, 8, 10, 13, 14, 17, 18, 19, 20, 22, 23, 25, 26, 28, 29, 30, 31, 32, 34, 35, 36, 38, 39, 41, 43, 44, 46, 48, 49, 50, 52, 53, 54, 56, 61, 64, 69, 70, 73, 74, 77, 79, 80, 82, 84, 85, 86, 91, 93, 96, 97, 107, 109, 111, 112, 113, 114, 115, 117, 118, 120, 123, 124, 128, 129, 130, 132, 133, 134, 138, 139, 142, 147, 148, 150, 151, 153, 160, 162, 163, 164, 165, 166, 167, 168, 176, 177, 179, 181, 185, 186, 188, 189, 191, 197, 199, 201, 205, 209, 210, 215, 219, 221, 223, 227, 231, 232, 233, 234, 235, 239, 241, 243, 244, 245, 246, 248, 249, 250, 258, 260, 261, 262, 264, 267, 268, 269, 270, 271, 272, 274, 277, 278, 280, 286, 288, 291, 292, 293, 298, 301, 310, 312, 313, 316, 323, 324, 326, 329, 334, 338, 341, 342, 345, 346, 347, 348, 350, 352, 355, 357, 359, 360, 362, 366, 367, 368, 370.
11. Numbers 98, 116, 121, 143, 154, 157, 187, 220, 247.
12. Numbers 11, 60, 65, 66, 87, 95, 104, 119, 125, 152, 170, 263, 273, 285, 296, 335, 344.

13. Manfred F. Bukofzer, *Music in the Baroque Era* (New York, 1947), p. 82. Bach's setting is that numbered 250 in the Breitkopf and Kalmus editions, but transposed down a degree, presumably to facilitate comparison.
14. Often the commitment to resolve the dominant of a half cadence at the beginning of the following phrase is ignored, resulting in a sense of surprise, of a fresh start. In this case, of course, the dominant still is interpreted as part of a standard cadence in spite of its failure to resolve "properly."
15. The figure 2138 was obtained by assuming that every fermata marked the end of a phrase. In addition, in No. 150 and No. 280, a rest in the bass obviously marks off a phrase as far as that voice is concerned, although no fermata is present, and No. 43, *Liebster Gott, wann werd' ich sterben,* has been left out of consideration because the phrases are not clearly marked off in it. And it should be borne in mind that numbers 88, 126, 178, 195, 204, 256, 257, 259, 282, 295, 302, 305, 306, 307, 308, 309, 318, 319, 328, 349, 353, 354, and 361 are duplicates of other harmonizations, as pointed out in footnote 6, and hence were not included in these calculations.
16. By the principle of what Meyer calls saturation. See his *Emotion and Meaning in Music* (Chicago, 1956), p. 135.
17. Number 360.7; therefore not included in this category.
18. See Chapter 3 above.
19. Omitting the two short chorales and the one sectional one leaves the number at 345.
20. See Friedrich Blume, "Umrisse eines neuen Bachbildes," *Syntagma Musicologicum,* ed. Martin Ruhnke (Kassel, 1963), pp. 466-479.

Chapter Six

1. It goes without saying that the diminuendo would have been quite impossible on the harpsichord, one of the instruments for which this piece may have been intended.
2. In preparing the examples for this movement, I have found it advantageous to reduce the score either to a bass or figured bass alone, or else to a bass along with the main voice or voices. It is for this reason that this particular passage takes on the appearance of a trio sonata.
3. See Manfred F. Bukofzer, *Music in the Baroque Era* (New York, 1947), pp. 220-221, for some descriptions of these so-called harmonic formulae.
4. In the following discussion, I shall refer only to passages in the opening section, although it is to be understood that corresponding passages can be found in the (identical) closing section.
5. The term *Well Tempered Clavier,* of course, properly applies only to the set of twenty-four preludes and fugues issued in 1722—what is now known as Volume I of this collection. The following discussions are restricted to the fugues in this so-called Volume I, although the same considerations also hold for the fugues in Volume II.

Energy — wind-tunnel turbines (?) (between buildings)
— large paddles in the Fraser —

6. The first two entries must be excepted, of course, because no episode precedes them, and because this whole process has not yet taken shape. The last section also is excepted, but only in order to be able to deal with it separately.
7. Bukofzer, *Music in the Baroque Era,* pp. 4-5.
8. Glen Haydon, "On the Problem of Expression in Baroque Music," *Journal of the American Musicological Society,* III (Summer 1950), 113-119.

Chapter Seven

1. Although some historians maintain that Beethoven is a transitional figure—half in the classic, half in the romantic era—this seems to be a minority opinion. Einstein goes so far as to imply that such a view is the result of a profound misunderstanding of Beethoven's art on the part of romantic musicians (A. Einstein, *Music in the Romantic Era* [New York, 1947]). The evidence presented in this essay and the one following would seem to indicate more of an affinity with Haydn and Mozart than with any of the romantics.
2. Friedrich Blume, "Die Musik der Klassik," *Die Musik in Geschichte und Gegenwart,* VII (1958), 1027-1090.
3. Since examples are often necessarily quite lengthy in this chapter and the one following, and are so readily accessible in print, I have usually refrained from inserting them into the text. Only where I felt that a brief snatch of music might call a particular effect to mind very quickly have I presented examples. The first movement of Beethoven's piano sonata opus 53 can serve as illustration for this particular assertion.
4. See, for example, opus 1 No. 2, or opus 64 No. 2.
5. It might be well to observe that we are often cheated of this overwhelming aesthetic experience by conductors who slow down the build-up to the reentry and the reentry itself, and add to the instrumentation in these passages (thereby lending emphasis to them that probably was not envisioned by Beethoven) but who resume the faster tempo at the bridge, thereby reducing its significance.
6. Robert Sondheimer does indeed go so far as to suggest that Haydn was not as good a composer as some of these men. The basis for his judgment, however, is emotional content—a criterion which would admit many amateurish scribblings into the ranks of masterworks. See Sondheimer's *Haydn, a Historical and Psychological Study Based on his Quartets* (London, 1951).

Chapter Eight

1. A similar conclusion is drawn in an unpublished dissertation by Donald M. Mintz, "The Sketches and Drafts of Three of Felix Mendelssohn's Major Works" (Cornell University, 1961).
2. Leonard B. Meyer, *Emotion and Meaning in Music* (Chicago, 1956).

3. See p. 222, above.
4. As pointed out in Chapter 6, the assertion that late-baroque composers presented only one emotion in a movement is open to question and must be qualified. Nevertheless, it is true that no late-baroque composer exploited changes of mood to the degree that the classical composers did.

Chapter Nine

1. Arnold Schoenberg, *Style and Idea,* trans. Dika Newlin (New York, 1950).
2. Arnold Schoenberg, *Harmonielehre* (Vienna, 1922).
3. Merle Armitage, *Schoenberg* (New York, 1937).
4. *Briefe,* Mainz, 1958.
5. *Style and Idea,* p. 104.
6. *Ibid.,* p. 104.
7. *Ibid.,* pp. 104-105.
8. *Ibid.,* pp. 104-105.
9. *Ibid.,* p. 109.
10. See, for instance, Friedrich Kainz, *Aesthetics—the Science,* trans. Herbert M. Schueller (Detroit, 1962), p. 355.
11. *Style and Idea,* p. 106.
12. *Ibid.,* p. 110 ff.
13. *Ibid.,* pp. 112-113.
14. *Ibid.,* pp. 113-114.
15. *Ibid.,* p. 143.
16. *Briefe,* pp. 178-179.
17. See, for instance, Ernst Krenek, "Tradition in Perspective," *Perspectives of New Music,* I (Fall 1962), 28, 31-32.
18. Jan Nordmark, "New Theories of Form and the Problem of Thematic Identities," *Journal of Music Theory,* IV (Nov. 1960), 210-217.
19. *Style and Idea,* pp. 112-113.
20. Nordmark, p. 217.
21. See Chapter 1, above.
22. See Chapter 3, above.
23. Armitage, *Schoenberg,* p. 270.
24. *Ibid.,* p. 270.
25. Except in such obvious practical matters as instrumental construction and tuning.
26. Hans-Heinz Draeger, "Curt Sachs as an Ethnomusicologist," *The Commonwealth of Music,* ed. Gustave Reese and Rose Brandel (New York, 1956), pp. 17-18.
27. *Ibid.,* p. 17.
28. *Ibid.,* pp. 17-18.
29. See Edward A. Lippman, "Hellenic Conceptions of Harmony," *Journal of the American Musicological Society,* XVI (Spring 1963), 3-35.
30. It is only in the tempered tunings of later times that a satisfactory resolution of this tension also could have been suggested by a move to a triad on G♭.

BIBLIOGRAPHY

Ambros, August Wilhelm. *Geschichte der Musik.* 3rd rev. ed. Leipzig: Leuckart, 1881-1893. 5 vols.

Antonowytch, Myroslaw. "The Present State of Josquin Research." In *International Musicological Society Report of the Eighth Congress, New York, 1961,* edited by Jan La Rue. Kassel: Bärenreiter, 1961. I, 53-65.

Apel, Willi. *Harvard Dictionary of Music.* Cambridge: Harvard University Press, 1951.

Armitage, Merle. *Schoenberg.* New York: G. Schirmer, 1937.

Bach, Johann Sebastian. *371 Four-part Chorales.* Breitkopf & Härtel edition. New York: Associated Music Publishers, [n.d.].

——— ——— New York: Edwin F. Kalmus, [n.d.]. 2 vols.

Besseler, Heinrich. *Bourdon und Fauxbourdon.* Leipzig: Breitkopf & Härtel, 1950.

——— *Die Musik des Mittelalters und der Renaissance.* Potsdam: Akademische Verlagsgesellschaft Athenaion, 1931.

——— "Von Dufay bis Josquin," *Zeitschrift für Musikwissenschaft,* XI (1928-29), 1-22.

Blume, Friedrich. "Die Musik der Klassik," *Die Musik in Geschichte und Gegenwart,* VII (1958), 1027-1090.

——— "Umrisse eines neuen Bachbildes." In *Syntagma Musicologicum,* edited by Martin Ruhnke. Kassel: Bärenreiter, 1963, Pp. 466-479.

Bukofzer, Manfred F. *Music in the Baroque Era.* New York: W. W. Norton, 1947.

Clement, M. L. "The Approach to the Cadence in High Renaissance Music." Master's thesis, University of California, 1943.

Crocker, Richard L. "Discant, Counterpoint, Harmony," *Journal of the American Musicological Society,* XV (Spring 1962), 1-21.

des Prez, Josquin. *Werken.* Edited by Alexander Smijers. Leipzig: Kistner & Sigel; later Amsterdam: G. Alsbach, 1921—. 51 vols. to 1964.

Draeger, Hans-Heinz. "Curt Sachs as an Ethnomusicologist." In *The Commonwealth of Music,* edited by Gustave Reese and Rose Brandel. New York: The Free Press, 1965.

Einstein, Alfred. *Music in the Romantic Era.* New York: W. W. Norton, 1947.

Hamm, Charles E. *A Chronology of the Works of Guillaume Dufay, Based on a Study of Mensural Practice.* Princeton: Princeton University Press, 1964.

Handschin, Jacques. "Les Etudes sur le XVe siècle musical de Ch. Van Den Borren," *Revue Belge de Musicologie,* I (1947), 93-99.

Haydon, Glen. "On the Problem of Expression in Baroque Music," *Journal of the American Musicology Society,* III (Summer 1950): 113-19.

Kainz, Friedrich. *Aesthetics—the Science.* Translated by Herbert M. Schueller. Detroit: Wayne State University Press, 1962.

Kenney, Sylvia. "English Discant and Discant in England," *The Musical Quarterly,* XLV (January 1959): 26-48.

——— *Walter Frye and the "Contenance Angloise."* New Haven: Yale University Press, 1965.

Krenek, Ernst. "Tradition in Perspective," *Perspectives of New Music,* I (1962), 27-38.

Leichtentritt, Hugo. *Geschichte der Motette.* Leipzig: Breitkopf & Härtel, 1908.

Lippman, Edward A. "Hellenic Conceptions in Harmony," *Journal of the American Musicological Society,* XVI (Spring 1963), 3-35.

Lowinsky, Edward E. *Secret Chromatic Art in the Netherlands Motet.* New York: Columbia University Press, 1946.

Machabey, Armand. *Genèse de la Tonalité Musicale Classique.* Paris: Richard-Masse Editeurs, 1955.

——— *Guillaume de Machault, La vie et l'oeuvre musical.* Paris: Richard-Masse Editeurs, 1955.

Machaut, Guillaume de. *Musikalische Werke.* Edited by Friedrich Ludwig. Leipzig: Breitkopf & Härtel, 1926-1943. 4 vols.

McHose, Allen I. *Basic Principles of the Technique of the Eighteenth and Nineteenth Century Composition.* New York: Appleton-Century-Crofts, 1951.

——— *The Contrupuntal Harmonic Technique of the Eighteenth Century.* New York: Appleton-Century-Crofts, 1947.

Meyer, Leonard B. *Emotion and Meaning in Music.* Chicago: University of Chicago Press, 1956.

Mintz, Donald M. "The Sketches and Drafts of Three of Felix Mendelssohn's Major Works." Ph.D. dissertation, Cornell University, 1961. Ann Arbor: University Microfilms, 1961.

Nordmark, Jan. "New Theories of Form and the Problem of Thematic Identities," *Journal of Music Theory,* IV (Nov. 1960), 210-17.

Obrecht, Jacob. *Opera Omnia.* Edited by Alexander Smijers. Amsterdam: G. Alsbach, 1953-1957—. Vol. 1—.

——— *Werken.* Edited by Johannes Wolf. Amsterdam: G. Alsbach, 1912-21. 30 vols.

Osthoff, Helmuth. *Josquin Desprez.* Tutzing: Schneider, 1962-64. 2 vols.

Perle, George. "Integrative Devices in the Music of Machaut," *The Musical Quarterly,* XXXIV (April 1948), 169-76.

Reaney, Gilbert. "The Ballades, Rondeaux and Virelais of Guillaume de

Machaut: Melody, Rhythm and Form," *Acta Musicologica*, XXVII (1955), 40-58.

—— "Voices and Instruments in the Music of Guillaume de Machaut," *Revue Belge de Musicologie*, X (1956), 3-17, 93-104.

Reese, Gustave. *Music in the Renaissance*. New York: W. W. Norton, 1954.

Salop, Arnold. "Intensity as a Distinction between Classical and Romantic Music," *Journal of Aesthetics and Art Criticism*, XXIII (1965), 359-71.

—— "Jacob Obrecht and the Early Development of Harmonic Polyphony," *Journal of the American Musicological Society*, XVII (Fall 1964), 288-309.

—— "On Stylistic Unity in Renaissance-Baroque Distinctions." In *Essays in Musicology, A Birthday Offering for Willi Apel*. Edited by Hans Tischler. Bloomington: University of Indiana, School of Music, 1968. Pp. 107-121.

—— "The Masses of Jacob Obrecht: Structure and Style." Ph.D. dissertation, Indiana University, 1959. Ann Arbor: University Microfilms, 1959.

Schoenberg, Arnold. *Briefe*. Mainz: B. Schott's Söhne, 1958.

—— *Harmonielehre*. Vienna: Universal Edition, 1922.

—— *Style and Idea*. Translated by Dika Newlin. New York: Philosophical Library, 1950.

Sondheimer, Robert. *Haydn, a Historical and Psychological Study Based on his Quartets*. London: Bernoulli, 1951.

Williams, Sara Jane. "The Music of Guillaume de Machaut." Ph.D. dissertation, Yale University, 1952. Ann Arbor: University Microfilms, 1964.

INDEX

Arnold Salop (1927-1967) received his B.A. (1952) from U.C.L.A., his M.A. in composition (1957) from Claremont Graduate School, and his Ph.D. in musicology (1959) from Indiana University. He served as assistant professor of musicology at George Peabody College for Teachers (1958-1960) and at Wayne State University (1961-1964), as associate professor of theory at the University of Mississippi (1964-1965), and as associate professor of musicology and theory at the University of Texas at Austin (1965-1967). He was known professionally both as a musicologist and as a composer.

The manuscript was prepared for publication by Sandra Yolles with the assistance of Mrs. Phyllis Salop and John W. Grubbs. The book was designed by Don Ross. The text type face is Linotype Caledonia designed by W. A. Dwiggins in 1937; and the display face is Garamond based on a design by Claude Garamond in the 16th Century. The text is printed on Westvaco Clearspring Book Antique Paper; and the book is bound in Columbia Mills Fictionette cloth and Elephant Hide over binders boards. Manufactured in the United States of America.